2nd edition

Woodland Stewardship

A Practical Guide for Midwestern Landowners

Find more University of Minnesota Extension educational information at www.extension.umn.edu.

Published by University of Minnesota Extension. Additional copies of this item can be ordered from the Extension Store at http://shop.extension.umn.edu/; or place credit card orders at 800-876-8636; or email questions to ShopExtension@umn.edu.

This material is available in alternative formats upon request. Contact your University of Minnesota Extension office or the Extension Store at 800-876-8636.

 Printed on recycled and recyclable paper with at least 25 percent (cover) and 30 percent (body) postconsumer material.

ISBN 978-1-888440-43-0

Acknowledgments

Authors

Melvin J. Baughman, Extension Forester, University of Minnesota

Charles R. Blinn, Extension Specialist, University of Minnesota

John G. DuPlissis, Forestry Outreach Specialist, University of Wisconsin – Stevens Point

Eli Sagor, Extension Educator, University of Minnesota

Angela S. Gupta, Extension Educator, University of Minnesota

David Drake, Assistant Professor, University of Wisconsin

Scott Craven, Professor, University of Wisconsin

David S. Wilsey, Extension Educator, University of Minnesota

Julie Miedtke, Extension Educator, University of Minnesota

Karen Potter-Witter, Professor and Extension Specialist, Michigan State University

Bill Cook, Extension Forester and Wildlife Biologist, Michigan State University

Paul Doruska, Associate Professor, University of Wisconsin – Stevens Point

Dean Current, Research Associate, University of Minnesota

Diomy S. Zamora, Extension Educator, University of Minnesota

Michael R. Reichenbach, Extension Educator, University of Minnesota

Gary Wyatt, Extension Educator, University of Minnesota

Graphic Designer – John Molstad

Project Manager – Arlene West

Peer Reviewers

The authors are very grateful for the time and expertise contributed by peer reviewers, but any oversights or errors in the final manuscript are solely the responsibility of the authors. Peer reviewers were: Andrew Arends, Tom Burk, Val Cervenka, Grant Domke, Bill Foss, Valiree Green, Kurt Hinz, Rick Horton, Dave Johnson, Dean Solomon, Lori Stevenson, and Martin Wiley.

Funding Sources

Minnesota Department of Natural Resources, Division of Forestry
Michigan State University – Renewable Resources Extension Act
University of Minnesota – Renewable Resources Extension Act

Contents

Contents (continued)

Contents (continued)

Contents (continued)

Chapter 1:

Preparing a Woodland Stewardship Plan

John G. DuPlissis, Forestry Outreach Specialist, University of Wisconsin – Stevens Point
Melvin J. Baughman, Extension Forester, University of Minnesota
Eli Sagor, Extension Educator, University of Minnesota

What will you do with your woodland? Some landowners choose to "let nature take its course." They believe that nature, left to its own processes, will be a better manager than they ever could be. While this may be true in some situations, many of the natural processes that formed today's woodlands have been impaired by human activity. Wildfires that once renewed certain types of woodland have been curtailed. Non-native insects and diseases have decimated populations of some tree species. Introduced plants and animals have replaced native species. Residential, commercial, and industrial development, along with its transportation system, has fragmented woodlands into smaller, more isolated pieces. Wildlife populations are substantially different from a century ago. Centuries of human influence and disruption of natural processes have impaired forest ecosystems. Doing nothing is not the same thing as "allowing nature to take its course." The alternative is to become a woodland steward by actively managing for wood, wildlife, or recreation while protecting the quality of your natural resources (soil, water, wildlife, trees, and other plants) for future generations to enjoy.

Your woodland is a renewable resource; however, trees are long-lived and take many years to mature. Decisions you make now about wildlife management, harvesting trees, or controlling invasive species will influence the character of your woodland for many years into the future. As a woodland owner you need to plan for the long term because whatever you do—or don't do—will have long-term effects.

Start by developing a woodland stewardship plan. This process will help you determine objectives; use your time, energy, and money efficiently; make informed decisions; avoid costly errors; and evaluate your progress.

What Is a Woodland Stewardship Plan?

A woodland stewardship plan typically is a written document that:

- Clearly states why you own your property and your management goals.

- Is tailored to help you meet your goals within the capability of the land.

- Is based on a clear understanding of ecological processes.

- Offers recommendations for sustainable forest management practices.

- Provides a timetable for carrying out the forestry practices needed to reach your objectives.

- Is concise, including information that is relevant and accurate.

- Avoids technical forestry terminology or defines all technical terms.

- Incorporates publications or other attachments to describe forest management practices and inform you about sustainable forest management.

- Explains where you can get help to follow through with the plan.

Creating a woodland stewardship plan is easier than you might think. A forester can do most of this work for you.

Work with a Forester

Forestry is a science that requires an understanding of how trees grow, reproduce, and respond to changes in the environment, as well as how to manipulate woodlands to meet a landowner's goals. Foresters are professionals with knowledge of forest ecosystems and processes and experience in managing forests. Work with a forestry professional to develop a stewardship plan for your property. Depending on your interests and resources, you also may need to work with other experts in fields such as wildlife, soil, water, and recreation. Some forestry services are free, while others require payment, but their value is enormous compared to the costly errors with long-term consequences that you could make on your own.

Your state department of natural resources and some soil and water conservation districts have foresters available to visit your woodland, answer your questions, and help you prepare a woodland stewardship plan. They also administer other planning, property tax incentive, and cost-share programs.

Private consulting foresters are independent contractors who help landowners prepare woodland stewardship plans, market timber, plant trees, or perform any other management practices. Consultants charge for their services, but in some states, the cost of woodland stewardship planning still may be paid for by a state agency.

Forest product companies employ foresters to buy timber from private lands. Some of these foresters also write management plans for woodland owners in exchange for the right to match the highest bid on your timber when your woodland is ready for a harvest.

Extension foresters at universities offer educational conferences, workshops, field tours, publications, web sites, and other materials to better inform you about forestry options.

▲

Forest Stewardship Plan Basics

The six steps that follow are designed to guide you through the forest stewardship planning process.

1. Identify Your Goals

The first step in developing a stewardship plan is to identify your woodland goals. How did you come to own your woodland property? What do you and your family do when you are there? What outcomes do you seek from owning your woodland? Sample goals may be to:

- Create habitat for a wide range of wildlife species.
- Maximize income from wood production.
- Provide the best possible deer habitat.

If you have multiple goals, prioritize them or determine where they apply to your land. Your broad, property-wide goals may require you to develop more specific objectives in different areas of your woodland. Sharing a list of clear, specific goals and objectives with a forester guides them when recommending appropriate management practices to you. Consider your management plan a living document that you can refine as you learn more about your woodland and its capabilities, or as your needs change.

2. Inventory and Evaluate Your Property

Work with a forester to inventory and evaluate your property. Begin by accurately locating your property boundaries and marking them with a fence, paint marks on trees, rock piles, stakes, or other means. Clear brush from your property lines to avoid trespassing when you or your neighbors carry out forestry practices. If the boundaries are not clearly identifiable, you may want to have your land surveyed.

Gather historical facts concerning previous land use or management activities that could have influenced the development of your woodland. Such activities might include livestock grazing, agricultural cropping, timber harvesting, tree planting, fires, and pest outbreaks. Foresters use information about these events and their timing to analyze the development of existing woodlands and to predict the results of future management practices.

A written woodland stewardship plan may include these components:

- Your name and contact information.
- Legal description of the property.
- Your management goals.
- Description of the ecosystem in which your property is located and ecological issues of local concern.
- Inventory of known or potential historic and cultural resources (for example, cemeteries, burial mounds, foundations). Your forester may be able to obtain this information from a state-wide database of such resources.
- Inventory of known or potential threatened, endangered, or special interest species that are or may be present on your property. Your forester may be able to obtain this information from a statewide database of such species.
- History of your property's management.
- Map or aerial photograph of the property (Figure 1-1), approximately to scale, showing the following:
  ◦ Property boundaries
  ◦ Woodland boundaries
  ◦ Land uses
  ◦ Roads and trails
  ◦ Utility wires, pipelines, or other rights-of-way or easements
  ◦ Buildings
  ◦ Water resources
  ◦ Unique natural, historical, or archaeological resources

Aerial photographs are especially helpful as a foundation for the map (Figure 1-2). They usually are available from local offices of the U.S. Department of Agriculture (USDA) or from your state forestry agency.

4

If the property is large and hilly, topographic maps may help you assess slope and aspect as they relate to woodland access and tree growth (Figure 1-3). Topographic maps are available from the U.S. Geological Survey, but also may be available online or sold on CDs and DVDs at outdoor stores.

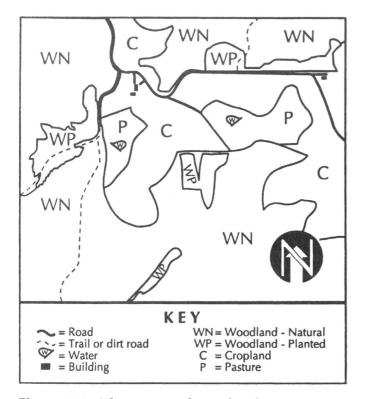

Figure 1-1. A base map shows land uses.

KEY

- = Road
- = Trail or dirt road
- Ⓦ = Water
- ■ = Building

WN = Woodland - Natural
WP = Woodland - Planted
C = Cropland
P = Pasture

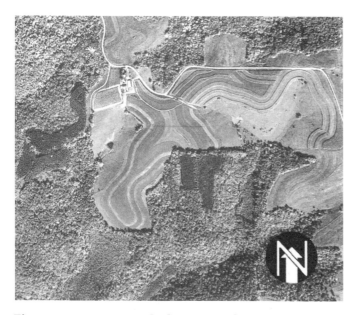

Figure 1-2. An aerial photograph helps identify land uses.

Figure 1-3. A topographic map shows elevation changes, roads, buildings, and other features.

- Soil type map (Figure 1-4) and interpretive information (Table 1-1) to help you determine the suitability of your land for different tree species, road or building sites, or other land uses. They may be available from local offices of the USDA Natural Resources Conservation Service.

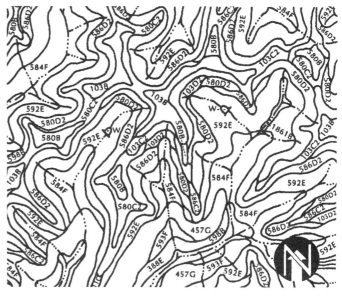

Figure 1-4. A soil type map.

Table 1-1. Typical soil interpretation for woodland management.

MAP SYMBOL & SOIL NAME	EROSION HAZARD	EQUIPMENT LIMITATION	SEEDLING MORTALITY	WINDTHROW HAZARD	PLANT COMPETITION	COMMON TREES	SITE INDEX	TREES TO PLANT
457G LaCrescent 45–70% slope	severe	severe	slight	moderate	moderate	northern red oak white oak American basswood	55 55 55	eastern white pine, white oak, American basswood, northern red oak, white ash
580B, 580C2 Blackhammer-Southridge 3–12% slope	slight	slight	slight	slight	Moderate	northern red oak American basswood white oak shagbark hickory	70 70 62 60	northern red oak, American basswood, sugar maple, white oak, eastern white pine, white ash, red pine
580D2 Blackhammer-Southridge 12–20% slope	moderate	moderate	slight	slight	moderate	northern red oak American basswood white oak shagbark hickory	70 70 62 60	northern red oak, American basswood, sugar maple, white oak, eastern white pine, red pine, white ash
584F Lamoille 30–45% slope	severe	severe	moderate	moderate	moderate	northern red oak American basswood green ash white oak shagbark hickory sugar maple	58 58 52 52 50 50	northern red oak, white oak, American basswood, eastern white pine, white ash
586C2 Nodine-Rollingstone 4–12% slope	slight	slight	slight	moderate	moderate	northern red oak white oak shagbark hickory American basswood sugar maple	65 60 60 70 60	northern red oak, white oak, American basswood, sugar maple, eastern white pine, white ash
586D2 Nodine-Rollingstone 12–20% slope	moderate	moderate	moderate	moderate	Moderate	northern red oak white oak American basswood sugar maple	65 60 70 60	northern red oak, American basswood, sugar maple, eastern white pine, white oak, white ash
592E Lamoille 20–30% slope	moderate	moderate	moderate	moderate	Moderate	northern red oak American basswood green ash sugar maple	55 55 52 50	northern red oak, white oak, American basswood, eastern white pine
592E Elbaville 20–30% slope	moderate	moderate	slight	slight	Moderate	northern red oak white oak American basswood sugar maple black walnut	65 60 65 65 65	northern red oak, black walnut, eastern white pine, white oak, sugar maple, American basswood

- Inventory of woodland resources such as:
  - Location of timber stands (Figure 1-5, pg. 6)
  - Estimates of timber quantity, quality, size, product potential, regeneration potential, and other characteristics by species and stands. (A stand is an area of woodland [usually 2 to 40 acres] that is sufficiently uniform in its tree species composition, spacing, and size; topography; and soil conditions that it can be managed as a single unit. Management practices such as planting, thinning, and harvesting are carried out more or less uniformly across a stand.)

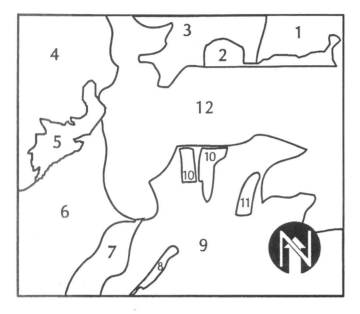

STAND NO.	DESCRIPTION
1	Red and white oak, basswood, sugar maple; 6- to 12-inch diameter; needs timber stand improvement.
2	Old field planted with red oak; 1 yr. old; let grow.
3, 9	Red and white oak; mixed sizes; needs group selection harvest and timber stand improvement.
4, 6	Red and white oak with pockets of aspen on upland; 10- to 16-inch diameter; let grow another 10 to 15 yrs., then harvest.
5	Red pine plantation; 26 yrs. old; 6- to 12-inch diameter; thinned recently; let grow.
7, 11	Red and white oak, basswood, and aspen; 5-yr.-old natural regeneration resulting from clearcut. Let grow 2 to 5 yrs. Then release oaks from competition and thin stump sprouts.
8	White pine plantation; 15 yrs. old; 4- to 8-inch diameter; let grow 5 to 10 yrs., then thin.
10	Red and white pine plantation; 20 yrs. old; 1- to 8-inch diameter; needs thinning.
12	Cropland and pasture.

Figure 1-5. A timber stand map and description.

- Site factors affecting tree growth including soil depth, texture, moisture, fertility, and chemical properties, and landscape position (such as north or south slope, ridge or valley).
- Location of trails, roads, and equipment landings.
- Water resources including perennial and intermittent streams, lakes, wetlands and seasonal ponds, seeps, and springs.
- Location of stream crossings.
- Wildlife habitat (including location and quality of food, cover, water, breeding, and nesting sites for significant wildlife species or groups of species).

More detailed descriptions of some timber inventory procedures are presented in Chapter 2: Conducting a Woodland Inventory.

Your woodland may be just one piece of a large forested landscape, but the cumulative effects of the management decisions you and other landowners make can greatly alter the forested landscape over time. Identify land uses on adjoining property and find out what plans your neighbors have for managing their land. This will help you to evaluate the potential impact of your woodland management activities on the whole forested landscape. Coordination among neighbors can produce a forested landscape that meets individual landowner objectives without adversely affecting the environment.

3. Develop Stand Objectives and Management Alternatives

An inventory shows the current condition of your woodland, but a forester can use the inventory to predict the future development of each stand by considering:

- Which tree species currently dominate the overstory (overhead canopy of trees)?
- Which species are present in the understory (trees, shrubs, and herbaceous plants beneath the overstory)?

- Considering site characteristics, which tree species show the greatest potential to dominate the site in the future? (A site is an area of woodland with relatively uniform growing conditions such as soil, moisture, and slope.)

- What undesirable tree species are currently competing for the resources on the site?

- How will the tree species that are present respond to different management practices?

- What damaging agents are present or likely to occur in the stand and how will they affect the stand in the future?

More than one management practice is usually available for each stand, but it may not be easy to reach your property goals, given the woodland resources and sites on your property. A forester will ask you to choose a management objective for each stand. Knowing your objectives will help narrow your choice of potential management practices for each stand. Such practices may include:

- Planting trees.
- Improving the timber stand (thin, weed, cull, prune).
- Harvesting timber.
- Fencing out livestock.
- Improving wildlife habitat.
- Installing erosion control structures on roads.
- Constructing access roads.
- Developing trails.
- Developing recreational facilities.
- Establishing fire protection or controlled burning.
- Controlling pests (insects, diseases, animals).
- Controlling weeds and brush.

4. Assess Management Constraints

Consider these management constraints when choosing which practices to implement:

- The amount of time you have available to do the work.
- Your experience and expertise levels.
- The availability of skilled contract labor.
- The equipment available.
- Your financial limitations.

- The availability of government financial aid.
- The potential economic return, including the tax implications (see Chapter 14: Financial Considerations).
- The presence of cultural resources and threatened, endangered, or special interest species that are regulated by state or federal law.
- The zoning laws or forest practice regulations in effect in your area.
- The prevailing attitudes of neighbors or the general public.

5. Choose Management Practices and List Them on a Schedule

Prepare an activity schedule, covering at least five to ten years, that lists management practices and the approximate dates when they should occur. If your woodland is large—perhaps several hundred acres—activities may occur every year. If it is smaller, management activities may occur less often, perhaps only once every ten years. Regardless of its size, inspect your woodland at least annually. Walk though the woodland and look for damage by pests, fire, or wind, unauthorized harvest, damaged fences, and soil erosion.

6. Keep Good Records

It will be easier to update your woodland stewardship plan and make sound decisions about the future when you keep accurate records of what you have done. Records also will be important when filing income tax returns, selling property, or settling an estate. Management records may include:

- Management plan.
- Timber inventory.
- Management activities accomplished (what, when, where).
- Sources of forestry assistance (name, address, telephone, e-mail addresses and web sites).
- Association memberships.
- Suppliers of materials and equipment.
- Contracts.
- Insurance policies.
- Forestry income and expenses.
- Deeds and easements.

Chapter 2:

Conducting a Woodland Inventory

John G. DuPlissis, Forestry Outreach Specialist, University of Wisconsin – Stevens Point
Charles R. Blinn, Extension Specialist, University of Minnesota
Bill Cook, Extension Forester and Wildlife Biologist, Michigan State University
Paul Doruska, Associate Professor, University of Wisconsin – Stevens Point
Melvin J. Baughman, Extension Forester, University of Minnesota

Good decisions require good information. An inventory of the woodland resources on your property is an important first step in developing a stewardship plan. Information gathered from the inventory provides you with a snapshot of the current condition and future potential of your woodlands.

Because woodlands are often viewed as a source of timber, a woodland inventory usually focuses on assessing trees as potential wood products. However, a woodland inventory is equally valuable for assessing wildlife habitat, planning trails for recreation, and understanding the quality of your soil and water resources. An inventory of your woodland should focus on what is most important to you and provide you with the information you need to make good decisions about the management of your land.

Your first step in conducting a woodland inventory should be to contract with a forestry professional to perform an inventory of your woodland. Since an inventory involves some time and expense, your forester must know your goals for the property and what resources are most important to you. A woodland inventory may include these and other features:

- Tree measurements:
  - Tree diameter
  - Tree height
  - Merchantable height
  - Tree defects
  - Tree volume
  - Tree grade
  - Biomass
- Stand measurements:
  - Stand volume
  - Stocking
  - Growth and yield tables
- Site quality:
  - Site index
  - Tree quality
  - Understory plant indicators

After analyzing this information, your forester will offer management alternatives for each stand. Knowing what is physically possible and financially realistic, you can select the management strategies that best meet your goals and resources.

Tree Measurements

Tree diameter, merchantable tree height, and grade can be used to determine the volume of useful wood in a tree.

Tree Diameter

Tree diameter is measured on the main stem 4.5 feet above ground on the uphill side of a tree. This is referred to as diameter at breast height (DBH). DBH usually is measured to the nearest inch using a diameter tape that is calibrated to permit direct tree diameter readings.

To measure tree diameter with a diameter tape, wrap the tape around the tree at breast height, perpendicular to the lean of the tree, standing on the uphill side of the tree (Figure 2-1). If there are branches or other protrusions at DBH, place the tape at the first unobstructed location above them. If the tree forks below DBH, consider each stem to be a separate tree and record separate measurements for each tree.

If you don't have a diameter tape, measure tree circumference by wrapping a normal tape measure around the tree at breast height, then dividing the resulting circumference in inches by 3.14 to determine DBH.

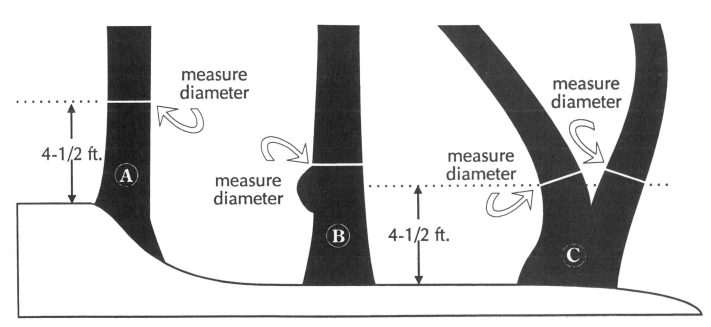

Figure 2-1. Measure stem diameter at breast height (DBH)

Tree Height

Total tree height is the distance in feet from the ground to the top of a tree. This height measurement is used mainly in conjunction with tree age to judge site quality, which is explained later in this chapter.

Merchantable tree height is the length of the main stem from the top of the expected stump to the upper limit of utilization in the tree. Stump height normally is 6 inches for softwood species and 12 inches for hardwood species, but varies depending on the volume table you use. The upper limit of utilization is where the main stem reaches a minimum usable top diameter, a main fork, or a serious defect such as a hole or a point of decay, or where excess limbs occur. Standards for merchantability vary widely depending on local product markets. The usual minimum top diameter inside the bark (DIB) is 4 inches for pulpwood, 8 inches for sawlogs, and 10 inches for veneer logs. Merchantable tree height usually is measured in 8-foot lengths called half-logs, sticks, or bolts, but may be measured to the nearest 2 feet on high-value trees. Your forester will determine a tree's height using a hypsometer, clinometer or a laser height finder (Figure 2-2). Measure the height of a leaning tree from a viewpoint where the tree is leaning to the left or the right, not from where it is leaning toward or away from you.

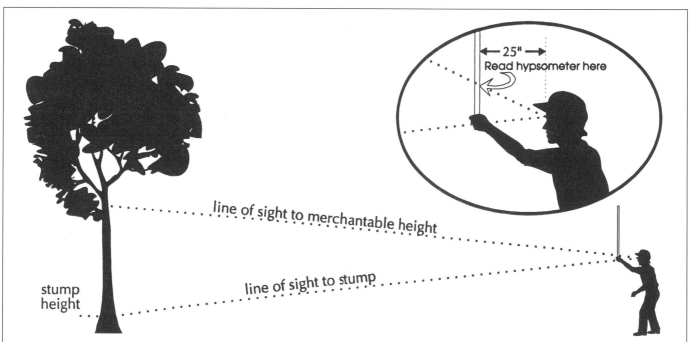

Figure 2-2. Measuring merchantable tree height with a hypsometer.

You can make a simple hypsometer by placing marks at 4-inch intervals along a stick or lath. Each mark represents one 8-foot bolt when the stick is used as follows:

1. Stand 50 feet from the tree center in a direction such that the tree does not lean toward or away from you.

2. With the stick in hand, extend your arm out 25 inches from your eye. Hold the stick vertically and in line with the stem of the tree being measured.

3. Find the upper limit of utilization. Remember that point.

4. Raise or lower the stick as needed until you can sight along the bottom of the stick to stump height. Then, moving your eyes, not your head, look up and read the stick measurement that corresponds to the upper limit of utilization point. Count the number of bolts between the stump and the merchantable height and record this number.

   If you are unable to get a good sight on the tree from a distance of 50 feet, stand 25 feet from the tree and divide the resulting height measurement by two.

Tree Defects

The main stem is the most useful part of a tree for conventional wood products such as pulpwood, posts, poles, and lumber. Defects that reduce the total volume of usable wood in the

Figure 2-3. Tree defects that reduce the total volume of usable wood.

tree include sweep, crook, cracks, decay, forks, and imbedded objects (Figure 2-3). Your forester will note the percentage of defect in each tree stem by product type. This percentage is then deducted from the overall estimate of tree volume. Because tree diameter decreases with increasing height in the tree, a defect occurring near the top of the tree will require a smaller percentage volume deduction than a similarly occurring defect near the base. Percentage deductions for tree defects are best estimated by a forester and recorded on a tally form. If the entire tree is unusable because of an excessive amount of defect, your forester will not measure it for wood products. This is a cull tree, and while not usable for wood products, it can be valuable for wildlife habitat.

Defects such as burls, bird pecks, dead limbs, insect holes, live limbs, and knots will not affect the total volume of usable wood, but they will reduce wood quality, or grade (Figure 2-4). Tree grade influences the types of products that can be made from a tree and therefore the stumpage price. Higher grade trees have fewer defects.

Tree Volume

To estimate the wood volume of a tree's stem, your forester will measure the tree diameter and merchantable height, then find the corresponding volume in a table.

Sawtimber and Veneer Trees

Trees that are large enough and of high enough quality to produce logs that can be sawed into lumber are referred to as sawtimber. To qualify as

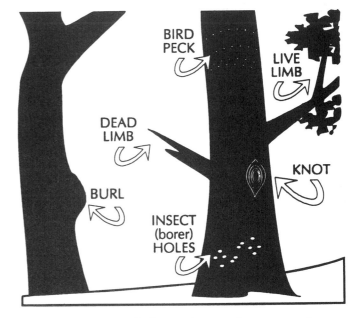

Figure 2-4. Tree defects that reduce wood quality.

sawtimber, trees should have at least one 8-foot bolt, be at least 10 inches DBH, and have a top diameter inside bark (DIB) that is the larger of either 8 inches or 50 percent of DBH. For example, to be a sawlog, a tree of 20 inches DBH should have a minimum top DIB of 10 inches. These specifications are typical, but individual buyers may have different specifications. Sawtimber trees must not contain too many defects that reduce wood volume such as decay, scars, cracks, bulges, bark distortions, holes, branch stubs, or crook.

Individual trees of many species (such as black walnut, white ash, sugar maple, red oak, white oak) that are of exceptional quality, have at least one 8-foot bolt, are at least 16 inches DBH, and contain bolts that have a top DIB of at least 10 inches often can be sold as veneer trees. Logs harvested from these trees will be sliced or peeled into thin sheets. Such trees are more valuable than sawtimber.

The basic unit for estimating wood volume for both sawtimber and veneer trees is the board foot. A board foot is a piece of wood of any shape that contains 144 cubic inches of wood (for example, 12 inches by 12 inches by 1 inch, or 6 inches by 6 inches by 4 inches). Timber value is often described in dollars per thousand board feet (MBF).

Formulas called log and tree rules have been developed to estimate the number of board feet in a tree or log. A tree rule refers to a table that estimates wood volume in a standing tree. A log rule refers to a table that estimates wood volume in a cut log. These rules differ in their assumptions about factors such as tree taper, board thickness, kerf (saw thickness), and minimum and maximum board width. They are never totally accurate, because:

- The assumptions on which they are based seldom occur.
- It is difficult to accurately measure volume losses from defects.

The Scribner rule (Table 2-1) is used most often in the Lake States.

Table 2-1. Tree volume in board feet (Scribner rule).

How to Use Table 2-1. As an example, a tree with a DBH of 22 inches and four bolts (32 feet) of merchantable height will yield about 286 board feet. If there were 10 percent defect in the tree, total tree volume would be reduced to 257 board feet. A reasonable range of volume estimates per acre is 1,000 to 15,000 board feet.

Number of 8-Foot Bolts

DBH In Inches	1	2	3	4	5	6	7	8	9	10	11	12
						Board Feet[1]						
9	14	—	—	—	—	—	—	—	—	—	—	—
10	16	34	52	65	—	—	—	—	—	—	—	—
11	—	37	58	79	100	117	—	—	—	—	—	—
12	—	42	64	89	114	139	164	181	—	—	—	—
13	—	48	71	97	129	156	185	214	244	—	—	—
14	—	—	80	109	140	177	207	240	273	306	334	—
15	—	—	90	122	156	195	233	268	305	342	380	417
16	—	—	102	136	174	215	260	299	340	382	424	466
17	—	—	118	158	201	249	301	345	393	442	490	538
18	—	—	135	180	230	285	344	395	450	505	560	615
19	—	—	153	205	262	323	490	447	510	572	635	697
20	—	—	177	230	294	364	439	503	573	644	714	784
21	—	—	—	258	329	406	490	562	641	719	797	876
22	—	—	—	286	365	451	545	625	711	799	885	973
23	—	—	—	317	404	499	602	690	786	882	978	1074
24	—	—	—	348	444	548	661	759	864	970	1075	1181
25	—	—	—	381	486	600	724	830	945	1061	1176	1292
26	—	—	—	416	531	655	789	905	1031	1157	1282	1408
27	—	—	—	452	576	711	857	983	1119	1256	1392	1529
28	—	—	—	489	624	770	928	1064	1212	1360	1507	1655
29	—	—	—	528	674	831	1002	1149	1308	1468	1626	1786
30	—	—	—	577	725	894	1078	1236	1407	1579	1750	1922

[1]Board foot volume is assumed to be the gross scale above a one-foot stump to a top DIB that is the larger of either 8 inches or 50 percent of the tree DBH. Volumes outside the tabulated range may be estimated by applying the following formula to an 8-foot bolt and then summing values to provide tree volume estimates:

Bolt volume (board feet) $= 0.395d^2 - d - 2$

Where d = small end inside bark diameter of the bolt, in inches.

Source: Burk, T. E., T. D. Droessler, and A. R. Ek. 1986. *Taper Equations for the Lake States Composite Volume Tables and Their Application.* University of Minnesota, Department of Forest Resources, St. Paul, MN 55108.

Pulpwood

Trees that are too small or too poor in quality to be sold for sawlogs are often sold for pulpwood. Ultimately, these trees are chipped or ground up to manufacture products such as paper, hardboard, and various types of structural board.

Minimum DBH for pulpwood trees is 5 inches. Minimum DIB is the larger of either 4 inches or 50 percent of tree DBH. (The minimum DIB for a pulpwood tree with a DBH of 12 inches, therefore, is 6 inches.) In the Lake States pulpwood commonly is cut to 100-inch lengths.

The basic unit for estimating pulpwood volume in trees is the cord. A standard cord is a closely stacked pile of logs containing 128 cubic feet of wood, bark, and air spaces between logs. A cord frequently is described as a stack of wood 8 feet long, 4 feet high, and 4 feet wide (Figure 2-5). The solid wood content (excluding bark and air space) of a cord varies from about 65 to 95 cubic feet depending on the diameter, roughness, and crookedness of the pieces. An accepted average value in the Lake States is 79 cubic feet of wood per cord.

Pulpwood also can be purchased by the ton. Different tree species have different wood densities. A 12-inch diameter red oak log will weigh much more than a 12-inch diameter aspen log because the oak log is much denser. For example, one cord of aspen weighs 2.4 tons, while one cord of red oak weighs 2.85 tons. Weight also varies depending on the season of the year because of the changing moisture content of logs.

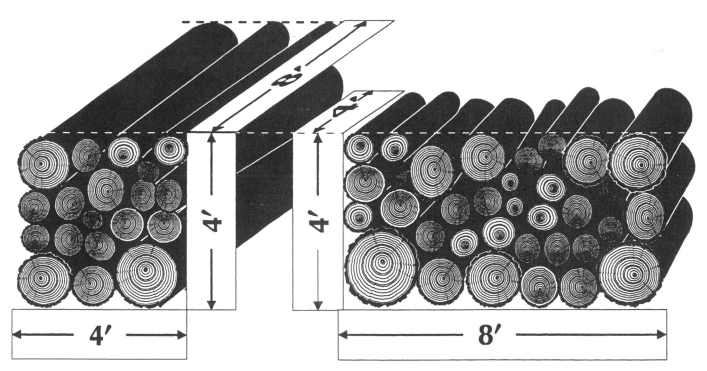

Figure 2-5. A standard cord of wood.

Table 2-2. Tree volume in cords.

How to Use Table 2-2. As an example, a tree with a DBH of 10 inches and 3 bolts (24 feet) of merchantable height will yield about 0.10 cords. If the tree contained 10 percent defect, then the tree volume would be reduced to 0.09 cords. A reasonable range of volume estimates per acre is 5 to 45 cords.

Number of 8-Foot Bolts

DBH In Inches	1	2	3	4	5	6	7	8	9	10	11	12
						Cords[1]						
5	.01	.02	.03	—	—	—	—	—	—	—	—	—
6	.02	.03	.04	.05	.06	—	—	—	—	—	—	—
7	—	.04	.05	.06	.08	.10	.11	—	—	—	—	—
8	—	.05	.06	.08	.10	.12	.14	.15	.17	—	—	—
9	—	.06	.08	.10	.12	.15	.17	.20	.22	—	—	—
10	—	.07	.10	.12	.15	.18	.21	.24	.27	.30	—	—
11	—	.09	.12	.15	.18	.22	.26	.29	.33	.37	.39	—
12	—	—	.14	.18	.22	.26	.31	.35	.39	.44	.48	—
13	—	—	.16	.21	.25	.31	.36	.41	.46	.51	.56	.61
14	—	—	.19	.24	.29	.35	.42	.47	.53	.59	.65	.71
15	—	—	.22	.27	.34	.41	.48	.54	.61	.68	.75	.82
16	—	—	.25	.31	.38	.46	.55	.62	.70	.78	.86	.93
17	—	—	.28	.35	.43	.52	.62	.70	.79	.88	.97	1.05
18	—	—	.31	.40	.49	.59	.69	.78	.88	.98	1.08	1.18
19	—	—	.35	.44	.54	.65	.77	.87	.98	1.10	1.21	1.32
20	—	—	.39	.49	.60	.72	.86	.97	1.09	1.21	1.34	1.46
21	—	—	—	.54	.66	.8	.94	1.07	1.20	1.34	1.47	1.61
22	—	—	—	.59	.73	.88	1.03	1.17	1.32	1.47	1.62	1.77
23	—	—	—	.65	.80	.96	1.13	1.28	1.44	1.61	1.77	1.93
24	—	—	—	.70	.87	1.04	1.23	1.39	1.57	1.75	1.92	2.10
25	—	—	—	.76	.94	1.13	1.34	1.51	1.70	1.90	2.09	2.28
26	—	—	—	.83	1.02	1.22	1.45	1.64	1.84	2.05	2.26	2.47
27	—	—	—	.89	1.10	1.32	1.56	1.76	1.99	2.21	2.44	2.66
28	—	—	—	.96	1.18	1.42	1.68	1.90	2.14	2.38	2.62	2.86
29	—	—	—	1.03	1.26	1.52	1.80	2.04	2.29	2.55	2.81	3.07
30	—	—	—	1.11	1.35	1.63	1.92	2.18	2.45	2.73	3.01	3.28

[1]Volume is standard unpeeled cords and includes the stem wood above a 1-foot stump to a top DIB that is the larger of either 4 inches or 50 percent of the tree DBH. Careful piling of harvested bolts is assumed, equivalent to 79 cubic feet of wood or 92 cubic feet of wood and bark per cord. Volumes outside the tabulated range may be estimated by applying the following formula to each 8-foot bolt and then summing values to provide tree volume estimates:

Bolt volume = $0.0003(d2 + D2)$

Where d = small end inside bark diameter of the bolt, in inches; D = large end inside bark diameter of the bolt, in inches.

Source: Burk, T. E., T. D. Droessler, and A. R. Ek. 1986. *Taper Equations for the Lake States Composite Volume Tables and Their Application.* University of Minnesota, Department of Forest Resources, St. Paul, MN 55108.

Woody Biomass

Woody biomass usually refers to any wood that can be used to produce energy. Buyers typically pay less for woody biomass than for veneer, sawtimber, and pulpwood; therefore, biomass usually is produced from small-diameter trees, branches, dead trees, downed logs, brush, and stumps. Woody biomass harvesting has the potential to expand forest management options by offering a market for low value trees and materials that interfere with the growth of better trees or that contribute to a fire hazard. Biomass harvesting guidelines have been or are being developed in each of the Lake States to ensure that biomass harvests help promote sustainable forest management. Biomass is commonly bought and sold on a tons-per-acre basis.

Stand Measurements

It is impossible to measure every tree in a stand, let alone an entire woodland. Each acre in a fully-stocked, mature woodland may have several hundred trees. Your forester will measure trees in sample plots and project those values to the whole stand. Sampling assumes that the measured trees represent all trees throughout the stand.

The number of sample plots needed is determined by the size of your woodland and the variability of tree species, sizes, and age classes. The number of sample plots generally will increase as the size of a property increases and as the number of the species, sizes, and age classes increases. If the trees contain highly valuable products, such as black walnut veneer, each tree containing that product may be measured. Your forester will determine the number of plots needed for management purposes in your woodland. Too many plots will waste time and money. Too few plots will yield imprecise estimates. Not every property needs a thorough inventory. If your woodland is less than 20 acres, it might be sufficient for a forester to simply walk through the woods with you to identify the different species and site characteristics, then recommend management alternatives based on the forester's experience in similar woodlands.

Sample plots should be randomly distributed across your property—not located in what appear to be "average" parts of your woodland or in those areas that are most convenient to reach. This is especially important on properties where tree size, species composition, and stand density vary.

Depending on the data to be collected, your forester may use fixed radius or variable radius plots. Fixed radius plots are circular plots that typically cover 1/10th acre (37.25 ft. radius) or 1/5th acre (52.67 ft. radius). Trees that fall within or on a fixed radius plot boundary can be included as part of the inventory. Fixed radius plots are generally used when inventorying all of the resources on your woodland property since they can be used to sample many stand attributes.

Variable radius plots are based on mathematical principles, but a simple wedge prism or angle gauge is used to determine which trees are in a plot (Figure 2-6). These gauges typically are calibrated to identify trees in 1/10th- or 1/5th-acre plots. Such gauges work best in stands where trees are pole-sized or larger.

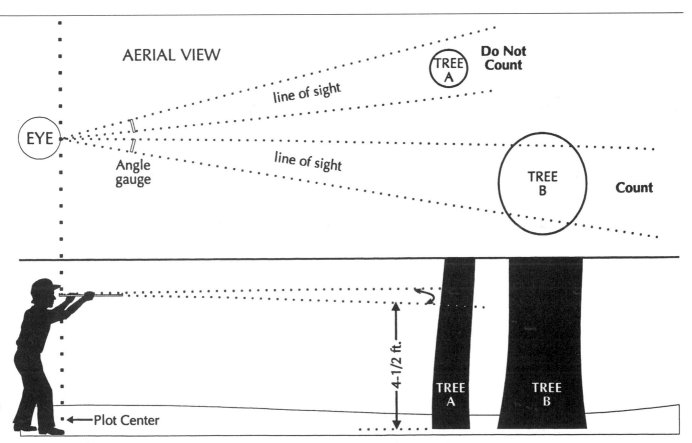

Figure 2-6. An angle gauge can be used to identify trees in a variable radius plot.

Figure 2-6 *(continued)*

A 10-factor, stick-type angle gauge consists of a rod 33 inches long with a piece of metal exactly 1-inch wide attached to one end and protruding above the stick about 1 inch. To use the angle gauge, stand in a fixed spot (plot center) with the "open end" of the stick near your eye and the 1-inch metal intercept pointed at a nearby tree. As you slowly pivot in a circle, keeping your eye over the plot center, look at each tree. Consider a tree to be within the plot if its stem at DBH (4.5 feet above ground) is wider than the 1-inch metal intercept.

Stand Density

Stand density is a measure of tree crowding. A stand may be under-stocked (too few trees), fully stocked (just the right amount of trees), or over-stocked (too many trees) for good tree growth. Stocking is a relative concept—a stand that is over-stocked for one management objective may be under-stocked for another. Knowing your stand's stocking level can help guide its management by helping you determine whether to let trees grow longer or to thin the stand now and provide more growing space around the residual crop trees. Foresters use several measures of stocking, including basal area, stocking charts, and crown cover.

Basal Area

The basal area of a tree is the cross-sectional area of its main stem in square feet measured 4.5 feet above ground. Basal area per acre is the sum of cross-sectional areas (in square feet) of all trees on an acre (Figure 2-7). The optimum basal area for a stand depends on its species composition and tree size or age. Look for basal area recommendations in Chapter 6: Managing Important Forest Types.

The wedge prism and angle gauge described in Stand Measurements (see pg. 15) can be used to measure basal area. When using a 10-factor wedge prism or angle gauge, count all the trees in the variable radius plot and multiply by 10 to determine basal area. For example, if there are 14 trees in a

plot, multiply 14 by 10 to determine that the basal area is 140 square feet per acre. Take several basal area measurements and average them to determine the average basal area for a stand.

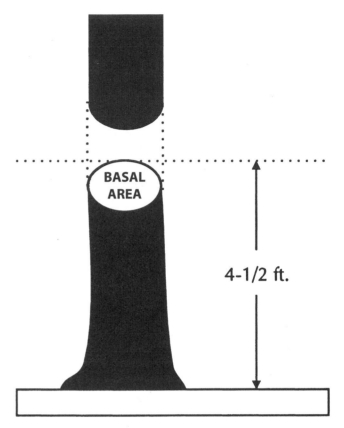

BASAL AREA

4-1/2 ft.

Figure 2-7. The basal area of a tree is its cross-sectional area in square feet measured 4.5 feet above ground.

Stocking Chart

A stocking chart uses information about a stand's basal area, trees per acre and their average diameter to recommend optimum stocking to sustain rapid tree growth. For example, Figure 2-8 (see pg. 18) is a stocking chart for red pine stands managed for maximum fiber production. Trees grow best when stocking is between the A and B curves. If a red pine stand had a basal area of 190 square feet and 350 trees per acre, those corresponding lines intersect at the A level. The closest average stand diameter is 10 inches. Follow the heavy black line for the 10-inch average stand diameter down to the B level and read the basal area and number of trees per acre at that point. We see that trees of this size

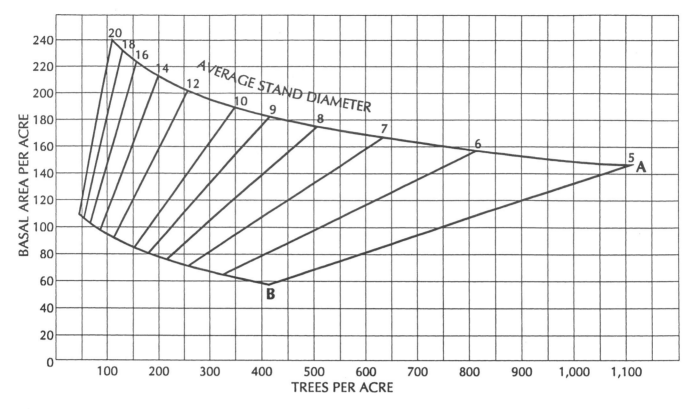

Figure 2-8. Stocking chart for red pine.

would grow faster if the stand were thinned back to approximately 85 square feet of basal area and 160 trees per acre. But a forester would point out that cutting 45 percent of the stand to reach that level is too much to cut at one time. The rule of thumb is to cut no more than 33 percent of the stand at any one time. It will take two thinnings over time to reduce this stand to a stocking level where red pines grow best. Stocking charts for selected tree species and forest types are shown in Appendix C. A forester can help you understand stocking charts and identify a target spacing for your stand.

Crown Cover

Crown cover refers to the percentage of sky area blocked by tree crowns when viewed from ground level. Some foresters use a mirror with grid lines on it to view the reflected canopy and measure crown cover, but most simply look upward at the sky from each plot center and estimate crown cover. Crown cover is used as a measure of stand density mainly when setting up a shelterwood harvest. This is a partial harvest aimed at allowing more sunlight to reach the forest floor where it can

sustain the growth of seedling trees (see Chapter 4: Regenerating Woodland Stands). For example, a shelterwood harvest may aim for a 75 percent residual crown cover after the harvest. More specific guidelines are in Chapter 6: Managing Important Forest Types for specific forest types that rely on shelterwood harvests for regeneration.

Growth and Yield Tables

Yield tables have been developed for some commercially important tree species showing the estimated volume of wood per acre that could be grown at different stand ages. Such tables usually estimate expected volumes in pure, even-aged stands on sites of different quality as measured by site index. Table 2-3 is a yield table for red pine. If you owned an even-aged red pine stand with a site index of 65, current stand age of 80 years, and basal area of 120 square feet, you could expect to have a volume of approximately 42.3 cords per acre. There also are computer programs that predict growth and yield at different stand ages based on inventory information.

Table 2-3. Volume in cords per acre[1] for even-aged red pine stands by site index, age, total tree height, and basal area.

Total Age in Years	Total Height in Feet	Basal Area Per Acre[2]					
		30	60	90	120	150	180
SITE INDEX 75		Cords Per Acre					
40	61	7.2	14.5	21.7	29.0	36.2	43.5
60	86	10.2	20.4	30.6	40.8	51.0	61.3
80	103	12.2	24.5	36.7	48.9	61.2	73.4
100	115	13.6	27.3	41.0	54.6	68.3	81.9
120	124	14.7	29.4	44.2	58.9	73.6	88.3
140	130	15.4	30.9	46.3	61.7	77.2	92.6
160	134	15.9	31.8	47.7	63.6	79.6	95.5
SITE INDEX 65							
40	53	6.3	12.6	18.9	25.2	31.5	37.8
60	74	8.8	17.6	26.4	35.1	43.9	52.7
80	89	10.6	21.1	31.7	42.3	52.8	63.4
100	100	11.9	23.7	35.6	47.5	59.4	71.2
120	107	12.7	25.4	38.1	50.8	63.5	76.2
140	112	13.3	26.6	39.9	53.2	66.5	79.8
160	116	13.8	27.5	41.3	55.1	68.9	82.6
SITE INDEX 55							
40	45	5.3	10.7	16.0	21.4	26.7	32.0
60	63	7.5	15.0	22.4	29.9	37.4	44.9
80	76	9.0	18.0	27.1	36.1	45.1	54.1
100	85	10.1	20.2	30.3	40.4	50.5	60.5
120	91	10.8	21.6	32.4	43.2	54	64.8
140	95	11.3	22.6	33.8	45.1	56.4	67.7
160	98	11.6	23.3	34.9	46.5	58.2	69.8
SITE INDEX 45							
40	37	4.4	8.8	13.2	17.6	22.0	26.4
60	51	6.1	12.1	18.2	24.2	30.3	36.3
80	62	7.4	14.7	22.1	29.4	36.8	44.2
100	69	8.2	16.4	24.6	32.8	41.0	49.2
120	74	8.8	17.6	26.4	35.1	43.9	52.7
140	78	9.3	18.5	27.8	37.0	46.3	55.6
160	80	9.5	19.0	28.5	38.0	47.5	57.0

[1]Cords = 0.003958 (BA x Height). Rough cords for trees 3.6 inches DBH and larger to a 3-inch top DIB.
[2]For trees 3.6 inches DBH and larger.
Source: Benzie, J. W. 1977. *Manager's Handbook for Red Pine in the North Central States (General Technical Report NC-33).* USDA Forest Service, North Central Forest Experiment Station, St. Paul, MN 55108. 22 pp.

Yield information can be used as a basis for financial analyses of different investment alternatives. Yield tables are not always accurate, but are helpful for comparisons. Your forester may be able to provide growth and yield information for your woodland.

Site Quality

As part of a woodland inventory, site quality should be evaluated to help predict how well important tree species will grow. The rate that a tree grows depends partly on genetic characteristics and partly on site factors, including soil fertility and texture, moisture, climate, slope, and aspect (direction a slope faces). Soil maps with interpretive information about tree growth are very useful when available, but soil maps are more commonly available for farmland, not for woodland. To judge site quality, foresters are more likely to evaluate the condition of existing trees, measure site index based on tree age and height, or identify understory plants indicating site quality.

Tree Quality

Experienced foresters know what a good quality tree of a particular species should look like on a good site. Mature trees on good sites tend to be taller, have straighter stems, fewer limbs on main stems, and long merchantable stem heights, compared to trees of the same species on poor sites. When a majority of mature trees on a site exhibit desirable characteristics, a forester would judge that site to be good quality.

The difficulty in judging site quality by the condition of existing trees is that a stand with poor quality trees may not indicate a poor site. Trees may be poor because the best quality trees were harvested through repeated cuts (high-grading), leaving trees that were genetically inferior or damaged. A stand may have been lightly stocked at one time and pastured. Open grown trees develop short stems with large crowns, but their poor quality appearance may be due to low stocking density, not to site quality. Previous wind or ice damage also may have damaged crowns of trees throughout a stand, leaving trees in poor condition.

Site Index

Foresters often judge site quality based on the total height that dominant and co-dominant trees will grow in a given time—usually 50 years in the Lake States. Trees are expected to grow taller on good sites than on poor ones in the same time period. This measure of site quality is called site index. Site index curves have been constructed for many tree species so that site quality may be determined for a stand of trees larger than saplings if average tree age and average total tree height are known.

Tree Age

Determine age on dominant or co-dominant trees (Figure 2-9) of a species that is to be favored by management and is common on the property.

If trees were planted in your woodland, look for records showing the year of planting to determine tree age. If some plantation trees were recently harvested, count the annual growth rings on a stump or log (Figure 2-10).

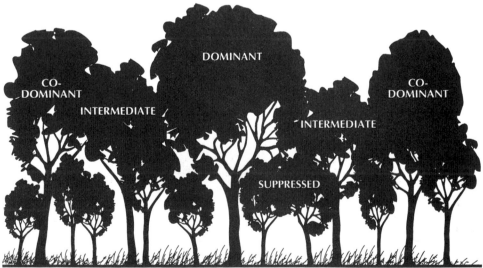

Figure 2-9. Tree dominance. The dominance of a tree refers to the position of its crown relative to other trees in the canopy. Dominant trees have relatively large crowns and are taller than most other trees in the stand. Co-dominant trees make up the general canopy level. Intermediate trees are slightly lower than the general canopy and have relatively small crowns. Suppressed trees are below the general canopy level.

Figure 2-10. A tree grows a new ring of wood each year.

To measure the age of a living tree without cutting it down to count rings, you can take a core sample at 4.5 feet above the ground using an increment borer (Figure 2-11). An increment borer is similar to a hand drill, but has a hollow drill bit. It extracts a core of wood about the size and shape of a pencil. This core shows annual growth rings as bands of light and dark wood. By counting the rings in the core and adding the number of years it took the tree to grow to a height of 4.5 feet, your forester can determine tree age.

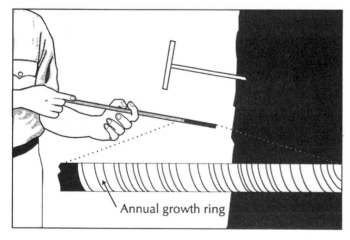

Figure 2-11. Tree core sample removed by an increment borer.

The age of conifers such as red (Norway) pine, white pine, and balsam fir that produce one whorl of new branches each year can be estimated by

counting whorls (Figure 2-12). This approach works best when the trees are young (<25 years) because it is easier to see each whorl. False whorls can develop if more than one spurt of growth occurs in a year.

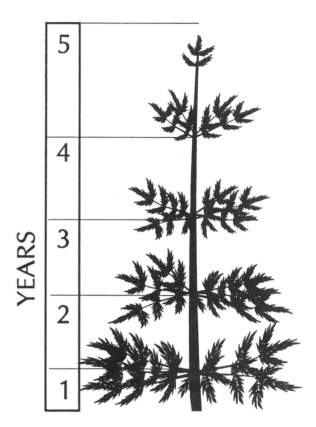

Figure 2-12. Count the whorls of branches to determine the age of a conifer.

Site Index Curves

If you know the average tree age and total tree height of a tree species of primary interest, refer to a set of site index curves for that species to determine site quality. Site index curves for red pine are shown in Figure 2-13. These curves were developed for use in pure, even-aged stands of red pine. A pure stand is one in which at least 80 percent of the trees are of the same species. An even-aged stand is one where the age difference between the youngest and oldest tree in a stand does not exceed 20 percent of the projected rotation length. A rotation is the number of years required to establish and grow trees to a specified size, product, or condition of maturity at which they can be harvested.

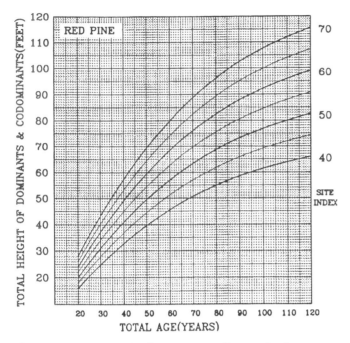

Figure 2-13. Site index curves for red pine plantations.

For example, if you measured several dominant and co-dominant red pines and determined their average age was 80 years and average total tree height was 90 feet, find 80 years on the bottom axis in Figure 2-13 above, then follow the vertical line upward from that point until it intersects the 90-foot level on the left vertical axis. Now follow the site index curve from the junction of those two lines to the right vertical axis, where you will find that the site index is 65. These trees would be expected to be 65 feet tall at age 50. The higher the site index, the better the site. Site index curves for common tree species are shown in Appendix B. Site index curves are reasonably accurate measures of site quality for stands older than 20 years. For younger stands, special equations are used to estimate site index.

Understory Plants as Site Indicators

Foresters increasingly use associations of understory plants to indicate site quality for particular tree species. Some understory plants grow on a wide range of sites, but those with more specific site requirements (for example, in moisture and

nutrients) are used for site classification. Understory plants tend to persist on sites regardless of past timber management, and the presence of a particular combination of understory species can indicate how well particular tree species will grow, even if those tree species are not currently found on a site. For example, if a combination of understory plants in north-central Wisconsin indicates a very dry to dry, nutrient poor site, a forester knows that site is best suited for growing jack pine, red pine, white pine, oaks, and red maple. Tree growth may not be particularly good on this poor site, but these tree species are the best adapted to it. Site type classifications have been developed for the Lake States, but their descriptions are beyond the scope of this book.

References

A list of online soil surveys by county is available at: http://websoilsurvey.nrcs.usda.gov/app/

A paper copy of an aerial photo can be obtained through your local Natural Resources Conservation Service office. You can find the office for the county you live in or where your property is located at http://offices.sc.egov.usda.gov/locator/app

Blink, C. R. and T. E. Burk. 1986. *Sampling and Measuring Timber in the Private Woodland* (NR-FO-3025). University of Minnesota Extension, St. Paul, MN 55108. 8 pp. Available online at: http://www.extension.umn.edu/distribution/naturalresources/DD3025.html

Carmean, W. H., J. T. Hahn, and R. D. Jacobs. 1989. *Site Index Curves for Forest Tree Species in the Eastern United States* (General Technical Report NC-128). USDA Forest Service, North Central Forest Experiment Station, St. Paul, MN 55108. 142 pp. Available online at: http://www.treesearch.fs.fed.us/pubs/10192

Martin, A. J. 1989. *What Is a Board Foot?* Department of Forest Ecology and Management, University of Wisconsin, Madison, WI. Forestry Facts No. 42. 2 p. Available online at: http://forest.wisc.edu/extension/Publications/42.pdf

Martin, A. J. 1989. *What Is Basal Area?* Department of Forest Ecology and Management, University of Wisconsin, Madison, WI. Forestry Facts No. 43. 2 p. Available online at: http://forest.wisc.edu/extension/Publications/43.pdf

Martin, A. J. 1989. *What Is a Cord?* Department of Forest Ecology and Management, University of Wisconsin, Madison, WI. Forestry Facts No. 44. 2 p. Available online at: http://forest.wisc.edu/extension/Publications/44.pdf

Native Plant Community Classification. Minnesota Department of Natural Resources. Available online at: http://www.dnr.state.mn.us/npc/classification.html

Making and Using Measurement Tools - Basal Area. 1998. University of Minnesota Extension. St. Paul, MN. Forest Management Practices Fact Sheet Managing Water Series # 12 FS-06981. Available online at: http://www.extension.umn.edu/distribution/naturalresources/DD6981.html

Table 2-4. Sample tally form for recording number of pulpwood trees by DBH and number of eight-foot bolts per tree.

Tract location _____   Tract name _____

Date _____   Species _____   Plot number _____

DBH (inches)	Number of eight-foot bolts							
	1	2	3	4	5	6	7	Totals
5								
6								
7								
8								
9								
10								
Totals								

The dot-dash tally method is a convenient way to record timber cruise data. Each dot or dash represents one tally tree with a specified DBH and merchantable height according to the following convention:

Table 2-5. Sample tally form for recording number of sawtimber trees by DBH and number of eight-foot bolts per tree.

Tract location (section, range, township) _____ Tract name _____

Date _____ Species _____ Plot number _____

DBH (inches)	Number of eight-foot bolts							
	1	2	3	4	5	6	7	Totals
10								
11								
12								
13								
14								
15								
Totals								

The dot-dash tally method is a convenient way to record timber cruise data. Each dot or dash represents one tally tree with a specified DBH and merchantable height according to the following convention:

Chapter 3:

How Trees and Woodlands Grow

Melvin J. Baughman, Extension Forester, University of Minnesota

To manage your woodland, it is helpful to know how individual trees grow and what factors influence the growth of the whole woodland.

Your woodland is more than a collection of trees. It is part of an ecosystem with trees, shrubs, herbaceous plants, insects, and animals that interact with each other and with the soil, water, and climate. Trying to change one part of this ecosystem will affect the other parts. Your woodland is ever changing due to many influences.

How Trees Grow

To survive and grow, trees need adequate amounts of carbon dioxide, water, sunlight, and nutrients. Factors that influence the availability or use of these elements include tree characteristics, site characteristics, and climate.

Parts of a Tree

Trees are composed mainly of carbon, but to ensure healthy growth, trees also need oxygen, hydrogen, nitrogen, potassium, calcium, magnesium, phosphorus, sulfur, and trace amounts of several other elements. In general, carbon dioxide and sunlight are absorbed by the leaves, water is absorbed by the roots, and nutrients are absorbed mostly by the roots but also by the leaves. Leaves are the food factories in a tree. They contain a green substance called chlorophyll that enables the sun's energy to convert carbon dioxide and water into sugar. Trees use sugar as a basic ingredient in all plant parts.

Tree growth occurs from buds on the ends of branches, from the tips of tiny roots, and in the cambium—a thin layer of cells beneath the bark that covers the whole tree. (Figure 3-1)

Cambium cells produce both inner bark and sapwood. Inner bark or phloem is spongy tissue that transports food from the leaves to other parts of the tree. Phloem cells live for a relatively short time, then die and become part of the outer bark, which insulates the tree from weather extremes and serves as a barrier against insects and disease. Sapwood or xylem is the pipeline that transports water from the roots up to the leaves. A new layer (ring) of sapwood grows each year. Light-colored bands of sapwood are called springwood—thin-walled cells that grow early in the year. Dark-colored bands of sapwood are summerwood—thick-walled cells produced in the summer when tree growth has slowed. Sapwood cells live for several years, then lose their vitality, die, turn a darker color, and become known as heartwood. Heartwood provides substantial physical support for the tree.

Effects of Tree Characteristics

A tree's genetics, crown size, and ability to tolerate shade and competition from other plants influence how well it will grow in different environments.

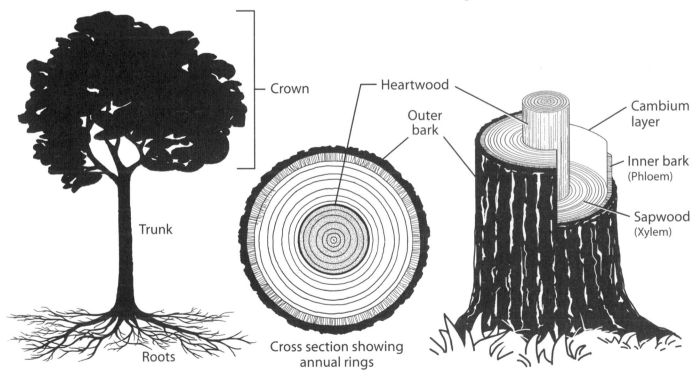

Figure 3-1. Parts of a tree.

Genetics affects many aspects of tree form and growth, including the rate of height and diameter growth, stem form, crown form, any tendency to self-prune, the angle of branch attachment, and tolerance to insects and diseases. You must decide which of these traits is important in helping you achieve your objectives for your woodland. For example, when relying on natural reproduction, kill or harvest undesirable trees during intermediate and final harvests. Permit only desirable trees to produce seed, stump sprouts, or root suckers. When growing trees for timber, poor-quality trees may be an acceptable seed source if their rough appearance is a result of stand conditions or damage not related to genetic characteristics. When planting seeds, seedlings, or cuttings, use planting materials from a reputable tree nursery that collects seed or cuttings from high quality trees growing as close to your planting site as possible. Depending on your needs, the seed source also may exhibit one or more of the form and growth characteristics listed above.

Trees with large crowns have more leaves and, therefore, normally grow faster in height and stem diameter than trees with small crowns. The live-crown ratio of a tree is the percentage of total tree height that has live branches on it (Figure 3-2).

For timber production purposes a live-crown ratio of approximately one-third often is optimum, but the optimum percentage varies by species. If the crown is too small, the tree will grow slowly. If a crown is too large, there will be too much wood in the limbs and too little in the more usable main stem.

Tree species differ in their tolerance for shade and competition (Table 3-1). Trees often are classified as very tolerant, tolerant, intermediate, intolerant, and very intolerant to shade. Some species tolerate more shade as seedlings than as larger trees. Species that are very tolerant will reproduce and grow in deep shade beneath a dense canopy. Species that are very intolerant will survive only if their seeds sprout in wide openings that receive direct sunlight. The size of canopy openings, ranging from the loss of a single tree to removal of many acres, greatly influences which tree species will reproduce and survive. You must know the shade tolerance of a species to determine the light conditions necessary for reproducing it. Tree species that regenerate in openings may be different from species forming the original canopy, thus changing the species composition over time according to the size of canopy openings created.

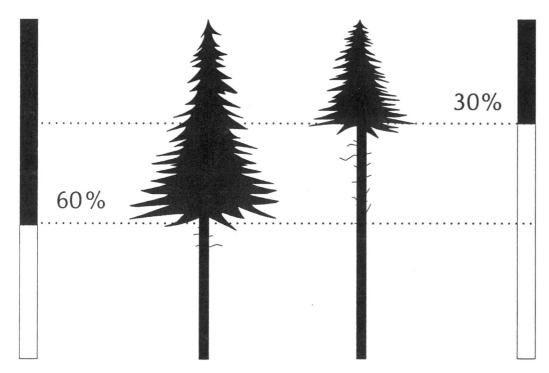

60%

30%

Figure 3-2. Live-crown ratio of a tree.

Table 3-1. Tree species by shade tolerance classification.[1]

Very Intolerant	Intolerant	Intermediate	Tolerant	Very Tolerant
Black Spruce	Black Cherry	Balsam Poplar	Balsam Fir	Beech
Black Willow	Black Walnut	Bitternut Hickory	Basswood	Eastern Hemlock
Eastern Cottonwood	Paper Birch	Black Ash	Bigtooth Aspen	Sugar Maple
Jack Pine	Red Maple	Bur Oak	Black Ash	
Quaking Aspen	Red Pine	Green Ash	Green Ash	
Tamarack	Silver Maple	Hackberry	Hackberry	
		Red Maple	Northern White-Cedar	
		Red Oak	White Ash	
		Shagbark Hickory	White Spruce	
		White Ash		
		White Oak		
		White Pine		
		Yellow Birch		

[1] Note: Some species occur in two columns because of their wide tolerance range.
Source: U.S. Department of Agriculture, Forest Service. 1990. *Silvics of North America, Volume 1 and 2* (Agricultural Handbook No. 654). U.S. Government Printing Office, Washington, DC 20402. http://www.na.fs.fed.us/Spfo/pubs/silvics_manual/table_of_contents.htm

Effects of Site Characteristics

Site characteristics that affect tree growth include soil depth, texture, moisture, fertility, pH, and topography.

Soil Depth, Texture, Moisture, Fertility, and pH

On the whole, deep soils are better for tree growth than shallow soils because they potentially have a greater nutrient supply and water-holding capacity. Rooting depth may be restricted by bedrock, coarse gravel, a hardpan layer, or excess soil moisture. Tree roots that absorb the most nutrients and water usually are found in the top two feet of the soil profile.

Soil particles are classified by size as sand (<0.002mm diameter), silt (0.002mm to 0.05mm), and clay (0.05mm to 2.0mm).

Soil texture refers to the relative proportions of sand, silt, and clay in a mass of soil. Soils with a high percentage of sand have large pore spaces between soil particles. Since they absorb and drain water quickly, they are droughty unless there is a shallow water table. Clay soils have a large water-holding capacity, but they absorb water slowly and water adheres so tightly to the soil particles that much of it is unavailable for plant use. Soils with a high percentage of silt have the most favorable texture for moisture absorption and drainage.

Soil fertility is based largely on the type of parent material from which the soil originated. Some of the most fertile soils originated from limestone, shale, and windblown deposits, whereas some of the least fertile soils originated from sandstone and granite. On the whole, fine-textured (clay) and medium-textured (silt) soils have a greater nutrient supply than coarse-textured (sandy) soils.

Most tree species grow well when the soil remains moist much of the year, but only a few species tolerate very dry or very wet conditions for long periods. Soil may be too dry for good tree growth where the soil is sandy, rocky, or shallow. Soil may be too wet where the soil is clay and the area has high rainfall or groundwater close to the surface. Soil pH is a measure of its acidity or alkalinity. Soil pH affects absorption of minerals by plant roots. A pH of 7 is neutral, neither acid nor alkaline. A pH below 7 is acidic; above 7 is alkaline. Most tree species grow best in a slightly acid soil, but the preferred pH varies by species.

Definitions of Basic Soil Texture Classes

Sand is loose and single-grained. Individual grains can readily be seen or felt. If you squeeze a handful of dry sand, it will fall apart when you release the pressure. If you squeeze a moist handful, it will form a clump that will crumble when touched.

Sandy loam contains a great deal of sand, but also has enough silt and clay to make it stick together when wet. Individual sand grains can readily be seen and felt. Squeezing a dry handful of sandy loam will form a clump that readily falls apart. If you squeeze a moist handful, a clump will form that will bear careful handling without breaking.

Loam has a relatively even mixture of different grades of sand, silt, and clay. It has a somewhat gritty feel, yet is fairly smooth and slightly plastic. If you squeeze a dry handful, it will form a clump that will bear careful handling. A clump formed by squeezing moist soil can be handled quite freely without breaking it.

Silt loam has a moderate amount of fine grades of sand and only a small amount of clay. More than half of the particles are silt. When dry, silt loam may appear lumpy, but the lumps can be readily broken, and when pulverized it feels soft and floury. When wet, the soil readily runs together and puddles. Whether dry or moist it will form clumps that can be freely handled without breaking, but when moistened and squeezed between thumb and finger to form a ribbon, it will break apart.

Clay loam is a fine-textured soil that usually breaks into hard lumps when dry. When moist clay loam is pinched between a thumb and finger, it will form a thin ribbon that will break readily, barely sustaining its own weight. Moist clay loam soil is plastic and will form a clump that will bear much handling. When kneaded in the hand, it does not crumble readily, but works into a compact mass.

Clay is a fine-textured soil that usually forms very hard lumps when dry and is quite plastic and usually sticky when wet.

Topography

Topography affects tree growth largely because of its influence on soil depth, moisture availability, and sunlight exposure.

Because gravity pulls soil particles and water downhill, soil depth, nutrient supply, and water supply usually are greater on lowlands, hillside benches, and coves than on steep hills. For similar reasons concave slopes are better for tree growth than convex slopes.

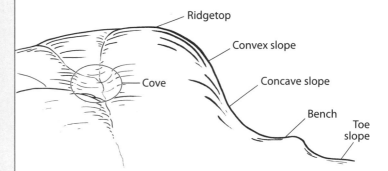

Figure 3-3. Landscape position

Aspect is the compass direction a slope faces when you are standing on it looking downhill. Aspect influences the intensity of sunlight reaching the ground, which in turn affects the moisture evaporation rate. Slopes that face north and east tend to be cooler and moister than slopes facing south and west. In the northern hemisphere the sun's rays shine more directly on south slopes, warming and evaporating moisture from them. West slopes are drier than east slopes because the sun shines on west slopes during the hottest part of the day, increasing water use by trees and evaporation from the soil. These effects become exaggerated as the slope becomes steeper or the hills become higher.

Effects of Climate

Trees are genetically programmed to grow within certain climatic conditions. The length of the frost-free growing season, temperature extremes, precipitation amounts, and the duration of droughts are a few elements of climate that influence tree growth. A single tree species also varies in its climatic requirements across its natural range. For example, quaking aspen naturally occurs from northern Alaska to northern Illinois, but a quaking aspen transplanted from Illinois will not flourish in Alaska.

Native trees have evolved and adapted to a specific climate. When tree seeds or seedlings in the Northern Hemisphere are moved a short distance northward for planting, they may grow faster than local trees because they are genetically programmed to begin growth earlier in the spring and to extend their growth longer in the fall. But when trees are moved too far north, they often cannot survive the winters, are damaged by late spring or early fall frosts, or find the growing season too short to consistently produce viable seed. Trees growing on the northern limits of their natural range usually should not be moved more than 50 miles north.

When planting stock is moved southward in the Northern Hemisphere, it often grows more slowly than native trees because such introduced trees are genetically programmed to begin growth later in the spring and end growth sooner in the fall. They also may not tolerate the higher temperatures and greater water demands of a warmer climate.

Plant hardiness zone maps have been created to show where tree species typically can be grown in North America based on the average annual minimum temperature. Search online to find a plant hardiness zone map. Zone boundaries have changed in recent years because of climate changes. Trees and tree seeds usually should not be moved from one zone to another. Plant hardiness zones should not be your only criteria for tree selection since they do not take into account other climatic factors affecting tree survival, such as summer temperatures, precipitation, number of frost-free growing days, humidity, and snow cover.

In the Lake States much of our winter snowfall runs off in the spring, summer rainfall is not evenly distributed over the growing season, and prolonged summer droughts occur periodically. Our native trees have adapted to this precipitation pattern. Where the prairie meets the forest, evaporation may exceed precipitation, greatly reducing tree survival. Some tree species will grow in droughty prairie regions, but may need supplemental watering, mulching, or weed control, especially when young.

Trees also influence the climate on a global scale. Since individual trees are composed mainly of carbon, woodlands are great reservoirs of carbon, a greenhouse gas. Carbon storage is becoming a recognized value for woodlands to help offset the impact of burning coal, oil, and natural gas, which releases carbon into the atmosphere, leading to global warming. Trees remove carbon from the atmosphere and store it in their woody tissues.

How Woodlands Grow

A tree seed germinates, a seedling emerges, it is browsed by a deer, it grows to a sapling, a bird nests in its branches. When it is a pole-sized tree, wind breaks a branch. When mature, it is felled by a logger. In the vacant space left behind, a seed germinates, but it's of a different tree species than the felled tree, and the forest changes.

This process of change, in which a collection of tree species is slowly replaced by a different collection of tree species is called succession. Forestry is the art and science of manipulating a woodland to achieve your personal goals. Forestry can speed up or slow down natural succession. Your management may affect the characteristics of your woodland for a century or much longer, so it is wise to consider the long-term impacts of your decisions. Doing nothing may not yield the outcome you want to see. Future owners and others who depend on your resources will live with the consequences of your management practices.

The basic unit of management is a stand. It is common practice for a forester to develop a set of management practices for each stand based on the owner's objectives. Woodland owners often have different objectives for different stands because their growth potential may be different.

▲ ————————————————————————————————

The growth potential of a stand is partly affected by the mix of tree species growing on it, but in the long term, growth potential is governed by the underlying site characteristics: soil, moisture, topography, and climate. Each stand in a woodland has an ecological trajectory, a natural pathway for change, that is heavily influenced by site characteristics. This pathway can be altered and the species composition of a stand changed via natural disaster (such as a fire or windstorm) or human activities (such as harvesting, thinning, or introducing invasive exotic species). To simplify management and reduce costs, you ordinarily should encourage growth of tree species that are naturally adapted to the site characteristics.

To further understand the concept of an ecological trajectory, let's assume you are walking through a 40-acre stand of quaking aspen and paper birch that is about 20 years old. The forester with you notices that part of this stand is on an upland with loamy-sand soil. He points to understory plants that indicate a moderately dry growing site. Besides the tall aspen, there are quite a few shorter red and white oaks, red maple, sugar maple, white ash and basswood. If nature takes its course and no natural disaster or human interference occurs while the hardwoods are maturing, this aspen stand will eventually succeed to a northern hardwood stand in which aspen is a minor component. But if a fire sweeps through the stand or it is clearcut when the aspen are mature, then hardwoods will be suppressed and aspen will continue to dominate the stand.

Another portion of the aspen stand you are exploring is on a lowland with silty clay-loam soil with a high percentage of humus (decaying organic matter). The forester points to shrubs and understory plants that indicate the site is moist to wet during much of the growing season. Beneath the canopy of aspen, balsam fir and white spruce are growing in abundance. In the absence of a natural disaster or clearcut, the ecological trajectory for this stand is toward a spruce-fir stand with a minor component of aspen. If a fire swept through this stand or it were clearcut when the aspen were mature, then aspen would quickly regenerate and the balsam fir and white spruce would again be suppressed.

Do not assume that the tree species currently growing on a site are those best adapted for long-term production. Ask a forester to evaluate the whole plant community (trees, shrubs, and understory plants) as well as soil, moisture, topography, and climate, then recommend which tree species will grow best on the site. Change stand boundaries as needed to encompass sites with relatively uniform growing conditions.

From the above discussion, you probably also realize that if no human management intervenes in a woodland, natural forces still cause change. Each tree species has a natural life span that may be shortened on a poor site or lengthened on a good site. Competition for nutrients, moisture, and sunlight leads to the death of individual trees. Fire, wind, insects, and disease can weaken and eventually kill trees.

Chapter 4:

Regenerating Woodland Stands

Melvin J. Baughman, Extension Forester, University of Minnesota
Eli Sagor, Extension Educator, University of Minnesota
John G. DuPlissis, Forestry Outreach Specialist, University of Wisconsin – Stevens Point

There are many reasons to harvest and regenerate a woodland stand:

- The trees are mature.
- There is low potential for future value growth.
- To improve wildlife habitat.
- To salvage and renew the stand after a severe windstorm, insect outbreak, fire, or other natural disturbance.

Choosing the right harvest and regeneration method, however, requires an intimate knowledge of the ecological processes underlying woodland stand development, as well as site conditions, stand size, timber value, current and desired tree species on the stand, landowner objectives, and other factors.

Most natural stands are composed of many tree species at various stages of growth. Woodlands constantly change as trees grow and die, moisture conditions vary, natural disturbances occur, people plant and cut trees, and so forth. Variations in stand age and origin, soil type, aspect, disturbance history, and species make every stand unique.

The various harvest and regeneration methods are not a discrete set of choices, but a spectrum of alternatives. At one end of the spectrum is the removal of all woody vegetation, leading to dramatic changes in soil temperature, moisture, and light conditions. These post-harvest conditions favor fast-growing species that need full sunlight such as aspen, jack pine, and red pine. At the other end of the spectrum is removal of single trees at scattered locations throughout the stand. This kind of harvest creates small canopy gaps favoring regeneration of shade-tolerant species such as sugar maple, balsam fir, and hemlock (where it exists). Between the two ends of the spectrum lies an infinite variety of treatments that vary by the number of trees harvested and how they are distributed around the stand.

Woodlands can be regenerated by natural or artificial means.

Natural Regeneration

Trees reproduce naturally from seed, root suckers, stump sprouts, or layering (Figure 4-1).

Seed

All tree species can reproduce from seed, but only a very small percentage of seeds will become established seedlings. Success depends on:

- The supply of viable seed.
- Effective seed dispersal.
- Seedbed condition.
- Weather.
- Competition from other plants.
- Damage from insects and diseases.
- Predation by animals.

The amount of seed available depends on tree species, age, health, and weather. Tree species with very large seeds (such as oak, walnut, and hickory) produce relatively few seeds, while species with small seeds (such as aspen and cottonwood) produce abundant seed. Very young and very old trees produce few viable seeds. Healthy trees with large crowns produce more seeds than trees that are unhealthy, have small crowns, or are suppressed by taller trees. Seeds from some tree species remain viable for only a few days after dispersal while seeds from other species may survive for several years on the tree or on the forest floor. The frequency of good seed crops depends on the tree species, overall tree health, and weather during pollination and seed growth. If your regeneration strategy relies on tree seeds to regenerate the new stand, time your harvest and regeneration treatments to coincide with a good seed year.

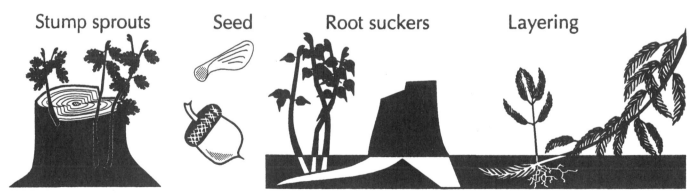

Figure 4-1. Natural regeneration methods.

Tree seeds are dispersed in a variety of ways. For example, aspen and cottonwood seeds are covered with cotton-like down and may be carried several miles by wind. Maple and pine seeds have wings allowing them to glide in the wind. Cherry seeds frequently are dispersed by birds that eat the cherries and drop the seeds far from parent trees. Walnuts, acorns, and pinecones are carried away and buried by squirrels. Seeds from willows and other shoreline species may be dispersed by water.

Each tree species requires certain seedbed conditions for seedling survival. For many species seed must be in contact with mineral soil so the seed can absorb enough moisture to germinate and grow. Seeds from other species may germinate on leaf litter, rotten logs, or moss, but if those materials dry out, the seedlings will die.

Soil temperature must be high enough so seeds will germinate, but not so high that the seedlings will be killed. Annual weather conditions and the amount of sunlight versus shade will affect soil temperature. Shade may be produced by living plants or harvest debris.

Competition from other vegetation may greatly affect seedling survival. Trees, shrubs, and herbaceous plants may rob delicate tree seedlings of needed sunlight and moisture.

Insects and animals consume large amounts of tree seeds and may eat most of the supply in poor seed years. Damping-off disease kills emerging seedlings too, but its effect varies greatly among tree species.

When you want to regenerate a stand by natural seeding, you will need to know how the species you wish to encourage disperses seed, how far its seed travels, how abundantly it produces seed, and what type of seedbed it needs for germination and seedling survival. This information will affect how you harvest and prepare the site. Chapter 6: Managing Important Forest Types provides basic regeneration information for important tree species.

Root Suckers

Some hardwoods (such as aspen and black locust) can regenerate from root suckers, usually after the parent tree has been cut down. Root suckers grow from live roots, not from exposed stumps. Trees that grow from root suckers are genetically identical clones of the parent tree. A single parent tree may produce several hundred suckers, creating a dense new stand (Figure 4-2). The number of suckers may be reduced if there is too much shade on the forest floor from residual trees left after a harvest; the parent tree is particularly large, old, or in poor health; or timber harvesting damages the root system by cutting or soil compaction.

Figure 4-2. Stand of aspen suckers.

Stump Sprouts

Oak, basswood, birch, maple, and some other hardwoods sprout from stumps. Like root suckers, stump sprouts are genetically identical to the parent tree. The difference is that stump sprouts grow from exposed stumps, not roots. The most vigorous sprouts arise from relatively young stumps cut close to the ground in late fall or winter when there are food reserves stored in the roots. Stumps often send up numerous sprouts, but these usually thin naturally to two or three main stems. You can speed up this process and encourage the strongest stump sprouts by cutting excess sprouts when the sprouts are five to ten years old (12 to 20 feet tall).

Layering

Layering occurs when a buried branch on a living tree takes root and develops into a new tree. The lower limbs of black spruce, balsam fir, and northern white-cedar sometimes touch the ground and become covered with organic matter. Roots develop on those buried branches. Layering is not usually an important reproduction method in forests, but may provide additional northern white-cedar for deer browse.

Artificial Regeneration

Artificial regeneration refers to the planting of seeds, seedlings, or cuttings. Artificial regeneration usually is more expensive than natural regeneration, but permits better control over species selection, genetic characteristics, and tree spacing.

Direct Seeding

Direct seeding is the process of sowing or planting seeds. It often is used to establish jack pine and black spruce, as well as some hardwoods, including black walnut. Direct seeding of black spruce is preferred to planting seedlings on sites with poor access, such as spruce bogs. The appropriate site preparation, moisture, and temperature requirements vary by species and are similar to those necessary for natural seeding. Often the seed is chemically treated to protect it from diseases, rodents, and birds.

Seedlings

Planting seedlings, either bare-root or container-grown stock, is the most reliable way to regenerate a stand, especially for conifers. Bare-root seedlings are dug from the nursery bed and shaken to remove most of the dirt around their roots. They frequently are designated as 1-0, 2-0 or 2-1 stock, with the first number referring to how many years they were grown in the original nursery seedbed and the second to how many years they were grown after being transplanted to another nursery bed. Transplants generally have a more fibrous root system and larger stem diameter than seedlings that are not transplanted. Transplants are recommended for regenerating slow-growing conifer species such as spruce and fir, and for harsh planting sites where survival is likely to be a problem.

Seedling costs vary depending on tree age, grade, species, and quantity ordered. Transplants survive very well, but are expensive and, therefore, are not widely used. One- or two-year-old seedlings are less expensive than transplants and are recommended for most hardwood and conifer plantings. Tree seedlings sometimes are graded and sold by height class, stem diameter, or root condition.

Container-grown seedlings usually are grown in a greenhouse in 1- to 2-inch diameter containers. Some biodegradable containers may be planted in the ground with the seedling in them. Other seedlings must be removed from the container before they are planted. Container-grown stock can be very useful for dry planting sites or for late season planting.

Cuttings

Cuttings are exact genetic replicas of the parent tree. They commonly are used to regenerate poplars, but also can be used to regenerate willow and green ash. Cuttings are usually 8- to 12-inch lengths of tree stems about 1/4- to 3/4-inch in diameter (longer cuttings may be used on drier sites). They are cut during the late winter from the previous year's growth of vigorous seedlings or stump sprouts. Cuttings usually have no visible roots, but when buried vertically with just an inch of the stem protruding above ground, they will form roots. Rooted cuttings also may be available for purchase. Cuttings grow best where the soil remains moist throughout the growing season.

Tree Spacing

When designing a plantation, you need to determine an appropriate spacing between mature trees. Consider the typical crown width of a tree species when individual trees reach a useful size. For example, when growing trees for timber, you'll need to allocate enough space so the individual trees will be just beginning to crowd each other when they are large enough to support a commercial thinning. A forester can help you determine the correct spacing depending on the species and purpose for the plantation.

Table 4-1 shows the number of trees needed per acre for various spacings. To calculate the number of trees per acre for other spacings, multiply the planned spacing (in feet) within rows by the spacing (in feet) between rows and divide that number into 43,560 (the number of square feet in an acre). For example, a plantation with trees 8 feet apart within rows and 10 feet apart between rows would require 545 trees per acre:

$$\frac{43,560}{8 \times 10} = 545 \text{ TREES PER ACRE}$$

Table 4-1. Number of trees per acre at different spacings.

SPACING (IN FEET)	TREES PER ACRE
4 x 4	2,722
5 x 5	1,742
6 x 6	1,210
7 x 7	890
8 x 8	680
9 x 9	538
10 x 10	436
11 x 11	368
12 x 12	303

Site Preparation

Site preparation often is necessary to create a good environment for natural or artificial regeneration. Its purpose may be to expose mineral soil for natural or artificial seeding or to reduce competition from undesirable vegetation or both. Site preparation may best be done before a stand is harvested (especially for hardwoods) if it is likely that large amounts of woody debris will remain after the harvest. Such debris would make it hard for site preparation equipment to reach the area. If woody debris will be piled or windrowed, it may be best to do site preparation work after the harvest. Ask a forester which treatments fit your conditions.

Mechanical scarification may be needed to expose the mineral soil and mix it with duff. This can be accomplished by whole tree harvesting (where the whole tree, branches and all, is skidded to the landing rather than just the main stem) and dragging harvested trees over a different route with each load or by dragging a tree top around the stand after harvest. Machines also are available for disking, scalping, rock raking, and trenching.

Burning may be prescribed to remove logging debris or a heavy layer of organic material (such as moss and leaves) or to suppress existing woody vegetation. Prescribed burning requires a burning permit and must be done by a competent and well-equipped fire crew. Fire will kill young conifers, but many hardwood trees and shrubs, particularly oak, will resprout after a fire. Burning may give seedlings a fair chance to compete with resprouting vegetation. Burning is occasionally done before a harvest, but more often is done afterward.

Herbicides are available to kill most any herbaceous or woody vegetation. However, they may not discriminate between your crop trees and weed trees. Foliar applications (spraying herbicide on the leaves) are commonly used for site preparation. Depending on the herbicide, target species, and stand density, herbicides may be applied as a spray (large droplet size) or mist (small droplet size). Backpack sprayers are appropriate for small areas while large areas will require tractor-drawn sprayers. Herbicides are sometimes applied before harvest (especially in hardwoods) to kill vegetation that will compete with natural or artificial seeding. Herbicide usually is applied to young conifer stands after harvest to reduce competition from hardwoods. It may make sense to delay such an application until one or more years after harvest. In addition to depleting root energy reserves, the delay gives woody vegetation a chance to sprout after logging, thereby exposing more leaf surface to contact with the herbicide.

To avoid killing desirable young hardwood trees, cut them off close to the ground before applying herbicide. They will resprout the next year. To avoid killing desirable herbaceous plants, apply herbicide late in summer or early fall after they have produced seed and their tops have naturally died back.

38

Planting

The best time to plant trees is in spring, soon after frost leaves the ground. At this time the soil is moist, the climate is somewhat mild, and normally there is ample rainfall. If you must plant in late spring or early summer, use container-grown seedlings, because they tend to experience less transplant shock than direct-sowed seedlings. Fall planting usually is less successful because root growth is slowing, frost heaving may occur over the winter (especially in clay or wet soils), and growth regulators in the tree may become imbalanced, leading to top dieback.

Take good care of seedlings before planting! Ask the nursery to ship them using the swiftest transportation method available. If you transport the seedlings yourself, protect them from wind and sun during transit. Inspect the seedlings upon arrival. They should be dormant (that is, the buds and roots should not have begun to break, and should have no mold, be moist and flexible, and show no significant browning (especially on conifer needles). If you cannot plant the seedlings immediately, store them in their original container at a temperature of 35° F to 45° F.

If you need to postpone planting bareroot seedlings for more than three to five days, remove them from the container and heel them into a trench (Figure 4-3). Store seedlings in this manner only so long

as they remain dormant. Once they begin to grow, take extreme care to prevent their roots from drying out when you dig them up, transport them to the planting site, and replant them.

While planting, keep the seedling roots moist, but do not immerse them in water for more than 30 minutes, as this can lead to root damage and loss of beneficial microorganisms. Exposing tree roots to hot sunlight and drying winds for three to five minutes may be fatal.

Plant trees by hand or machine following these rules:

1. Plant only when soil moisture is adequate to ensure survival.
2. Make a planting hole large enough to easily accommodate the seedling root system.
3. Place roots in the planting hole without twisting, curling, or bending them. If necessary use a hatchet or heavy knife to trim any long roots on small bundles of trees.
4. Plant the tree in a vertical, upright position to lessen the chance of it growing a crooked stem.
5. Plant the tree at the same depth that it grew in the nursery. Look for the root collar where the root meets the upper stem (Figure 4-4).
6. Firm the soil around the roots to eliminate air pockets.
7. Water seedlings thoroughly after planting.

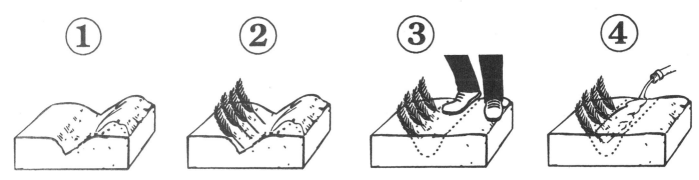

Figure 4-3. Heel-in bareroot seedlings for temporary storage. (1) In a cool, shady location, dig a V-shaped trench that is deep enough so the earth will cover the entire root system and part of the lower stem. (2) Remove the seedlings from their container and spread them along the sloping side of the trench in two or three layers. (3) Pack soil around the roots. (4) Water as necessary to keep roots moist.

Figure 4-4. Plant seedlings only as deep as the root collar.

There are two general methods of hand planting trees. One of these is the hole method. Dig a hole with a shovel, mattock, grub hoe, or mechanized auger. Make it large enough to accommodate the tree roots without bending them. Place the tree in the hole, distribute the roots evenly, and pack soil firmly around the roots. This method usually results in a high rate of seedling survival, but it is slow and not practical for planting large numbers of trees.

Using a planting bar or other tool is a faster method of hand planting a large number of trees. Insert a spade, planting bar (dibble), hoedad or similar tool into the soil and move it back and forth to form a V-shaped slit. Remove the tool and insert the tree seedling deep enough into the slit that it will be buried to the root collar. Remove the planting bar and reinsert it about three inches behind the seedling. Pull the bar away from the seedling to

firm soil around the roots, then push it toward the seedling to seal the top of the planting hole. For a still better seal, create a third slit a couple of inches away and seal its top by pressing down firmly with your boot (Figure 4-5). Using this method, you can plant 1,000 to 3,000 seedlings a day, depending on your experience and the condition of the planting site.

Using a tree-planting machine pulled behind a tractor (Figure 4-6) is faster than either hand planting method if the terrain is relatively level and clear of stumps, woody debris, and large rocks. The planter has a box to hold seedlings, a seat for the person planting, a coulter to break through the soil surface, a V-shaped blade to open a trench into which the operator places a seedling, and packing wheels that firm the soil around the seedling. Some machines have spray attachments to apply herbicides for vegetation control. A person sometimes follows the machine on foot to straighten seedlings or replant any that were planted too shallow. A three-person crew using one of these machines can plant about 10,000 trees in an eight-hour day.

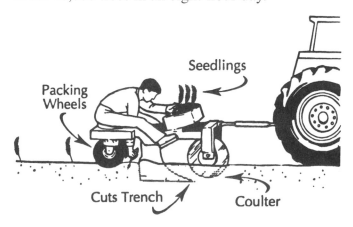

Figure 4-6. Tree-planting machine.

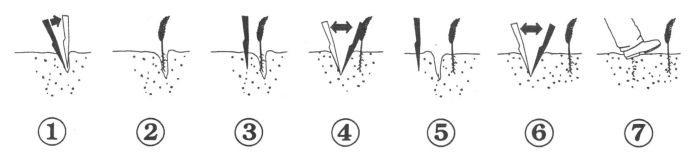

Figure 4-5. Planting a seedling with a bar.

Harvest and Regeneration Systems

A harvest and regeneration method (also called a silvicultural system) is a combination of timber harvesting and site preparation practices that prepare a site for natural or artificial regeneration. There are many different methods along a continuous spectrum to fit different site conditions, stand sizes, timber values, current and desired future tree species, landowner objectives, and other factors. Depending on the method you choose, the reproducing stand will be even-aged or uneven-aged.

Although the focus is often on the harvest, equally important are the conditions established by the harvest. These conditions, along with follow-up care and tending of the new stand, will determine the future development of the woodland. For this reason, foresters prefer the term "regeneration methods" (or systems) over "harvesting methods." A regeneration method focuses on the future stand. A harvest method focuses only on the arrangement and means by which mature trees are removed.

Even-aged Regeneration Systems

Even-aged harvest and regeneration systems require complete removal of the overstory resulting in a new stand where nearly all the trees are the same age. Even-aged systems usually are economical to implement because the landowner can remove a large volume of wood at one time for sale and they offer many options for site preparation. Even-aged systems are appropriate to:

- Create an even-aged stand.
- Regenerate tree species that need full sunlight and that can survive with high soil temperature and intense light.
- Regenerate shallow-rooted species in exposed locations where scattered trees left standing after a harvest would be uprooted or broken by wind.
- Regenerate species that naturally reproduce from seeds scattered by wind from adjacent stands, root suckers, stump sprouts, or seeds

released from cones after fire.
- Salvage merchantable material when whole stands are over-mature or severely damaged by insects, disease, wind, or fire.
- Clear the site for conversion to another species by planting or seeding.
- Provide habitat for wildlife species that thrive in a high-density, even-aged stand.

These systems offer some, but not all, of the growing conditions that naturally occur following a major fire or windstorm.

Clearcutting

Clearcutting involves harvesting all the trees in a stand regardless of their species or marketability (Figure 4-7). Clearcutting simulates regeneration conditions after a catastrophic windstorm, fire, or other disturbance. This method creates conditions optimal for regeneration of light-demanding species adapted to growth in full sunlight.

Traditionally, unmerchantable trees in a stand that was being clearcut would be felled or killed standing. Only desirable seedlings and saplings (advance regeneration) would be left to grow. Today, however, retaining scattered trees or patches inside clearcuts is becoming more common. Residual trees and patches provide vertical habitat for some wildlife species, particularly raptors, which use the residual trees as perch sites. Residual trees also provide some age, size, and perhaps species diversity and may improve the visual quality of a clearcut. On the other hand, residual trees may be

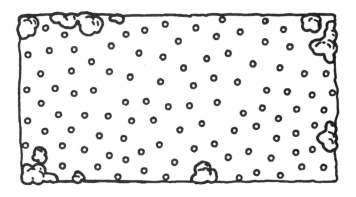

Figure 4-7. Clearcutting system.

subject to wind damage and can interfere with the regeneration of desirable species that do not tolerate shade. For these reasons, residual trees often are left in patches rather than distributed uniformly throughout the clearcut. Clearcuts typically are larger than two acres, but vary greatly in size and shape.

As in all regeneration systems, sources of regeneration must be determined before harvesting, but they may include seedlings already present before the harvest (advance regeneration), natural seed on the forest floor or on tree branches at the time of harvest, natural seed produced by adjacent stands, direct seeding, replanting, or stump sprouts and root suckers sprouting after harvest.

Clearcutting is not appropriate where the removal of a mature overstory would allow the water table to rise and inhibit the regeneration of a new stand.

Seed Tree

This system leaves mature trees of desirable species scattered throughout a harvested stand at intervals close enough to furnish seed to the entire cut area (Figure 4-8). Residual stocking (unharvested trees left standing) is not sufficient to protect, modify, or shelter the site in any significant way. Once the new stand is established (typically three to ten years after the initial harvest), seed trees may be harvested or left to grow through the next generation. This system is appropriate only for tree species that produce wind-dispersed seed. To obtain maximum seed production, seed trees must be healthy, large-crowned, and wind-firm. Seed trees usually are left singly, but may be left in small groups for wind protection. The number of seed trees required depends on the species' ability to produce seed and the distance that seed can be dispersed reliably by wind. In most cases three to ten seed trees per acre are left.

The initial tree harvest should occur after seeds have been dispersed in a year when there is a good seed crop. Site preparation usually is necessary before the harvest to create a receptive seed bed.

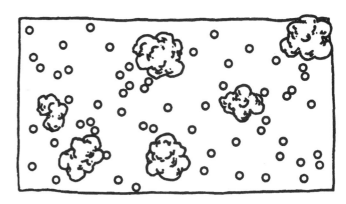

Figure 4-8. Seed-tree system.

The seed-tree system has several disadvantages:

- Diseases carried by the seed trees could be quickly transferred to new seedlings.
- Seed trees may be killed by wind, fire, or insects before they produce seed.
- The wood product value of the seed trees will be lost if it is not economical to harvest them after regeneration occurs.
- New seedlings may be damaged by equipment used to harvest the seed trees.
- A good seed crop may not occur for several years, allowing undesirable shrubs and trees to invade the stand.
- There is little control over the spacing or number of seedlings throughout the stand.

Shelterwood

This system involves making two or three cuts in a stand to stimulate advance regeneration before a final clearcut. In a three-cut system, the first is a heavy thinning that removes undesirable species and poorly formed or diseased trees while leaving the best trees with plenty of growing space to expand their crowns, grow vigorously, and produce seed. This cut can be eliminated if intermediate thinnings have achieved the same results. The second cut is a thinning made when there is a good seed crop. It usually leaves 50 to 70 percent crown cover, but allows enough sunlight to reach the forest floor that seeds from shade-tolerant species can

42

germinate and survive.

Site preparation (prescribed fire, mechanical, or herbicide) usually occurs just before or after this harvest to expose mineral soil for the seedbed and set back undesirable shrubs and trees. The final cut is made three to ten years after the previous cut, when advance regeneration is well established. It

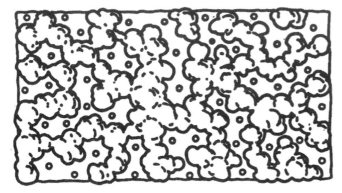

Uniform Shelterwood

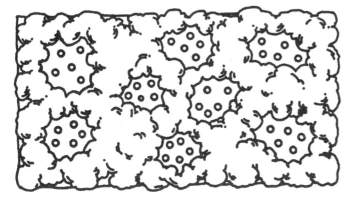

Group Shelterwood

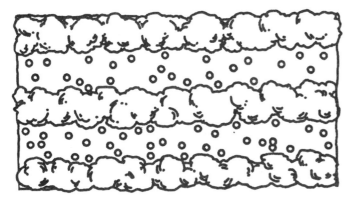

Strip Shelterwood

Figure 4-9. Shelterwood system.

clears remaining mature trees, releasing the young stand to grow in full sunlight. It also may result in stump sprouting or root suckering to supplement the established seedlings. There are several variations in the pattern of trees cut (Figure 4-9.)

The shelterwood system is used to develop advance regeneration before a final harvest. It is most appropriate for species that are intermediate to tolerant of shade, where residual trees are not subject to wind damage or epicormic branching, where logging damage to residual trees can be minimized, and where the increased cost of several partial cuts is acceptable. If naturally developing advance regeneration is not adequate, supplemental planting can be used.

Uneven-aged Systems

Uneven-aged systems promote a variety of species, ages, and sizes within a stand. In this system, light cuts at 5- to 25-year intervals encourage regular growth and prevent severe disturbances to the stand. Each cut may include thinning, harvesting, and understory treatments that create small canopy gaps where shade-tolerant tree species can regenerate. Some sapling and pole-sized trees may need to be cut to release the best stems from competition and encourage fast growth in the reduced understory light.

The goal is to achieve an optimum distribution of size and age classes so that that each class contains enough quality trees to replace those harvested in the next larger size class. Uneven-aged systems typically produce high quality wood because there are frequent opportunities to remove poor trees, allowing the best trees to grow longer. The visual quality of such stands may be superior to even-aged systems.

Two disadvantages of uneven-aged systems are that relatively small volumes of wood are harvested during each cut and repeated entries to the stand with heavy equipment can damage residual trees and hinder regeneration.

In an uneven-aged system, trees of all sizes are removed in each cut according to these general guidelines:

- Trees at high risk from insects, disease or other hazards
- Trees that directly compete with crop trees
- Cull trees
- Low vigor trees
- Unwanted species (to remove seed sources)
- Improve spacing (including thin dense sapling patches and stump sprouts)
- Mature trees

Tree diameter often is used as a measure of tree maturity. Consider these factors when determining an optimum maximum diameter for harvesting trees in an uneven-aged system:

- Higher quality sites normally allow trees to be grown to a larger diameter before growth rates decline significantly and decay becomes a major factor in tree value.

- Uneven-aged stands normally contain a variety of tree species, each with a different growth rate and life span that affect the optimum maximum diameter for the species.

- Each type and quality of wood product desired (such as pulpwood, sawtimber, and veneer) requires trees within a range of diameters.

- As a high-quality tree gets larger, it becomes more economically valuable due to its larger volume and higher grade. Grade is a measure of tree quality that determines the types of products (including veneer, high quality lumber, and low quality lumber) for which its wood is suitable. Attaining veneer size and grade can greatly increase a tree's value. Deciding whether to cut a large, valuable tree or let it grow longer must be weighed against the uncertainty of it still being alive and healthy for the next harvest.

- Your goals as the landowner affect the maximum diameter classes to keep. You may choose to extend a tree's life to enhance non-timber resources (such as aesthetics, wildlife food and shelter, and old growth character istics). Extending a tree's life may increase the

volume of valuable sawtimber and veneer, but there is also an increased risk for reduced growth rates and damage.

You will need to consider additional criteria to enhance wildlife habitat, water quality, and aesthetic values.

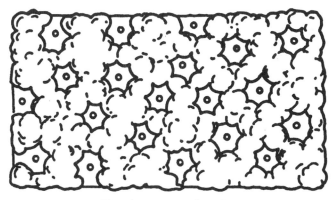

Single-tree selection

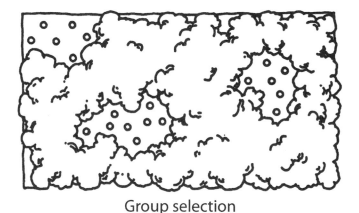

Group selection

Figure 4-10. Selection system.

Single-Tree Selection

In this system, individual trees of various sizes and ages are periodically removed to provide space for seedling development and to promote the growth of the remaining trees (Figure 4-10). Although both shade tolerant and intolerant species may regenerate in the newly created gaps (see shade tolerance table, Table 3-1, Chapter 3, p. 28), over time intolerants will die out and tolerants will survive. One major disadvantage of this system is that residual trees of all sizes can be damaged by logging equipment, especially while dragging logs from scattered sites out of the stand.

Group Selection

Under this method, trees are removed in small groups ranging from 1/50th acre (34-foot diameter circle) up to 1/2 acre (167-foot diameter circle). Smaller openings favor the regeneration of very shade-tolerant species, while larger openings may allow regeneration of species rated intermediate to tolerant of shade. Less logging damage may occur on residual trees than in the single-tree selection system, but such damage is still a concern.

Influence of Climate Change

You may wonder whether your woodland management plans should be altered in anticipation of the changing climate. The world's leading scientists and institutions agree that our climate is changing, but the impacts on forests in any given region are still uncertain. For instance, the scientific community is unable to say whether the Lakes States region is likely to get warmer and wetter or warmer and drier. Likewise, it is uncertain how temperatures are likely to fluctuate within a year. Will both seasonal highs and lows increase or will the pattern of temperature fluctuation vary? Whatever the exact nature of regional climate change, it is likely to stress trees and cause some mortality in existing mature stands. Because each species will respond differently to changing conditions, maintaining a wide diversity of species and age-classes in your woodland and across the surrounding landscape is a prudent management approach.

Reference

USDA Forest Service, *Woody Plant Seed Manual*, Agricultural Handbook 727, www.nsl.fs.fed.us/ nsl_wpsm.html

Chapter 5:

Woodland Improvement Practices

Eli Sagor, Extension Educator, University of Minnesota
Melvin J. Baughman, Extension Forester, University of Minnesota
John G. DuPlissis, Forestry Outreach Specialist, University of Wisconsin – Stevens Point

This chapter focuses on ways to improve existing stands of trees. Removing undesirable species and poor quality trees, increasing tree growth rates, improving wood quality, and protecting trees from pests are common goals. You can continually improve your woodland with small steps in short time blocks. Practices are organized by tree size classes: seedling (less than 1-inch stem diameter), sapling (1- to 4-inch stem DBH), poletimber (5- to 9-inch DBH), and sawtimber (10-inch DBH and larger).

Seedling Stands

Seedling stands (in which the trees' stems are less than 1 inch in diameter) typically have large numbers of very small trees that face fierce competition from herbaceous and woody plants, extreme weather, pests, and heavy equipment operations in the stand. Herbaceous plants, shrubs, and trees compete with the tree seedlings for sunlight, moisture, and nutrients. Removing or reducing this competition may be necessary to ensure seedling survival and growth.

Seedling release can be done manually by hoeing or mulching, mechanically by mowing or cultivating, or chemically by using herbicides. For any of these, you must be able to locate the tree seedlings among their competition. If you are planting seedlings where you may need to do follow-up weed and brush control within a year, place a wire flag next to each seedling or periodically along the tree rows to help you locate the seedlings later.

Mowing is practical on old field plantations where trees are in straight rows with regular spacing, but mowing must be done frequently and it still allows weeds and woody brush to survive. Some form of cultivation offers better weed control than mowing. Hand hoeing weeds is practical only when you have just a few seedlings to manage. Cultivate field plantings with a tractor-drawn rotary hoe, harrow, disk, or in-row tiller such as a Weed Badger, Kimco, or Green Hoe. Seedling damage may occur if the tillage equipment cuts any seedling roots or if the equipment runs over seedlings due to operator carelessness or irregular tree spacing. Wet ground may prevent either mowing or cultivating when they are needed the most. You can use a hand-held brush hook or motorized brush saw to cut small woody shrubs and trees in small areas, but remember that many species, especially hardwoods, will resprout after cutting.

Mulch is usually effective at controlling weeds and conserving soil moisture. Its moisture conserving benefit is most helpful on the prairie and woodland fringe where precipitation is a limiting factor for tree growth. Many types work, including sheets of plastic or woven fabric, wood chips, straw, ground corncobs, paper sacks, or other organic materials. Mulch is difficult to transport and apply, so it may be appropriate only for relatively small plantations in open fields. Organic mulches may provide habitat for small rodents that can eat bark off trees in the winter.

The most common method of releasing seedlings from herbaceous or woody competition is to use herbicides. Usually a single application provides season-long control. Herbicides may be applied aerially or from the ground. Ground application using backpack or hand-held sprayers is more common on small plantations. For larger plantations, spray equipment can be mounted on skidders or other large equipment. Herbicides may be applied in spots around trees, in bands down tree rows, or be broadcast across an entire area. Spot and band treatments leave some herbaceous vegetation to help control soil erosion.

Select an herbicide labeled for the types of plants to be killed and those to be protected. Read the label carefully and follow the directions for application rates, timing, and precautions to take. Different herbicides kill vegetation in different ways. Some are growth regulators, while others destroy chlorophyll or essential plant tissues. Herbicides must be applied at a time when the target species are most susceptible. When applying herbicides by hand in hardwood plantings, hold a shield around important seedlings to prevent herbicide contact. To protect hardwood seedlings that resprout readily (such as oak), cut them off at ground level before applying herbicide to the area. They will sprout again after the herbicide danger has passed.

Use caution when applying herbicides so that spray does not drift onto adjacent areas or contaminate surface or ground water. Use drift-control additives if there is any possibility of wind-drift. Soil-activated herbicides can flow downslope and kill nontarget vegetation. Carefully observe environmental protection warnings on the label and maintain adequate buffer strips near water and nontarget areas.

▲ _____

Seedlings and saplings also may need liberation—the removal or killing of large, undesirable trees that would interfere with the development of a new stand beneath the canopy. (See "Deadening Unmerchantable Trees" on pg. 50.)

Tree shelters are hollow tubes about 4 to 6 inches in diameter and 2 to 6 feet tall that are placed over seedlings and held in place by stakes. Each seedling requires its own shelter, so they are expensive and cumbersome to install, but you can remove and re-use them.

Plastic shelters create a miniature greenhouse over each seedling that raises the humidity and carbon dioxide levels to increase the rate of tree height growth. They also may increase tree survival on difficult planting sites with low rainfall. When held snug to the ground, they keep rodents away from seedlings. Tall shelters prevent deer browsing—one of their most useful purposes. Hollow tubes may attract birds that fall inside and cannot escape, but placing a plastic net over the top of the tube will keep birds out. Shelters should be left in place until trees have grown through the top of the shelter. Shelters designed (and installed) to prevent rodent damage near the ground should be left until bark is thick enough to resist rodent damage. However, non-biodegradable shelters must be removed once trees have outgrown them in order to prevent damage or even tree death.

Woven wire shelters held in place by stakes protect seedlings from deer and rabbit browsing, but do not modify the atmosphere around the seedlings.

Where equipment will be operated to harvest mature trees, desirable tree seedlings must be protected from damage as much as possible. Strategies to protect the seedlings might be to:

- Tell equipment operators where seedling stands are located so they can try to avoid them.
- Harvest during the dormant season when hardwood seedlings have stored food reserves in their roots and thus have the capacity to resprout the next spring.

- Harvest when the ground is frozen to prevent seedlings from being uprooted.
- Harvest in winter when there is heavy snow cover.

Sapling and Poletimber Stands

Competition among trees eliminates poor quality and low-vigor trees throughout the life of a stand. In sapling and poletimber stands, focus your management on identifying potential crop trees and encouraging their growth. Typical objectives are to:

- Improve species composition.
- Control stand density.
- Improve tree quality.
- Increase tree growth rate.
- Harvest trees before they die.

Weeding is the practice of removing undesirable tree species that take up valuable growing space. Culling is the removal of trees that have no commercial value because of poor form, damage, or other physical defects. Thinning involves selectively cutting trees of a desirable species to give the remaining trees more growing space. Pruning removes limbs to straighten saplings or to allow knot-free wood to develop on poletimber trees. These practices collectively are called timber stand improvement (TSI). In TSI, your first step is to pick the objective, then determine which trees should be left in the stand and how to maximize their growth and potential.

For general woodland health:

- Retain tree species best suited for your site.
- Retain a diversity of tree species to protect biodiversity as a hedge against serious pest problems.
- Remove trees with insect and disease problems.
- Remove trees with severe damage to bark or crowns.
- Thin the stand to sustain vigorous growth on the best trees, thereby helping them resist insects, diseases, and weather extremes.

- Remove invasive, exotic species that may take over the stand and suppress the regeneration and growth of desirable native species.

If timber production is your goal, determine what products you wish to grow (for example, fuelwood, pulpwood, sawtimber, or veneer), then learn what tree species, size, and wood quality are required for those products. During TSI (Figure 5-1), encourage the growth of potential crop trees that:

- Are desirable species in the marketplace.
- Have tall, straight stems.
- Have few branches on the main stem.
- Have healthy crowns in dominant or codominant positions in the canopy.
- Are relatively free of insect and disease problems.
- Show no signs of bark damage or wood decay.

If your goal is to improve wildlife habitat, decide which wildlife species or groups of species you want to encourage and learn about their habitat needs. Use TSI to create appropriate habitat, such as:

- Food (fruit, nuts, seeds, buds)
- Shelter (hollow trees, thickets, brush piles, dead standing trees, downed logs, large woody debris in streams)
- Escape cover (dense thickets, hollow trees, large trees)
- Breeding sites (permanent openings, dense thickets, mixed hardwood and conifer stands)
- Nesting sites (several horizontal layers of vegetation—ground cover, understory, mid-story)

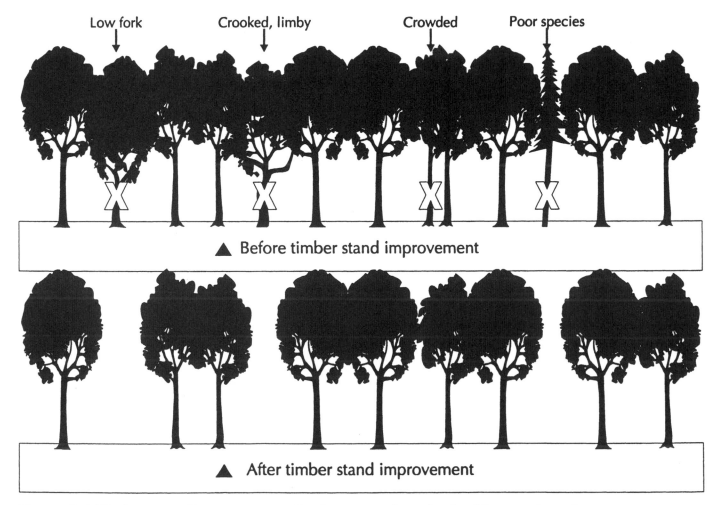

Low fork · Crooked, limby · Crowded · Poor species

▲ Before timber stand improvement

▲ After timber stand improvement

Figure 5-1. Timber stand improvement for fast growth and valuable wood products.

If visual quality is a concern during TSI:

- Remove trees or prune off lower branches to provide a pleasing vista.
- Save trees with beautiful flowers, fall leaf color, or interesting bark.
- Protect trees with interesting shapes.
- Save large trees.
- Encourage species diversity, especially a mix of hardwoods and conifers.

TSI may be commercial or pre-commercial, depending on whether cut trees can be sold for a profit. Pre-commercial TSI, however, is often economical in the long run because it sustains tree growth, shortens the time to harvest, and improves tree quality.

The following TSI recommendations are aimed at sustaining a healthy forest primarily for timber:

- Where stump sprouts occur on desirable species, wait until they are 3 to 5 years old, then thin them with loppers or a handheld, motorized brush saw to one or two vigorous, straight stems that are more than 10 inches apart.
- Thin sapling stands with a motorized brush saw, leaving 1-inch diameter stems 3 feet apart.
- When thinning dense sapling and small pole-sized stands, it may be more practical and economical to remove whole rows or swaths of trees than to selectively remove scattered trees. Follow a stocking chart (Appendix C) for the main crop species to determine how many trees to leave. In stands with large pole-sized trees and enough space between trees to maneuver logging equipment, selectively harvest trees, leaving the best and largest trees. Leave potential crop trees with dominant or codominant stems. Intermediate and suppressed trees have fallen behind in the competition for growing space and are unlikely to ever become quality dominant trees, even after release.

Sawtimber Stands

Commercial thinning is the principal TSI treatment in sawtimber stands.

Optimum stand density varies by forest type because of the different growing space requirements of the tree species found in them. Manage stand density by the crop-tree release method or with the help of a stocking chart (Appendix C).

A simple method for regulating stand density is to identify potential crop trees and remove any surrounding trees that are interfering with the crown of the crop trees. Based on your stand objectives, leave the most desirable species and best quality stems with dominant and codominant crowns.

When applying the crop-tree release method, leave crop trees at least 20 to 25 feet apart. If crop trees are scarce or unevenly distributed, leave two trees as close as 10 feet but treat them as one tree when thinning. Remove trees with crowns that encroach on the crop trees. (Figure 5-2)

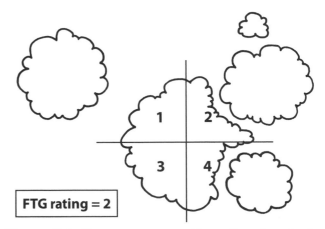

FTG rating = 2

Figure 5-2. Free to grow rating. Quadrants 1 and 3 are free to grow, for a FTG rating of 2.

The free to grow rating is a simple way to evaluate the level of crown competition. Ideally, crop tree crowns should be free to grow on all four sides; however, in dense, young stands, no more than two crowded sides should be released at once. Additional release can shock a tree, leading to epicormic sprouting and degraded tree form. Provide additional crown release in later treatments.

In general, do not remove more than one-third of the basal area from a stand at any one time. A heavier thinning may lead to wind damage, sunscald, and epicormic branching on residual trees. Epicormic branches (also called water sprouts) arising from dormant buds beneath the bark on hardwood trees create knots and lower wood quality.

A more sophisticated method for regulating tree spacing (that is, stand density) is to apply guidelines from a stocking chart if one is available for your forest type (see Chapter 2: Conducting a Woodland Inventory).

It is common practice to spray a spot or band of paint on trees to be removed during TSI.

Trees growing below the main canopy will not affect crop tree growth, but cut them if they are of marketable size or of undesirable species. Do not damage crop tree crowns, stems, or roots while thinning stands. Repeat thinning every 15 to 20 years.

During a commercial thinning, it may be necessary to remove more trees than you prefer to, including some high quality trees, to enable logging equipment to reach the trees to be removed and to provide enough wood volume to attract a logger. A professional forester can help you understand these tradeoffs and plan your harvest appropriately.

Deadening Unmerchantable Trees

During a TSI operation, you can kill undesirable trees by chemical or mechanical means. If the trees are cut mechanically and you expect them to resprout, treat the stumps with an herbicide labeled for that use.

When undesirable trees have no commercial value, it often is faster and easier to kill them standing rather than to cut them down. Trees can be killed by girdling, frilling, herbicide injection, or basal spray (Figure 5-3). Dead standing trees are useful to many wildlife species and cause little damage to the remaining trees when they break up. For safety purposes, trees that could fall across roads or trails or on buildings should be felled rather than killed standing.

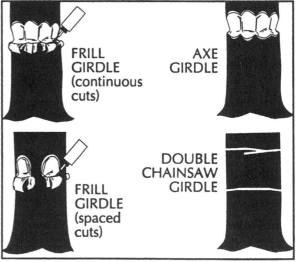

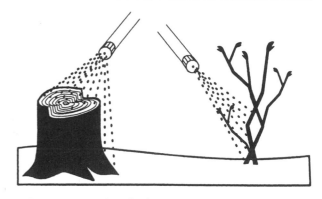

Fig 5-3. Methods for killing undesirable trees.

Girdling involves the complete removal of a 3- to 5-inch band of bark around the trunk with a hatchet or chain saw. Girdling also can be accomplished by encircling the main stem with two parallel chain saw cuts that are 1 inch deep and 3 to 5 inches apart. This is time-consuming, hard work; a tree may not die for several years; and live shoots may sprout below the girdle. Girdling often is used if sprouts are needed for wildlife browse and the resulting sprouts will not interfere with more desirable tree seedlings. Girdling is easier to do in spring when bark separates easily from the wood.

A frill girdle is a single line of downward axe or hatchet cuts that completely encircle the trunk and are then sprayed with an herbicide. Treatments during the growing season are more effective than treatments in winter or at the time of heaviest sap flow. The effectiveness also will vary with the concentration of the chemical used.

An herbicide injection can be used on trees over 5 inches in diameter. Some injectors are modified hatchets, while others resemble pipes with chisel points on one end. An injector cuts through the bark and injects a measured amount of herbicide into each cut. Space cuts 1 to 3 inches apart and apply this treatment any time from May through early fall.

To kill scattered shrubs or small trees, spray the lower 12 to 15 inches of the stem with an approved herbicide until it runs off. Apply chemicals during the growing season, and note that control may be poor on root-suckering species.

Do not apply chemicals near desirable plants or contaminate surface or ground water.

Pruning

Individual tree quality can be improved by pruning. It is time consuming and expensive, so undertake pruning with a careful eye on costs. Prune only 50 to 100 crop trees an acre that have the form and vigor to produce high quality sawtimber or veneer.

Corrective Pruning

Perform corrective pruning only on high-quality hardwood seedlings or small saplings, (primarily black walnut) to encourage a single straight leader (Figure 5-4). Most trees will correct themselves. Those that do not are probably genetically inferior and no amount of pruning will correct their form.

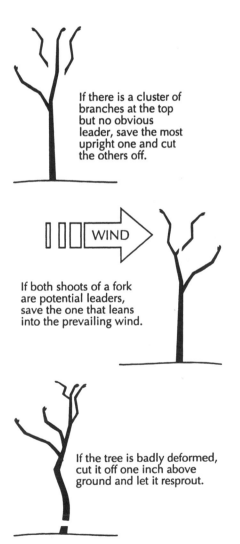
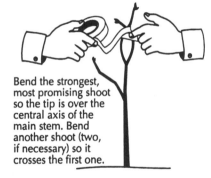
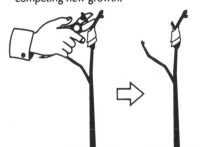

If there is a cluster of branches at the top but no obvious leader, save the most upright one and cut the others off.

If both shoots of a fork are potential leaders, save the one that leans into the prevailing wind.

If the tree is badly deformed, cut it off one inch above ground and let it resprout.

If the tree has a widely forked or multiple top, straighten the most promising leader by using one or more lateral shoots as support:

Bend the strongest, most promising shoot so the tip is over the central axis of the main stem. Bend another shoot (two, if necessary) so it crosses the first one.

Fasten the shoots together with three wraps of one-inch masking tape. Large or widely divergent shoots may need more layers of tape.

Cut off the tip of the supporting shoot(s) just above the wrapping to eliminate potentially competing new growth.

Figure 5-4. Corrective pruning.

Clear-stem Pruning

The purpose of clear-stem pruning is to remove lower branches on the stem to produce knot-free wood (Figure 5-5). Clear-stem pruning is justified when it raises the tree grade enough to increase its stumpage value beyond the pruning cost. Clear-stem pruning may be appropriate for red pine, white pine, black walnut, red oak, sugar maple, and yellow birch. Have a forester teach you appropriate pruning techniques, especially before you prune young hardwood trees.

You can begin clear-stem pruning when trees are just 10 feet tall, and should complete it before trees reach 8 inches DBH. Prune at least 9 feet high, but remove no more than one-third of the live crown at any one time. Additional pruning through the pole stage should increase the total clear stem up to 17 feet, if 16-foot logs are the objective.

Prune during the late dormant season just before spring growth begins. Pruning at this time helps prevent diseases from invading the pruning wounds before they dry out or glaze over with pitch. Do not prune oaks from mid-April through mid-July because oak wilt may enter the pruning cuts. The dormant season also is a comfortable time to work in the woods because it is cool, visibility is good, and there are few insect pests. If possible, time pruning to coincide with thinning so the accelerated tree growth quickly grows over pruning cuts and maximizes knot-free wood production.

Do not prune higher than 1/3 of total tree height or remove more than 50% of live crown.

CORRECT   INCORRECT

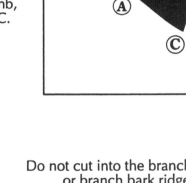

To prune a large limb, cut in order A, B, C.

Do not cut into the branch collar or branch bark ridge. Minimize the size of the cut surface.

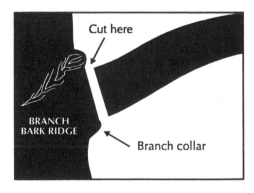

When removing a dead limb, leave callus ridge intact.

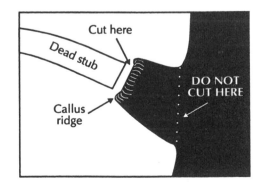

Figure 5-5. Clear-stem pruning.

Cut branches close to the trunk, but do not cut into the branch collar—a swelling of the main stem around the base of the branch. Cutting into the branch collar wounds the main stem and may lead to decay in the tree.

Tree paint and wound dressings do not promote healing. Use them only when an emergency such as storm damage requires that trees (particularly oaks) be pruned in May or June.

Work safely. Wear the appropriate personal protective equipment for the tool being used. At the very least, wear a hard hat, eye protection and gloves. Sharp tools cut cleanly and require less effort to use than dull ones. Tools commonly used for pruning include hand pruning saws, pole saws, shears, and pole pruners (shears). Using a chain saw is dangerous for pruning because you must hold it above shoulder level where it is difficult to control. A chain saw easily damages trees by cutting into the branch collar and by nicking bark on the main tree stem near the pruning cut.

Chapter 6:

Managing Important Forest Types

Melvin J. Baughman, Extension Forester, University of Minnesota

Foresters and scientists have developed several methods for classifying woodlands. These classifications help describe tree species that are currently present, or the combination of vegetation that would naturally occur on the site if it were undisturbed for a long period of time, or the site quality for growing particular tree species.

The "forest type" classification is based on the predominant tree species over an area of woodland. Forest types are named for one to three tree species that comprise at least 20 percent of the basal area in a mature stand or a predominance of stems in seedling and sapling stands. Forest type classification has been standardized across the United States, but each forest type has many variants. A forest type designation recognizes the combination of tree species currently in a woodland, but that type may not be the best type to grow on the site where it exists. We use forest types in this book because they are relatively easy for landowners and foresters to recognize and you do need to base management decisions on what tree species are present, even if you are trying to move the stand toward another combination of tree species that is better suited to the site.

A "plant community" classification considers site factors in designating the trees and other plants most likely to occupy a site if it were undisturbed for a long period of time.

A "vegetative habitat type" (also known as "site type" or "native plant community") classification identifies forest sites along a soil moisture-nutrient gradient. It takes into consideration soil texture, fertility, and moisture and leads to recommendations for tree species best suited to each site type. Site types are recognized by characteristic understory plants rather than tree species and site types are named for one or more understory plants.

An "ecological classification" system is based on climate, geology, landforms, landscape position, soil and vegetation. This hierarchical system first defines large-scale ecosystems that are multistate in scope (a province), then subdivides those ecosystems into smaller and smaller parts, down to a few acres (ecological land type phase) as the criteria are refined.

This chapter describes management of important forest types in the Lake States—Minnesota, Wisconsin, and Michigan. These descriptions are brief and may not provide adequate information for managing specific stands because so many site types and species combinations exist. A forester should inspect your woodland and prepare stand management plans before you implement any forestry practices.

Range maps help you determine what tree species are likely to be found in your area. A species usually grows better and its wood has greater commercial potential in the heart of its range, as opposed to the edge of its range where environmental factors limit its growth.

Site index curves help you determine whether the growth potential on your land is high or low for a species. To determine the site index for a species on a particular site, you need to know the average age and total tree height for trees of that species on the site, then refer to site index curves such as those in Appendix B.

Aspen

The aspen forest type, dominated by quaking aspen (also called "poplar" or "popple") and bigtooth aspen, covers more area than any other forest type in the Lake States (Figure 6-1). Paper birch and pin cherry are common associates. Balsam poplar (balm of gilead) is found on moist sites. Aspen is very intolerant of shade and relatively short-lived.

Figure 6-1. Range of quaking aspen.

Stands can be invaded readily by more shade-tolerant species. On dry sites, aspen may be replaced by red pine, red maple, or oaks; on sites with intermediate moisture, by white pine; on fertile sites by northern hardwoods, white spruce, and balsam fir; and on the wettest sites by balsam fir, black spruce, black ash, and northern white-cedar.

Products and Uses

Aspen species are used principally for paper and particleboard, but also for lumber, studs, veneer, plywood, shingles, matches, novelty items, biomass fuel, and animal feed. Aspen stands are important habitat for ruffed grouse, woodcock, snowshoe hare, beaver, porcupine, white-tailed deer, moose, and black bear.

Site Conditions

Aspen grows on a wide range of soils from shallow and rocky to deep loamy sands and heavy clay. Good soils are well-drained, loamy, and high in organic matter, calcium, magnesium, potassium, and nitrogen. The best sites have soils with silt-plus-clay content of 80 percent or more. Aspen prefers a water table from 2 to 8.2 feet deep. It grows poorly on sandy or droughty soils and on heavy clay.

Site index commonly is used to evaluate site productivity when aspen stands are at least 20 years old and have not been damaged by fire or overtopped by other species (Appendix B-1: Site index curves for quaking aspen). Manage aspen for timber only where the site index is 60 or better.

Regeneration

Regeneration from seed is possible, but unreliable. Good seed crops occur every four to five years on 50- to 70-year-old trees. Seeds ripen in May to June and are dispersed long distances by wind and water. They require a water-saturated seedbed for germination. A moist, bare mineral soil is best.

Aspen stands most commonly regenerate from root suckers that grow from lateral roots after a stand has been harvested or killed by fire or wind. Because aspen is very intolerant of shade, optimum root suckering occurs when the stand is completely clearcut. Do not leave more than 20 mature trees an acre after harvesting. If logging does not destroy undesirable trees and shrubs, remove them by felling, girdling, basal spraying, or controlled burning. Root suckering is most prolific when:

- Clearcutting is done when the soil is relatively dry or frozen to avoid damaging the lateral roots within 4 inches of the soil surface that produce the suckers. This is especially important on clay soils with a high water table.
- Harvesting occurs during the dormant season when food reserves stored in the roots are at a maximum, especially on fine-textured soils.
- Soil temperature is 74° F. (High soil temperature inhibits suckering.)
- Parent trees are healthy and have high carbohydrate reserves. Grazing, repeated cropping, killing of sucker stands, and insect defoliation will lower carbohydrate reserves.
- There is no excess soil moisture (to impede aeration) or severe drought.

If a stand is harvested during the growing season, root suckers will begin to grow immediately after trees are felled. Do not drive heavy equipment across young sprouts or they will be killed. To protect new sprouts begin logging at the rear of the stand, then progress toward the log landing.

Harvest stands for pulpwood at age 45 to 55 and for sawtimber at age 55 to 65. Harvest earlier if more than 30 percent of the trees are diseased (indicated by the presence of fungal conks or bark cankers).

Old, decadent stands with low vigor and stands with fewer than 50 mature aspen trees an acre may be difficult to regenerate. Encourage maximum suckering by harvesting these stands during the dormant season when the ground is frozen or relatively dry. If an old stand does not have a merchantable volume of wood, you may kill the old trees and stimulate suckering by felling the trees, by shearing them with a sharp blade on a bulldozer when the soil is frozen, or by setting a prescribed fire.

Two years after clearcutting there should be at least 5,000 aspen root suckers an acre. Some stands may have up to 30,000 root suckers an acre. The more the better, since aspen stands naturally thin themselves. If root sucker density following the clearcut appears low, ask a forester to judge whether the stand is adequately stocked. If stocking is not adequate, wait at least 10 years, then clearcut the stand again. Following this second clearcut, sucker density should improve to a satisfactory level.

Aspen will not compete well with other hardwoods such as maple, basswood, ash, and oak. Over time the aspen will die from disease and be replaced by more shade-tolerant species. Clearcutting a mixed species stand favors aspen regeneration. Removing aspen during thinning will favor other hardwood species.

Where you find mature aspen with an understory of white spruce and balsam fir (two shade-tolerant conifers), clearcutting aspen and purposely damaging the conifers will reproduce mainly aspen. In contrast, carefully harvesting the aspen while leaving the conifers undamaged will enable aspen root suckers to survive in scattered patches. In 40 to 50 years the conifers and aspen will mature. Clearcutting then will regenerate a stand of mainly aspen with a few scattered conifers.

Intermediate Treatments

Once an aspen stand has regenerated, trees grow rapidly. A densely stocked stand thins naturally; artificial thinning is unnecessary to produce pulpwood and may increase losses from hypoxylon canker, poplar borer and rot. Dense stands also promote natural pruning. Artificially thinned stands may produce more sawtimber and veneer than unthinned stands, but thin to grow these products only when disease incidence is low and the site index is 70 or higher. One thinning at about age 30 leaving approximately 240 trees an acre may be appropriate. Row thinning of sapling stands has produced faster volume growth on residual trees, but results are inconsistent. Take great care to avoid wounding residual aspen trees, since decay and discoloration can enter trees through those wounds.

Pests and Diseases

Aspen is highly susceptible to fire damage. Major insect pests are leaf-feeding forest tent caterpillar, large aspen tortrix, and gypsy moth, plus various wood borers that weaken and degrade the stem. Several species of fungi cause stem cankers or white rot that reduce the volume of usable wood.

To reduce losses from these pests, do not grow aspen for timber where the site index is less than 60. Stands growing on poor sites are highly susceptible to pests. Try to regenerate 30,000 suckers an acre and maintain a high number of stems an acre to discourage poplar borer and hypoxylon canker. Do not thin aspen; wounds on residual trees will favor establishment of poplar borer and hypoxylon canker.

To minimize pest damage, harvest trees by age 40, unless the site index is at least 75 and veneer is the desired product. If fewer than 15 percent of the trees are infected with hypoxylon canker, stands may grow longer than 40 years. If 15 to 25 percent of the trees are infected with hypoxylon canker, harvest early and regenerate aspen. If more than 25 percent of the stand is infected, consider converting to an alternate forest type or species. Harvest early if white rot affects more than 30 percent of the basal area.

Repeated defoliation by forest tent caterpillar will weaken the trees, increasing their susceptibility to disease. Insecticides may be required to protect the stand during prolonged outbreaks.

Balsam Fir

The balsam fir type occurs across the northern Lake States (Figure 6-2). Common associates include black spruce, white spruce, paper birch, quaking aspen, bigtooth aspen, yellow birch, American beech, red maple, sugar maple, eastern hemlock, eastern white pine, tamarack, black ash, and northern white-cedar.

Figure 6-2. Range of balsam fir.

Products and Uses

Balsam fir is used mainly for pulpwood and small sawtimber. Wood waste is burned for energy. Fir stands provide summer shade for moose, deer, and bear and winter cover for moose and deer. Timber wolves, pine marten, fisher, lynx, and bobcat are associated with this type of woodland. Hares, spruce grouse, and songbirds use these stands for cover and a food source. Balsam fir boughs are extensively clipped for wreaths and small trees are cut for Christmas trees.

Site Conditions

Balsam fir grows on a wide range of inorganic and organic soils and on wet to dry sites. It is most common on wet to moist sites, where soil moisture is adequate throughout the growing season and standing water may be present during part of the season. On moist sites balsam fir is gradually replaced by northern hardwoods such as sugar maple. On wet sites it usually is dominated by black spruce and tamarack. Good sites are found on well-drained loams and moderately well-drained silt loams, clay loams, and clays. It grows where pH is 5.1 to 6.0, but does best with pH 6.5 to 7.0 in the upper organic layers. A site index (Table 6-1) is most reliable when measuring dominant balsam firs that have not been previously suppressed in even-aged stands or by assessing the site

index of associated species (Appendix B-2: Site index curves for balsam fir in the Lake States). The balsam fir site index is unreliable in uneven-aged stands.

Table 6-1. Comparative site index for balsam fir and common associates.

Balsam fir	Quaking aspen	Paper birch	Black spruce	Northern white-cedar
Site index in feet				
60	70	70	60	40
50	60	55	50	35
40	50	40	40	30
30	35	25	30	25

Source: Johnston, W. F. 1986. Manager's handbook for balsam fir in the north central states. General Technical Report NC-111. USDA Forest Service, North Central Forest Experiment Station. P. 5.

Regeneration

Beginning at age 30, balsam fir produces good seed crops every two to four years. Wind disperses seed for 80 to 200 feet from mature trees. If enough moisture is available, seeds will germinate on almost any seedbed and seedlings will survive for several years with only 10 percent of full sunlight. The best seedbed is medium-textured mineral soil with some shade. Thick duff with no shade is a poor seedbed. Scarification that incorporates duff will improve the seedbed.

Because balsam fir is very shade tolerant, it can be managed in uneven-aged stands, especially on moist-wet sites. Use a two-stage shelterwood harvest, leaving 60 percent crown cover where advance regeneration is not adequate and where residual firs are known to be windfirm (resistant to strong winds).

Balsam fir also can be managed in even-aged stands by clearcutting in alternate or progressive strips or patches. Use clearcutting where the shelterwood system will lead to excessive mortality from rot, wind, or spruce budworm or where advance regeneration of fir is well established before the cut. Cut strips perpendicular to, and progressing toward, the prevailing wind. Cut strips up to three chains wide with seeding from both sides or two chains wide with seeding only from the windward side.

Excessive slash from harvesting will hinder growth of advance regeneration and provide too much shade over a seedbed. Reduce slash by full-tree skidding.

Balsam fir is seldom planted because of low market demand and the relative ease of regeneration by natural seeding.

Depending on site conditions and the tree species mix that is present, a balsam fir stand can be converted to other forest types. In a mature stand of fir with some aspen, clearcut to produce a stand of aspen suckers with scattered firs. If advance fir regeneration is sparse, place harvest areas within two to three chains of seed-bearing firs. Firs will grow up with the aspen. Once the aspen has matured, cut the aspen, being careful to preserve the firs for longer growth. Some aspen will regenerate in the openings, sustaining a two-species stand. When the firs mature, repeat the cycle by clearcutting.

Where balsam fir forms an understory beneath paper birch, clearcut the birch to release the fir. To reduce spruce budworm problems, maintain some overstory birch by clearcutting progressive strips or small patches. To ensure a birch component in the new stand, scarify the soil in scattered openings and leave seed-bearing birches within three chains.

In a balsam fir stand with at least three to five paper birch seed trees an acre, you can retain a birch component by clearcutting the stand in progressive strips or small patches or using shelterwood cutting. Cut strips one to two chains wide and patches one acre or less. Scarify about 50 percent of the harvest area to prepare seedbeds for fir and birch. Whole-tree skidding when the soil is not frozen or snow covered will scarify the site. About eight years after the harvest, thin the new stand to manage the mix of fir and birch.

In northern hardwood stands with a balsam fir component where the site index for sugar maple is greater than 55, control fir advance regeneration to favor hardwood reproduction and clearcut mature fir if hardwood advance reproduction is adequate. Adequate stocking is 5,000 hardwood seedlings three to four feet tall or 1,000 saplings two to four inches DBH. If hardwood reproduction is not adequate, remove the firs in two or more shelterwood harvests to favor hardwoods.

On less well-drained hardwood sites (with a sugar maple site index of less than 55) manage balsam fir along with other hardwoods. These include yellow birch (plus eastern hemlock in Michigan and Wisconsin) on somewhat poorly drained sites and black ash and red maple on poorly drained sites. To grow only pulpwood, clearcut where fir advance growth is adequately stocked and use shelterwood harvest where it is not. To grow both pulpwood and sawlogs, thin young stands to obtain the desired mix of fir and hardwoods. Then harvest the fir at about age 50 and leave the hardwoods until they mature (at roughly age 100). When the hardwoods are mature, reproduce all species as described above. Selection cutting is suitable where a high proportion of fir is desired.

Where balsam fir occurs with pine on dry to moist-dry sites (usually sandy soils), encourage red pine (or jack pine on very dry sites) by eliminating all fir when harvesting pines.

Balsam fir often forms an understory in mature white pine stands on moist to moist-wet sites. This understory may improve wildlife habitat or esthetics, but for timber production the fir should be removed to facilitate regeneration of white pine or other conifers.

On moist to moist-wet sites where balsam fir is mixed with white spruce, spruce is preferred because of its higher timber value, longer life, and greater tolerance to spruce budworm defoliation. If a mature fir stand has more than 500 well-distributed white spruce that are three feet or taller an acre, clearcut the stand to release the spruce, but take care to minimize logging damage. If spruce regeneration is not adequate, either use shelterwood cutting and scarification to encourage spruce or clearcut the stand and plant white spruce. As the new stand grows, weed out balsam fir during thinnings.

▲

On moist-wet to wet sites where balsam fir is mixed with northern white-cedar and black spruce, minimize the fir component. Broadcast burn (controlled ground fire) harvest sites to eliminate woody debris and undesirable small trees and shrubs to create a good seedbed for white-cedar and spruce.

Intermediate Treatments

The degree to which competing vegetation should be controlled depends on the management objective and type of site. Mixed species stands enhance wildlife habitat and aesthetics and reduce the potential for spruce budworm damage. On wet and moist-wet sites, balsam fir will eventually grow above associated hardwoods, but on moist sites with northern hardwoods, balsam fir will be suppressed. Balsam fir responds well to release when trees are still young and vigorous (for example, with current annual height growth of six inches or more, a fairly pointed crown, and smooth bark with raised resin blisters). A single herbicide release or cleaning about eight years after a harvest or when stand height averages 6 to 10 feet will help ensure balsam fir dominance.

Research is not available to determine desirable balsam fir stand densities in the Lake States, but a stocking chart for even-aged spruce-fir stands from the Northeast offers some guidance (Appendix C-1: Stocking chart for even-aged spruce-balsam fir stands).

Pests and Diseases

The spruce budworm is the major insect pest of balsam fir. Budworm survives best on older trees and in dense stands. To minimize damage, manage fir on a 40- to 50-year rotation, keep large forest areas well diversified by age class, thin stands to maintain vigorous growth, and maintain a high spruce and hardwood component. Insecticide use may be warranted in high value stands that have been defoliated for two consecutive years and that cannot be harvested within five years.

Heart rot and root rot are major diseases. To minimize damage follow budworm management practices to sustain vigorous stands and avoid scarring trees during intermediate cuttings.

Windthrow—trees uprooted or broken by wind—can be a serious condition, especially on wet, shallow soils. Minimize windthrow by maintaining a well-stocked, vigorous stand. Do thinning and shelterwood cutting only on sites where fir is known to be windfirm. When making a partial cut, ensure the windward side is protected by a zone of uncut timber at least one chain wide and make cutting boundaries straight. In mixed stands with hardwoods, maintain a well-distributed hardwood component. If damage becomes severe, conduct a salvage harvest.

Birch

Paper birch forms either small pure stands or mixtures. Quaking and bigtooth aspen and pin cherry are its most common associates. It also may be mixed with yellow birch, red maple, northern red oak, white pine, jack pine, white spruce, and balsam fir. This forest type occurs throughout the northern Lake States (Figure 6-3).

Figure 6-3. Range of paper birch.

Products and Uses

The main uses for paper birch are paper, fuelwood, dowels, and novelty items, but it also is used for lumber and veneer. Birch trees can be tapped in the spring to obtain sap for syrup, wine, beer, or medicinal tonics. Its showy white bark and bright yellow fall foliage make it an attractive landscape tree. Young stands provide an important source of browse for deer and moose. Songbirds feed on its seeds while ruffed grouse and squirrels eat male flower buds and catkins.

Site Conditions

Paper birch is a pioneer forest type that revegetates land disturbed by fire, clearcutting, and other factors. It grows on almost any soil and topographic situation, ranging from steep, rocky outcrops to flat acid bogs with peat soil. Paper birch tends to grow best on deep, well-drained to moderately well-drained, nutrient rich glacial deposits. It grows poorly on very dry and very wet sites.

Regeneration

Paper birch is intolerant of shade and usually is regenerated by clearcutting or shelterwood systems. Although small birches produce vigorous stump sprouts when cut, merchantable-size trees do not sprout well and sprouts are normally of low quality. Natural seeding is the most common source of regeneration. The optimum seedbearing age is 40 to 70 years. In mature stands, good seed crops occur every other year on the average, but some seeds are produced in most areas every year. Its light seeds are dispersed readily by the wind; however, the majority of seeds fall within the stand where they are produced. If a clearcut has to be more than 300 feet wide, leave seed trees throughout the site to get adequate seed dispersal and provide for the survival of seed trees and protection of new seedlings. Remove seed trees within two years after acceptable regeneration.

Paper birch germinate best on mineral soil, so site preparation by disking or burning is recommended. Germination on humus is reduced by about 50 percent, but initial height growth is better on humus than on undisturbed sites, probably because of greater nutrient availability. Germination on undisturbed litter is relatively poor.

Shaded sites produce about twice as many seedlings as full-sun sites, so harvest by narrow, progressive clearcut strips, small patch clearcuts, or a two-cut shelterwood system (especially on hot, dry sites). In a shelterwood system, the first cut should thin the canopy and provide more sunlight to the forest floor. A year later, disk the site to lightly bury the birch seeds, help control competing vegetation, and incorporate organic matter. Disking is especially helpful following a good seed fall. After the stand is sufficiently stocked with seedlings, clearcut canopy trees to release the new seedlings.

To establish birch on old field sites, remove the sod, plant bare-root or container-grown seedlings, and protect them from girdling by rodents and browsing by deer.

Intermediate Treatments

Young paper birch grows rapidly, but the growth rate declines significantly in old age. The species is short-lived, reaching maturity in 60 to 70 years. It usually lasts only one generation and then is replaced by more shade-tolerant species. Poor sites may be clearcut for firewood every 40 years or converted to another species. Good sites can be managed for sawlogs on 50-year or longer rotations. On good sites that are clearcut and regenerate to aspen, pin cherry, and paper birch, the faster growing aspen and pin cherry will outgrow and suppress the birch.

Birch often grows in two-story stands. When paper birch has an understory of white spruce or balsam fir, the conifers will eventually dominate the stand, but birch will retain a presence. When paper birch has an understory of northern hardwoods (such as, sugar maple, red maple, basswood, ash, and some oaks), the birch will be replaced by the hardwoods over time. To retain a higher percentage of birch, thin mixed species stands to release the birch. Gradual thinning over time is recommended. The heavier the thinning, the greater the height and diameter growth response of paper birch. However, heavily thinning a stand that has not previously been thinned may cause many of the remaining trees to die. Stands approaching maturity seldom respond well to thinning.

Pests and Diseases

Bronze birch borer is the most serious insect pest of paper birch. Usually it attacks overmature trees or weakened trees. The most serious defoliators are the forest tent caterpillar, birch skeletonizer, birch leafminer, birch leaf-mining sawflies, birch case-bearer, and gypsy moth. Defoliation alone seldom kills healthy trees, but it reduces their growth rate and makes birch susceptible to other damaging agents, particularly bronze birch borer.

Birch also is affected by decay-causing fungi, stem cankers that ruin the tree for timber purposes, and root-rotting fungus.

Over-browsing by deer and moose at the seedling stage reduces the amount of dominant birch in regenerating stands or impairs the quality of sur-vivors. Porcupines damage larger trees by feeding on the inner bark and girdling large branches in the crown and upper trunk. The yellow-bellied sap-sucker pecks rows of holes through the bark; these become the point of entry for decay organisms and ring shake (separation). Hares and other small mammals may seriously damage planted seedlings.

Because paper birch bark is thin and highly flam-mable, even large trees may be killed by moderate fires.

Paper birch is very susceptible to logging damage during partial harvest treatments using mechanical techniques.

Black Ash–American Elm– Red Maple

This forest type occurs throughout the Lake States (Figure 6-4) with varying proportions of ash, elm, and maple. American elm has declined in impor-tance because of the prevalence of Dutch elm disease. The most common associates are balsam poplar, balsam fir, and yellow birch, but also may include eastern white pine, tamarack, black spruce, northern white-cedar, white spruce, quaking aspen, slippery elm, paper birch, and American basswood. Management recommendations in this section focus on black ash.

Figure 6-4. Range of black ash.

Products and Uses

Black ash is used for lumber, veneer, fuelwood, and baskets. The need for more basket-grade trees has resulted in greater interest in managing black ash, especially around Native American communi-ties. Its seeds are an important food to game birds, songbirds, and small animals, and the twigs and leaves provide browse for deer and moose.

Site Conditions

Black ash typically grows in bogs, along streams, and in poorly drained areas that often are season-ally flooded. It is most common on peat and muck soils, but also grows on fine sands that are under-lain by sandy till (mixed clay, sand, gravel, and boulders) or on sands and loams that are underlain by clayey till. It can tolerate semi-stagnant con-ditions, but for best growth, the water should be moving so the soil will be aerated even though saturated. It tolerates pH from 4.4 to 8.2. In the northern Lake States the type frequently grades into northern white-cedar on wetter sites and into hemlock-yellow birch on better-drained areas. In northern Wisconsin it grades into tamarack or black spruce stands.

Regeneration

Black ash reproduces from stump sprouts when trees are less than 12 inches DBH, from root suckers after trees are cut, and from seeds. It produces good seed crops about every four years. Because of seed dormancy requiring cold treatment, black ash seed does not normally germinate under natural conditions until the second year, and seed may remain viable for eight years.

Regenerate stands that are 15 to 18 inches DBH or 110 to 130 years old. A partial or complete removal of the overstory without advance regeneration will allow a rise in the water table, leading to a lack of seedling regeneration and stump sprouting.

If there are fewer than 5,000 desirable seedlings an acre, make a shelterwood cut, leaving 75 percent crown cover of the best quality trees. When stocking reaches 5,000 seedlings an acre, reduce the crown cover to 50 percent. When seedlings are 2 to 3 feet tall (at about three to five years), clearcut the remaining trees when the ground is frozen and preferably covered with at least a foot of snow to reduce damage to seedlings.

To reinforce natural regeneration, plant 1-0 or 2-0 seedlings. (e.g. 1 or 2 year old seedlings).

Intermediate Treatments

Black ash is a small, slow growing tree, commonly reaching just 8 to 10 inches DBH when mature. It is intolerant of shade.

In pole-sized stands, release crop trees about 5 to 7 feet beyond their crowns. Delay later thinnings until the crowns close and the lower branches have self-pruned, then thin to 90 percent crown cover. During thinnings, remove undesirable species and trees with poor stem form, suppressed crowns, or signs of disease or damage.

Pests and Diseases

Trunk rot and butt rot are the most serious diseases affecting black ash. Emerald ash borer is an invasive insect species that infests and kills all species of ash. It occurs in parts of Michigan, Minnesota, and Wisconsin and is moving westward. Contact your state forestry agency for recommendations if your ash trees are dying or if you suspect they may be infested with emerald ash borer. Do not import or export firewood beyond the local area to minimize insect movement in the wood. Deer browse heavily on young black ash and if poplars are scarce, beaver will cut down ash.

Black Spruce

Black spruce commonly grows in pure stands on organic soils and in mixed stands on mineral soils. Mixed stands often include northern white-cedar, white spruce, balsam fir, and tamarack. It is found throughout the northern Lake States, but especially northern Minnesota (Figure 6-5).

Figure 6-5. Range of black spruce.

Products and Uses

Black spruce is grown almost exclusively for pulpwood. The spruce grouse depends on this forest type for most of its food and cover. Several songbirds use this forest type in summer.

Site Conditions

Black spruce usually grows on wet organic soils, but productive stands are found on a variety of soil types from deep humus through clays, loams, sands, coarse till, boulder pavements, and shallow soil over bedrock. The most productive black spruce stands are on dark brown to blackish peats, which usually have a considerable amount of decayed woody material. The best sites occur where the soil water is part of the regional groundwater system and is enriched by nutrients flowing from mineral soil areas. The poorest sites occur where the soil water is separated from the groundwater system, and where there is 2 feet or more of poorly decomposed, yellowish-brown sphagnum moss. When found on mineral soil, black spruce grows best where the slope is gentle and moisture is plentiful, either from a shallow water table or seepage along bedrock. Site index curves for black spruce are in Appendix B-3.

Regeneration

Rotation lengths for black spruce range from 60 to 140 years, but usually should not exceed 100 years on organic soils or 70 years on mineral soils because of butt rot and subsequent wind damage.

Black spruce stands 40 years or older have a nearly continuous seed supply. Good seed crops occur every two to six years, but partially closed cones remain on trees and disperse seed over several years. Under natural conditions, most seed is dispersed after a fire. Reproduction by layering (root development from low-hanging branches) is common in swamps and bogs.

A good seedbed is moist, but not saturated, and free from competing vegetation. Moist mineral soil usually provides a good seedbed, but exposed mineral soil may be too waterlogged or subject to frost heaving in low-lying areas. Living sphagnum moss makes a good seedbed, but some moss species may outgrow and smother spruce seedlings. Other mosses, especially feather mosses, tend to dry out after clearcutting and make poor seedbeds. Moss seedbeds should be removed by fire or machine or compacted by machine.

Clearcutting blocks or strips is the best method for harvesting and reproducing black spruce.

The best growing sites on organic soil usually are brushy and require broadcast burning of slash to reduce shrub competition. To avoid heavy slash that covers desirable residual trees or good sphagnum moss seedbeds, use whole-tree harvesting or burn the slash. Fires that completely remove the surface organic layer usually provide good seedbeds. Seedbed scarification also increases the number of surviving black ash seedlings.

Natural seeding can be effective with large, wind-firm stands. Cut progressive strips perpendicular to the prevailing wind to maximize seed dispersal and minimize wind damage. Cut these strips into the wind, up to six chains wide where natural seeding occurs from both sides, or four chains wide where natural seeding occurs only from the windward side.

Rely on natural seeding along the outer portion of large stands while considering direct seeding of interior areas. On well-prepared sites, sow two to three ounces of seed an acre between March and mid-May of the first year following burning or other site preparation. Treat seed with bird repellent and fungicide.

Natural seeding, especially on nonbrushy sites, often results in stands that are too dense for optimum pulpwood growth. To avoid overstocking, count the trees three years after site preparation. If there are at least 600 healthy, well-spaced black spruce seedlings an acre that are at least 6 inches tall, clearcut the adjacent area of mature spruce to eliminate further seeding into the new stand.

Planting seedlings is more reliable than seeding, but also more expensive. Black spruce can be planted successfully using 3-0 or container-grown seedlings. Transplants (2-2) are expensive but useful where serious weed competition is expected.

Intermediate Treatments

Thinning overstocked sapling and poletimber stands is generally not economical and may lead to increased wind damage. Although black spruce is shade tolerant, on good sites a dense overstory of undesirable shrubs or hardwoods may severely suppress seedling growth. In these situations control brush with herbicide to release the spruce.

Pests and Diseases

Eastern dwarf-mistletoe is the most serious disease affecting black spruce. It causes branch deformations (witches' brooms, or dense clusters of abnormal small branches), reduces growth, and eventually kills trees. Mistletoe survives only on living trees and spreads slowly. To kill mistletoe, cut all trees in infected areas plus a border strip one to two chains wide; then burn the site with a hot fire. To prevent mistletoe infections, clearcut and burn all mature stands where feasible to eliminate undetected mistletoe sources.

Wind may cause substantial breakage and uprooting in older black spruce stands, especially where butt rot is present and where stands have been opened up by partial cutting. Minimize wind damage by using the rotations recommended above and clearcutting narrow strips that progress over time toward prevailing winds.

Black Walnut

Black walnut (Figure 6-6) generally is found scattered among other tree species. Pure stands are not common, but do occur. Common associates include yellow-poplar, white ash, black cherry, basswood, beech, sugar maple, oaks, and hickories. Its leaves and roots actively secrete material toxic to some trees, shrubs, and herbaceous plants.

Products and Uses

Wood products from black walnut include sawlogs, veneer logs, gun stocks, and smaller novelty pieces. Nuts are excellent for human consumption. Frequent nut crops make it an excellent tree for wildlife, especially squirrels. Nut shells are used as an abrasive in grinding and polishing.

Site Conditions

Walnut grows best on lower north- and east-facing slopes, stream terraces, and floodplains. It is common on limestone soils and grows well on deep loams, loess soils, and alluvial deposits that are fertile and moist, but well-drained. Poor sites for walnut include steep south- and west-facing slopes, narrow ridgetops, and poorly drained sites. Soils with acid clayey subsoils, coarse sand or gravel layers, or bedrock within 2.5 feet of the surface are not suitable for walnut. Site index curves for black walnut plantations are in Appendix B-4.

Figure 6-6. Range of black walnut.

Regeneration

The rotation length for black walnut is 50 to 80 years. It naturally regenerates from seed and stump sprouts if trees are less than 20 to 30 years old. Since black walnut trees normally are a minor component of a woodland, natural regeneration is unreliable and planting seedlings is recommended.

Black walnut is intolerant of shade. To prepare a woodland site for planting, cut or kill with herbicides all woody vegetation larger than 0.5-inches in diameter. On grassy and weedy sites apply herbicides in the year before planting to kill existing vegetation in planting strips or blocks. Plant seedlings at a spacing of 10 by 10 feet for timber production and 15 by 15 feet for a combination of timber and nuts. In field plantings for timber, planting a conifer (such as white or red pine) in every third row may increase the survival rate, growth rate, and improve the stem straightness of walnut trees. Plant seedlings in the spring as soon after the ground thaws as possible. Use seedlings at least 1/4-inch in diameter, measured 1-inch above the root collar.

Seeds are easier and less expensive to plant than seedlings, but must be protected from squirrels and other rodents. Mechanical barriers (such as hardware cloth and tin cans) are most reliable, but they are expensive and time consuming to install.

Sow seeds in either fall or spring. Husks do not need to be removed for fall planting. Spring planting eliminates overwinter feeding by rodents, but requires that the seed be stratified before planting to break dormancy. (Stratification involves subjecting seed to cold temperatures and regulating moisture for several months.)

Intermediate Treatments

Control weeds for at least three years after planting to maximize the sunlight, moisture, and minerals available to walnut seedlings and to reduce plant cover that encourages rodents. Control weeds by mowing or cultivation in open field plantings or by herbicides. In most situations herbicides are more cost effective and reliable than mowing or cultivation.

Corrective pruning can improve seedling form if tip dieback or stem forking has occurred. Do not prune too heavily; young stems have a strong natural tendency to grow upright. Clear-stem pruning is recommended to help produce knot-free wood.

Fertilization generally is not needed on a good black walnut site unless a specific nutrient is deficient. Foliage analysis will reveal any nutrient deficiencies. Weeds are the usual benefactors of fertilizers.

Thin the stand lightly and frequently, perhaps every 10 years, to maintain rapid, uniform growth. If you planted conifers along with the walnuts, remove the conifers when they compete for crown space. When thinning, provide at least 5 feet of space around three-quarters of the crowns of crop trees. Select crop trees early by choosing those with straight stems, one dominant leader, well-formed crowns, and no apparent signs of disease or injury. Kill competing trees by felling or girdling and treating them with an herbicide.

Pests and Diseases

The major pests of black walnut are walnut caterpillars and bud borers. Pesticides usually are not economical. The major diseases that infect black walnut are anthracnose and fusarium canker. Fungicides may be necessary to control anthracnose for the purpose of improving nut production, and insecticides may be necessary to control caterpillars. Anthracnose can be managed by controlling weeds that weaken the trees. Fusarium canker can be controlled by restricting pruning to late winter. Fire is highly damaging to black walnut.

Incorrect pruning can lead to serious problems, including fusarium canker, bark necrosis, and sunscald.

Bur Oak

The bur oak type occurs across Minnesota, Wisconsin, and southern Michigan (Figure 6-7, pg. 68). Because it tolerates a wide range of soil and moisture conditions, bur oak associates with many other trees. Northern pin oak and black oak are associates on sandy sites; white oak and hickories are found with it on other dry upland sites. Chinkapin oak and eastern redcedar are associates on hot, dry hillsides in southwestern Wisconsin. Associates on lowland sites include shagbark and other hickories, black walnut, eastern cottonwood, white ash, American elm, swamp white oak, American basswood, black ash, silver maple and sycamore. Because of its fire and drought resistance, bur oak is the most common tree on oak savannahs along the prairie-forest transition zone in Wisconsin and Minnesota.

Products and Uses

Bur oak wood is commercially valuable for sawlogs and veneer, although high quality timber is

68

not common. Their acorns are a prime food for squirrels, wood ducks, white-tailed deer, and small mammals.

Figure 6-7. Range of bur oak.

Site Conditions

Bur oak is one of the most drought resistant North American oaks. On uplands it often is associated with soils of limestone or sandstone origin. It is found on droughty sandy plains, black prairie loams, and on loamy slopes of south and west exposure. Toward the western edge of its range, it is more abundant on moist north-facing slopes than on south-facing slopes. It often dominates severe sites with thin soils, heavy claypan soils, gravelly ridges, and coarse-textured loessial hills. Bur oak is also an important bottomland species throughout much of its range.

On the prairie edge it is a pioneer tree, commonly succeeded by northern pin oak, black oak, white oak, and bitternut hickory. On moist sites it is replaced by the more shade tolerant sugar maple, American basswood, and American beech.

As a bottom-land species, bur oak is relatively intolerant of flooding. First-year mortality may be 40 to 50 percent if seedlings are submerged for two weeks or more during the growing season. For shorter periods of growing-season submersion, seedling mortality is only 10 to 20 percent.

Regeneration

Bur oak is slow-growing, but commonly lives 200 to 300 years or longer. The minimum seed-bearing age is about 35 years and the optimum is 75 to 150 years. Good seed crops occur every two to three years. Acorns are disseminated by gravity, squirrels, and to a limited extent by water. Germination usually occurs soon after seedfall (August through November), but acorns from some northern trees may remain dormant through winter and germinate the following spring. Acorn germination and early seedling development is best on moist, mineral soil with no litter cover.

Bur oak stands are self-sustaining on dry sites, but planting seedlings and controlling grass and brush will aid regeneration. Bur oak will be difficult to sustain on moist bottomland sites where other species grow faster, but planting seedlings during regeneration phases will help sustain some bur oak in the species mix. Although mature bur oaks have thick, fire-resistant bark, it is important to prevent fires from burning over the area until trees mature and develop thick bark.

Burning or cutting pole-size or smaller bur oaks results in vigorous stump sprouting, but sprout quality and form are poor.

Intermediate Treatments

Bur oak is intermediate in shade tolerance. Use intermediate cuttings to manage species composition according to the site. Prairie burning on upland sites is a common practice to kill invading brush and sustain prairie grasses. Mature bur oaks with thick bark withstand burns quite well.

Pests and Diseases

Bur oak is attacked by several defoliating insects, including oak webworms, oak skeletonizers, a leaf miner, variable oakleaf caterpillars, June beetles, and oak lacebugs. Oak wilt is a less serious problem in bur oak than in members of the red oak group, although the disease sometimes spreads through root grafts, killing entire groves. Bur oak is susceptible to attack by root rot, canker, and dieback diseases. It tolerates urban pollution better than most oaks. Young trees are susceptible to fire, but older trees develop thick bark that is fire resistant.

Eastern White Pine

Eastern white pine often occurs in pure stands, especially in the eastern portion of its range (Figure 6-8), but may have a balsam fir understory in the northern Lake States. It is a pioneer species on abandoned agricultural land and in the northern Lake States may succeed red pine. On drier, sandier soils it approaches permanence as a sustainable forest type. On heavy-textured soils, white pine usually is succeeded by sugar maple-beech-yellow birch, white pine-hemlock, sugar maple-basswood, or white oak types.

Figure 6-8. Range of eastern white pine.

Products and Uses

Eastern white pine is used mainly for lumber. Some songbirds, squirrels, and small mammals feed on its seeds. Bark and foliage are consumed by beaver, snowshoe hares, rabbits, porcupine, red and gray squirrels, mice, and white-tailed deer. Bears use large white pines as escape cover for their cubs and they use young dense stands for shelter during inclement weather.

Site Conditions

White pine grows on nearly all the soils within its range, but competes best on well-drained sandy soils of low to medium site quality. On medium-textured soils (sandy loams), it will out-produce most other native species in both volume and value. White pine also grows on fine sandy loams and silt-loam soils with either good or impeded drainage when there is no hardwood competition during the establishment period—as on old fields and pastures, burns, and blowdowns. Do not plant white pine on heavy clay soils, poorly drained bottomland sites, and upland depressions. Avoid planting in depressions, bases of slopes, narrow V-shaped valleys, or small openings in dense forests that favor the collection of cool, moist air that encourages the spread of white pine blister rust. Site index curves are in Appendix B-7.

Regeneration

White pine commonly lives 200 years and may live up to 450 years. Sawlog rotations usually are 80 to 120 years, but longer rotations are feasible to produce a stand with old-growth characteristics.

Reliable seed production begins when trees are 20 to 30 years old, and good seed years occur every three to five years. Seeds mature in August and September and are dispersed within a month by wind (200 feet within a stand, 700 feet in the open) and squirrels.

Seeds can germinate and survive on both disturbed and undisturbed litter layers. Under full exposure to sunlight, favorable seedbeds include moist mineral soil, polytrichum moss, or a short grass cover of light to medium density. Unfavorable seedbeds include dry mineral soil, pine litter, lichen, and very thin or very thick grass cover. Unfavorable seedbed conditions can be corrected by scarification or overstory shade; however, dense, low shade, such as that cast by slash piles or hardwood brush, hinders seedling survival.

Regenerate white pine by clearcutting, seed tree, shelterwood, or group selection. If there is abundant advanced reproduction, remove the overstory to release the white pines. Clearcutting during or just after heavy seed crops often results in well-stocked stands on light soils. Clearcutting in small patches or stands with seed dispersed from adjacent stands is also possible. Because of competition from other vegetation and poor seed crops, mechanical site preparation and planting may be necessary with clearcutting.

A two-cut shelterwood system probably is the most reliable method for natural regeneration. Ten years before the final harvest, remove 40 to 60 percent of the overstory (no more than 30 to 40 percent of the basal area), preferably ideally in the year before or during a good seed year. Harvest during snowless months to scarify the site and expose mineral soil. Remove hardwood regeneration during the harvest since hardwoods may seriously compete with pine seedlings. After 5 to 10 years, if white pine seedlings are abundant, clearcut the residual overstory. (Delay this harvest until the new white pines are 20 to 25 feet tall if you expect white pine weevil to be a problem.) If white pine regeneration is not satisfactory, you may need to again thin the overstory, control advance hardwood regeneration, and wait another 5 to 10 years before the final harvest. Consider planting white pine seedlings to increase the density to 500 to 600 seedlings an acre.

Mechanical site preparation and planting are required on bare land or in white pine stands that do not naturally regenerate. Plant 2-0 or 3-0 seedlings at rates up to 600 to 800 trees an acre (closer where heavy white pine weevil damage is expected). Plant under a light forest canopy to reduce weevil and white pine blister rust damage.

Intermediate Treatments

White pine is intermediate in shade tolerance. It will tolerate up to 80 percent shade, but achieves maximum height growth in as little as 45 percent full sunlight. In the seedling stage it is very susceptible to competition because its height growth is slow. If white pine survives to the sapling stage, it becomes a stronger competitor.

Pure natural stands of white pine almost never stagnate. Stagnation occurs when all trees grow at about the same rate, then growth slows due to competition. Because of differences in vigor, age, and site, differentiation into crown and diameter classes usually occurs. You do not need to thin white pine seedling and sapling stands, but if a hardwood overstory develops, partially remove it to maintain 50 percent of full sunlight on the white pine. When trees average six to eight inches DBH, begin thinning and remove the hardwood overstory. Use the stocking chart for eastern white pine in Appendix C-3 as a thinning guide. When stands reach the A level, cut them back to the B level. Basal area after thinning should be about 100 square feet for young stands and 150 square feet for older stands.

Since white pine has persistent branches (that is, the lower branches do not self-prune as the tree ages), prune potential crop trees to a height of 17 feet to develop clear wood. Prune in the dormant season, removing limbs less than two inches in diameter. Maintain at least a 30 percent live-crown ratio. You can remove at least 25 percent of the live crown in open stands and up to 50 percent in closed stands without losses in height growth. Frequent light prunings are preferred to a single heavy pruning. Depending on local markets, pruning may not be economical.

Pests and Diseases

The most serious pests are white pine blister rust, white pine weevil, root rot, and deer browsing.

White pine blister rust can kill trees of any age. A local forester can advise you about the blister rust hazard in your area. Do not plant white pine in high-hazard zones. In medium and low-hazard zones, begin clear-stem pruning early to minimize the disease. Start pruning when white pines are more than two feet tall and continue until you have removed all branches within nine feet of the ground. Cut off infected limbs (shown by cankers

▲

or flagging of dead needles) wherever they occur. Trees with cankers on the main stem or on a branch within four inches of the main stem cannot be saved.

White pine weevils tunnel into the terminal leader, causing crooked or forked stems. If damage is present in small trees, clip wilted terminals in July and destroy the clipped terminals to remove weevils.

Reduce white pine weevil and blister rust damage by regenerating white pines under an overstory of hardwoods and releasing them slowly. When the pines are about 20 to 25 feet tall, remove the overstory.

White pines are a favorite food of deer. Protect seedlings with a budcap (Figure 6-9) or deer repellent.

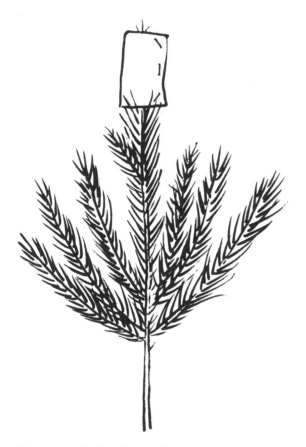

Figure 6-9. Bud capping protects young white pine from deer. Place a budcap on the main leader in fall. Cut lightweight paper into 4-inch by 6-inch pieces. Fold the paper around the leader, covering the top bud; fasten it with three staples that catch needles. Repeat annually until the trees are at least 4 feet tall.

Hemlock–Yellow Birch

This type occurs mainly in northern Wisconsin, Michigan's Upper Peninsula, and the northern portion of lower Michigan (Figure 6-10). Eastern hemlock and yellow birch are the principal species, with hemlock usually dominating. Common associates include red maple, sugar maple, and American basswood.

Figure 6-10. Range of eastern hemlock.

Products and Uses

Hemlock is used for paper and lumber. Yellow birch lumber and veneer are used in making furniture, paneling, plywood, cabinets, boxes, woodenware, handles, and interior doors. It is one of the principal hardwoods used in the distillation of wood alcohol, acetate of lime, charcoal, tar, and oils. Yellow birch is good browse for deer and moose. Other wildlife feed on the buds and seeds. Hemlock stands are essential for shelter and bedding of white-tailed deer during winter. The type also provides important cover for ruffed grouse, turkeys, and many other animals.

Site Conditions

Hemlock and yellow birch grow best on moist, well-drained sandy loam, loamy sand, and silt loam soils. Older stands typically occur on soils with a high water table and varying texture that develop a thick humus layer under a relatively low, dense overstory. As the site becomes drier, the type merges with sugar maple, sugar maple-beech-yellow birch, or beech-sugar maple. On wetter sites, hemlock-yellow birch frequently merges into the hemlock and white pine-hemlock types and on the wettest sites with the black ash-American elm-red maple type.

Regeneration

Eastern hemlock is a slow-growing, long-lived tree that grows well in shade. It may take 250 years to reach maturity and some specimens survive over 800 years.

Hemlock begins producing seed at age 15 and good seed crops occur every other year. Seeds fall from mid-October through early winter, but are dispersed only about one tree height in distance. Hemlock requires a warm, moist site for stand establishment, but successful regeneration is difficult to achieve. Seed viability is low. Seeds require temperatures of about 44° to 64° F for 45 to 60 days to germinate (longer than most tree species require). Seeds are severely damaged after only two hours of drying, and seedlings are subject to damping-off and root rot fungi.

Yellow birch begins producing good seed crops at age 40 in dense stands, and good crops occur every two to three years. Seeds are dispersed by wind primarily in October. Good seed fall occurs at least 330 feet from seed-bearing trees and seed can disperse much farther when blown across crusted snow. Yellow birch seedlings and small saplings reproduce from sprouts when cut, but sprouting from larger stems is very poor.

Regeneration of this type is most successful on moist flats or sites providing some protection from extended periods of sunlight. Use a shelterwood system that leaves 70 to 80 percent crown cover for optimum hemlock regeneration or 45 to 50 percent crown cover for optimum yellow birch regeneration. Kill advance regeneration and remove litter with a spring fire or scarify the site, mixing organic and mineral soil over 50 to 75 percent of the area. Plan treatments to coincide with good seed crops because the effects of scarification last only two or three growing seasons.

Without these conditions most eastern hemlock and yellow birch regeneration occurs on rotten logs, stumps, and mounds that normally have warmer surfaces and better moisture retention than the forest floor.

Seedlings develop slowly even under ideal growing conditions, with stable moisture in the upper soil horizon throughout the growing season. Once the root system has reached a soil depth not radically affected by surface drying, usually after the second year, seedlings grow more rapidly without interference from overhead shade. Supplemental seeding would enhance natural seeding under most conditions. Seedlings are fully established when they are 3 to 5 feet tall, and then can be released completely from overhead competition.

Survival and height growth of planted hemlock (3-0 stock) and yellow birch (2-0 stock) usually is good in small openings or under a partial overstory. To artificially seed birch, stratify seed for 4 to 8 weeks at 41° F in moist peat or sand. Spread 0.5 lb an acre of birch seed about a week after site preparation in May, or sow unstratified seed before January.

Intermediate Treatments

Both hemlock and yellow birch are very slow growing species, but hemlock is longer lived, commonly surviving to 400 years of age.

Eastern hemlock is the most shade tolerant of all tree species in North America and can withstand suppression for 400 years. Yellow birch is intermediate in shade tolerance. Within five years of regeneration, yellow birch seedlings may require release from faster growing species. In the sapling stage, thin stands to provide 6 to 8 feet of open space around the best dominant and codominant trees. Continue periodically releasing dominant and codominant trees through the small sawlog stage. However, excessive release of hemlock may reduce growth, increase mortality, and contribute to windthrow. Heavy release of yellow birch results in epicormic branches that degrade the stem.

In mixed stands of hardwoods and hemlock, where the proportion of hemlock is 15 percent or more, it is feasible to manage for hemlock at various residual stocking levels. Hemlock does not require as much growing space as hardwoods, so residual stocking is greater in stands where hemlock predominates. Stands with less than 15 percent hemlock should be managed for hardwoods.

When thinning stands exceeding 200 square feet an acre of basal area, remove no more than one-third of the total basal area at one time. Excessive cutting results in reduced growth and increased mortality and contributes to windthrow. In addition, hardwood encroachment interferes with the successful establishment of hemlock. Fully stocked stands with basal areas of less than 200 square feet an acre can be thinned to a minimum of 120 square feet an acre.

Yellow birch prunes itself well so long as its crown is allowed to close within five or six years after release. It can, however, be pruned to 50 percent of its height without reducing growth. Prune small, fast-growing trees with small knotty cores to limit discoloration and decay.

Pests and Diseases

Young hemlock seedlings are often damaged by desiccation, damping-off fungi and root rot. In the Eastern United States, the hemlock woolly adelgid is a serious insect pest that feeds on needles. It is expected to reach the Lake States sometime in the future. Young hemlock and birch are susceptible to fire damage. The bronze birch borer is the most serious insect pest of yellow birch. Mature and overmature trees left severely exposed after logging and in lightly stocked stands are more subject to attack than are trees in well-stocked stands. Yellow birch is a preferred food of snowshoe hare and white-tailed deer. Overmature birch are subject to canker diseases, root rots, and stem decay. Birch is not a preferred host for leaf-feeding insects, but severe outbreaks that last several years will kill birch.

Jack Pine

Jack pine (Figure 6-11) usually grows in pure stands, but may be mixed with northern pin oak, red pine, quaking aspen, paper birch, and balsam fir. On moist sites in the northern Lake States, jack pine may succeed to red pine to eastern white pine to hardwoods (such as sugar maple, basswood, and northern red oak).

Figure 6-11. Range of jack pine.

Products and Uses

Jack pine is used mainly for pulpwood, poles, and small sawlogs. It is moderately useful deer browse. Dense, young stands provide cover for snowshoe hares. Dense sapling and poletimber stands offer some wildlife shelter, but not as much as most other conifers. The Kirtland's warbler, an endangered species of bird that nests only in Michigan, requires homogeneous jack pine stands that cover more than 80 acres and and have trees that are 5 to 20 feet tall with branches that reach the ground. Older jack pine stands usually are less dense than other conifer stands, permitting the growth of understory shrubs and herbaceous plants that provide food and cover for wildlife.

Site Conditions

Jack pine commonly grows on level to gently rolling sand plains. It occurs less commonly on eskers, sand dunes, rock outcrops, and bald rock ridges. It grows best on well-drained loamy sands where the midsummer water table is 4 to 6 feet below the surface. Jack pine does well on moderately acidic soils, but it will tolerate slightly alkaline conditions. It grows poorly on shallow bedrock and heavy clay soil. Jack pine survives and grows better than other tree species on dry sandy soils. On better sites, convert the stand to species that are more productive and valuable for wood products. Site index curves for jack pine are shown in Appendix B-9.

Regeneration

Although jack pine is short-lived, stands sometimes survive for 100 years. Plan a rotation age of 40 to 50 years for pulpwood and 60 to 70 years for poles and sawtimber. Mature trees range from 8 to 12 inches DBH.

Jack pines typically begin producing seeds when they are 5 to 10 years old under open-crown conditions, but later when growing in dense stands. The best seed production occurs in trees that are 40 to 50 years old. Seed production is fairly regular and increases until crown competition becomes a factor. Some seed is usually produced every year and total crop failures are rare. Jack pine cones in parts of the range are serotinous—that is, they remain closed at maturity. Serotinous cones open most readily during dry weather when the temperature is at least 80° F, although many remain closed until they are exposed to fire or high temperatures (122° F) near the ground after wind breakage or logging. Nonserotinous cones may disseminate seeds during any season. Jack pine seeds are dispersed by wind about two tree heights.

Seedling survival is highest on mineral soil and burned seedbeds where competition from other vegetation is not severe, the water table is high, and there is light shade primarily from scattered slash. Heavy slash must be reduced by full-tree skidding, burning with a hot fire, chopping, disking, or dragging. Shrubs and other competition can be controlled by full-tree skidding, machine scalping, disking, roller-chopping, bulldozing, shearing, rock or root raking, or using herbicides. Clearcutting creates the best conditions for regeneration, but seed tree or shelterwood systems may be appropriate depending on the stand and site conditions.

Clearcut where a new stand will be established by planting improved seedlings, direct seeding, or scattering serotinous cones from high-quality trees. The sun's heat near the ground surface will open serotinous cones and release the seed. If the mature stand is not a suitable seed source, burn the site to destroy slash and plant or seed the area using a desirable seed source.

The seed-tree system may work satisfactorily where you have 10 well-distributed, desirable quality seed trees an acre with an abundant supply of nonserotinous cones. After the harvest, burn the area to consume slash, kill competition, and prepare a favorable seedbed. Burn slash as soon as possible after harvest to minimize the risk of seed trees windthrowing before they cast seed. Jack pine slash requires a month of warm, dry weather to cure sufficiently to burn. Early spring fires permit seeding during the most favorable season, but late fall burning and seeding may be almost as effective if rodent populations are low.

Consider the shelterwood system in well-stocked stands with nonserotinous cones. Treat competition and slash as described earlier. Cut the stand to leave 30 to 40 square feet of basal area an acre in desirable seed trees. Remove the shelterwood overstory when there are 600 seedlings an acre or within 10 years.

Direct seeding in early spring may be successful where the water table is within a few feet of the surface or there is frequent precipitation during germination and early seedling development. Coat the seed with bird and rodent repellents and sow it at the rate of 20,000 viable seeds an acre.

▲

Where direct seeding has failed, or on deep, dry sandy soils, plant bare-root seedlings in spring or container-grown stock into early summer. Plant at a 6- to 8-foot spacing.

Jack pine is a pioneer type on nearly all sites except dry, sandy soils. On better sites facilitate the successional trend by harvesting jack pines in several cuts to encourage the growth of other species, or clearcut and plant another species, usually red pine or white spruce, depending on the site.

Intermediate Treatments

Jack pine is very intolerant of shade. On better sites with substantial hardwood competition, control brush with herbicides when it threatens to overtop jack pines.

Most natural jack pine stands are understocked. To prevent stagnation in dense seedling and sapling stands with more than 2,000 trees an acre, weed out undesirable trees, leaving 800 to 1,000 uniformly spaced crop trees. In very dense seedling stands (for example, with 10,000 trees an acre) it is less expensive to mechanically clear strips about 8 feet wide and leave strips about 2 feet wide. On good sites (with a site index of 60 or more) where sawtimber is desired, thin pole-sized stands to 80 square feet of basal area an acre or follow the stocking chart in Appendix C-4. Do not remove more than one-third of the basal area during any one thinning. Pruning is not recommended.

Pests and Diseases

Common insect pests of jack pine include bark beetles and jack pine budworm. Stem rusts, heart rot, root rot, and stem cankers are important diseases. Fire damages trees of all sizes. Deer browsing, snowshoe hare girdling, and porcupine bark stripping may cause significant mortality when animal populations are high.

Drought and injuries increase losses to insects and diseases. To minimize pest problems, keep stands growing vigorously. Thin regularly, removing suppressed and low-vigor trees while avoiding damage to residual trees. Harvest stands by age 50 (or by

age 70 where the site index is greater than 70). Do not reproduce jack pine where the site index is less than 55.

To avoid bark beetle damage, do not harvest or thin the stand from January through August unless you destroy all slash greater than two inches in diameter within three weeks of cutting. Destroy the slash by piling and burning, chipping, or burying. Avoid wounding trees during thinning. If trees are damaged by fire, windstorms, or logging, harvest them, remove the logs from the woodland, and destroy the slash within three weeks.

Maple–Beech–Yellow Birch

This collection of forest types, often called northern hardwoods, includes several mixes: sugar maple, sugar maple-beech-yellow birch, sugar maple-basswood, beech-sugar maple, and red maple. The dominant species varies with the type, as named, but common associates, depending on the site and geographic range of species, include white ash, green ash, black ash, black cherry, northern red oak, white pine, balsam fir, American elm, hackberry, bitternut hickory, white spruce, ironwood, eastern hemlock, northern white-cedar, paper birch, aspen, and pin cherry. Beech and hemlock occur in eastern Wisconsin and Michigan (Figure 6-12).

Figure 6-12. Range of sugar maple.

76

Products and Uses

This collection of forest types includes numerous tree species. Sawlogs, veneer logs, pulpwood, and firewood are the major wood products from them. Maple syrup is made from sugar maple sap. These forests provide habitat for a variety of wildlife, including deer, bear, squirrel, ruffed grouse, and woodcock.

Site Conditions

Northern hardwoods grow on sands, loamy sands, sandy loams, loams, and silt loams, but they grow best on moist, moderately to well-drained, fertile, loamy soil. Beech favors drier sites while yellow birch favors moister sites. The poorest sites occur on soils that are infertile, dry, shallow, or swampy. Site index comparisons among hardwoods are shown in Appendix B-8.

Regeneration

Northern hardwoods include species that are long-lived and shade tolerant that form self-perpetuating climax plant communities.

The major species produce abundant seeds, but sometimes at irregular intervals. Beech, elm, basswood, and red maple sprout prolifically from stumps. The stumps of young trees sprout more prolifically than those of older trees. Only the sprouts of basswood and sprouts from seedlings and saplings under 2 inches DBH on other species are desirable for reproduction.

Sugar maple, beech, hemlock, and balsam fir are very shade tolerant. Basswood, northern white-cedar and white spruce are tolerant. Yellow birch, white ash, red maple, red oak, bitternut hickory, and white pine are intermediate. Green ash and hackberry are intermediate to intolerant. Black ash, paper birch, aspen, and black cherry are intolerant of shade.

Selection, shelterwood, or clearcutting methods can be used successfully in these types of stands, depending on the species mix of the current stand, advance regeneration, site quality, and desired future species mix.

If high-quality, very shade tolerant species are desired, use single-tree selection or group selection methods. Harvest about every 15 years, leaving roughly 70 square feet of basal area. Do not leave less than 50 or more than 95 square feet of basal area in trees of more than 10 inches DBH. Alternatively, mark the stand for harvest as shown in Table 6-2. Cut mainly trees that have no potential for further economic growth or that interfere with the growth of better trees, then cut mature trees. This system produces an uneven-aged stand.

Table 6-2. Desirable stocking an acre for uneven-aged management of northern hardwoods.

DBH in Inches	Residual Number of Trees Per Acre	Basal Area in Square Feet
5	21	2.9
6	15	2.9
7	12	3.2
8	9	3.1
9	8	3.5
Subtotal	65	16.0
10	7	3.8
11	6	4.0
12	5	3.9
13	5	4.6
14	5	5.3
Subtotal	28	22.0
15	4	4.9
16	4	5.6
17	3	4.7
18	3	5.3
19	3	5.9
Subtotal	17	26.0
20	2	4.4
21	2	4.8
22	2	5.3
23	1	2.9
24	1	3.1
Subtotal	8	20.0
Total	118	84.0

SOURCE: Hutchinson, J. A. (ed.). 1985. Northern Hardwood Notes (Note 4.03). U.S. Government Printing Office, Washington, DC 20402.

To achieve an even-aged stand dominated by sugar maple, use a two-cut shelterwood system. Harvest in winter, preferably when there is snow cover to protect advance regeneration, and leave 60 percent crown cover after the first harvest. Leave good quality dominant trees for a seed source. Remove intermediate and codominant trees, defective trees, and undesirable species. Make the second cut after advance regeneration is 2 to 4 feet high. If you prefer a greater variety of species, use a two-cut shelterwood system following these guidelines:

- Eliminate all reproduction present before cutting.
- Harvest in any season except summer.
- Scarify the site during harvest.
- Leave 70 to 80 percent crown cover.
- Remove undesirable seed sources.
- Make the second cut after advance regeneration is 3 to 4 feet high.

To encourage yellow birch, focus on cool, moist sites. Discriminate against sugar maple in the residual overstory when marking the stand for shelterwood harvest. In open sawlog stands, after leaf fall, but before logging, scarify at least 50 percent of the site to mix humus with mineral soil while destroying advance regeneration; then harvest. In dense stands where mechanical scarification is not practical and on wetter sites, harvest to leave about 70 percent crown cover, then use prescribed fire to remove the litter and destroy advance regeneration.

Planting seedlings is rarely necessary, but is appropriate for open fields or under a shelterwood stand to change the species composition. In open fields plant only in fertile, well-drained soil. Thoroughly disk before planting, plant tap-rooted species such as white ash and northern red oak, plant only when there is good soil moisture, and control weeds for one to three years after planting. Under shelterwoods, kill undesirable understory plants and plant in the most open areas immediately after site preparation.

Where aspen is mixed with more shade-tolerant northern hardwood species, decide whether to encourage aspen or the other species. If there is an overstory of aspen and an understory of hardwoods, you can favor the aspen by clearcutting the stand when aspen are marketable to stimulate aspen root suckering. Favor hardwoods by removing the aspen when the understory hardwoods are 1 to 3 inches DBH, taking great care to avoid damaging the hardwoods. If the aspen has little commercial value, consider killing it with herbicides and letting it stand.

If aspen and other hardwoods are of equal size, favor aspen by clearcutting the stand. To encourage hardwoods, thin or harvest the stand leaving 70 to 85 square feet of basal area an acre in trees 4.6 inches DBH and larger, discriminating against aspen, or follow the stocking chart for even-aged management of northern hardwoods (see Appendix C-5).

Intermediate Treatments

When following the single-tree selection system in an uneven-aged stand, use Table 6-2 to determine the approximate basal area and number of trees to leave after each harvest. Remove poor quality trees and undesirable species during the harvest.

In an even-aged sapling stand, release yellow birch saplings between 10 and 20 years of age by removing competing trees with crowns within 5 feet of the birch. Thin basswood and red maple sprouts to two or three of the straightest, least-defective stems.

Periodically thin even-aged pole stands. There are different stocking charts depending on the percentage of different tree species in the stand. Appendix C-5 may be an appropriate stocking chart for many stands. As a general rule, do not reduce the basal area of trees 4 to 6 inches DBH or more to less than 60 square feet or leave more than 85 square feet. However, if basswood or hemlock are a significant part of the stand, the residual basal area can be increased.

Pests and Diseases

Logging equipment may damage remaining trees. In the next harvest remove trees with wounds larger than 50 square inches. Canker diseases affect yellow birch and sugar maple. Frost cracks also degrade sugar maple in the northern part of its range. Organisms causing rot and stain enter trees through damaged roots, stems, and branches. To reduce volume and quality losses from these sources, train heavy equipment operators to avoid damaging trees, maintain healthy stands, remove infected stems, and keep rotations less than 120 years.

Northern Pin Oak

Northern pin oak occurs in pure stands or in varying mixtures with white oak, black oak, bur oak, northern red oak or jack pine. It also may be associated with red pine, eastern white pine, quaking aspen, bigtooth aspen, red maple, black cherry, and paper birch. It occurs mainly in east central Minnesota, central and northern Wisconsin, and central Michigan.

Products and Uses

Timber quality tends to be poor, but northern pin oak is marketed as a red oak for lumber, railroad ties, and firewood. Northern pin oak acorns are important food for deer, turkeys, squirrels, ruffed grouse, and many other birds and small mammals.

Site Conditions

Northern pin oak commonly grows on dry, acid, sandy soils with a very thin organic layer in sand plains and on gravelly slopes. On better quality sites, conversion to other oaks, red pine, jack pine, or white pine is recommended for timber production.

Regeneration

As a minor forest type and a species with low economic value, little information is available about northern pin oak regeneration and management. It is intolerant of shade and will not reproduce under its own shade. Other oaks and white pine are less light demanding and tend to succeed it.

Acorns drop in the fall and germinate the following spring. The interval between good seed crops is estimated to be two to five years. Acorn weevils and wildlife consume a large portion of the acorn crop, especially in poor seed years. Acorns fall below the canopy, but are dispersed much further by squirrels, blue jays, and other animals. Northern pin oak naturally regenerates on dry sites where few other tree species can survive. Natural regeneration is unreliable under poor site conditions, but can be increased by clearcutting oaks in the fall soon after a good acorn crop has dispersed. Scarify the site during logging by dragging a tree top across the site to help bury acorns. Planting acorns or seedlings of oak or pine is recommended to help ensure regeneration.

Intermediate Treatments

Stand density is likely to be low because of poor site quality, but use intermediate harvests to thin dense patches, remove low quality trees, and adjust species composition. While northern pin oak is a satisfactory species for wildlife, in stands where your goal is timber production, favor other oaks and pines over northern pin oak during thinnings.

Pests and Diseases

Oak wilt is a serious disease. Avoid wounding trees from April through July when insects that transport the disease are most active.

Northern White-Cedar

The northern white-cedar type occurs in the northern Lake States (Figure 6-13) where common associates on wetter sites are balsam fir, tamarack, black spruce, white spruce, black ash, and red maple. Yellow birch, paper birch, quaking aspen, bigtooth aspen, balsam poplar, eastern hemlock, and eastern white pine are common on better drained sites.

Products and Uses

The rot- and termite-resistant wood is used principally for products in contact with water and soil, such as rustic fencing and posts, cabin logs, lumber, poles, and shingles. Smaller amounts are used for paneling, piling, novelties, and woodenware. Cedar leaf oil is distilled from boughs and used in medicines and perfumes; boughs are also used in floral arrangements. The northern white-cedar type is valuable for white-tailed deer shelter and browse in winter. It is also used by snowshoe hare, porcupine, red squirrel and in summer by several songbird species.

Figure 6-13. Range of northern white-cedar.

Site Conditions

Northern white-cedar grows on a wide variety of organic soils and mineral soils, but it grows best on limestone-derived soils that are neutral or slightly alkaline (pH of 5.5 to 7.2) and moist but well-drained. It does not develop well on extremely wet or extremely dry sites. It is usually dominant in swamps with a strong flow of moderately mineral-rich soil water. The organic soil (peat) is usually moderately to well decomposed, 1 to 6 feet thick, and often contains much rotted wood. It also can dominate peat ridges in bogs that have a sluggish movement of water weakly enriched with nutrients. On upland sites with mineral soil, it occurs on seepage areas, limestone uplands, and old fields.

Site index curves for northern white-cedar are in Appendix B-10. Manage for timber only where the site index exceeds 25.

Regeneration

Rotation lengths range from 70 years for posts up to 160 years for poles or small sawlogs. For optimum deer shelter, plan rotations of at least 110 years.

Northern white-cedar reproduces successfully from both seed and layering. Good seed production begins at age 30, but peaks after age 70. Most seeds drop from mid-September to late October, but some drop during winter. They are wind-dispersed up to 200 feet.

Germination and seedling development is best where there is a constant moisture supply, warm temperatures, and pH of 6.6 to 7.2. On undisturbed areas, seedbeds on rotten logs and stumps account for more than 70 percent of the seedlings. On undisturbed areas, seedlings prosper on both upland and swamp burns. Burning must be fairly severe to expose favorable mineral soil seedbeds on uplands or to improve moss seedbeds in swamps. White-cedar seedlings also reproduce well on skid roads where compacted moss stays moist. Light slash cover is better than none, but heavy slash cover hinders seedling establishment.

Moisture is often the most important factor during the first few years, but expect seedlings to be tallest when grown in about half sunlight and expect shoots and roots to be heaviest in full light. In areas with frequent hot, dry spells, partial overstory shade is necessary to reduce losses from drought and herbaceous competition.

Northern white-cedar can send out roots from any part of a branch or stem if moisture conditions are favorable. Layering frequently occurs in swamps, especially on poor sites with abundant sphagnum moss. Sprouts from roots or stumps are rare.

Northern white-cedar is shade-tolerant and can be managed under single-tree selection or clearcutting systems. A clearcut or shelterwood harvest followed by natural seeding is the usual regeneration method. If advance reproduction is not present, a combination of clearcut and shelterwood strips is recommended to optimize natural seeding. Strips vary from one chain wide where seedbearing trees are less than 35 feet tall to two chains where these trees are more than 60 feet tall. Use either alternate or progressive strips. If you use alternate strips, clearcut one set, then cut the adjoining strip in two stages using the shelterwood system about 10 years later. For the first stage of the shelterwood, leave a basal area of 60 square feet an acre in uniformly spaced dominant and codominant trees of desirable species. Select residual trees for good seed production, wind-firmness, and timber quality. The second stage of the shelterwood, the final clearcut, should occur about 10 years after the seed cut. If you use progressive strips, work with sets of three—the first two being clearcut at one-year intervals and the third one cut in two stages as previously described.

You may need to control associated trees before the final harvest if you want to obtain 50 to 80 percent white-cedar on good sites managed for timber or deer habitat. Kill undesirable trees (especially hardwoods) that reproduce by root suckers or stump sprouts at least 5 and preferably 10 years before reproduction cutting.

Rely on residual stems to reproduce a stand only if there are at least 600 stems an acre of relatively young (less than 50 years old) and healthy white-cedars remaining. Remove heavy slash that buries residual stems or seedbeds. Full-tree skidding in winter will remove most slash and is recommended where residual trees will be relied on for reproduction. Either full-tree skidding or burning may be used for slash disposal in clearcut strips.

Intermediate Treatments

A mixed species stand with 50 to 80 percent white-cedar is best for multiple-use purposes. Young stands of white-cedar that are overtopped by shrubs or hardwoods may benefit from an herbicide release, providing there is no surface water nearby that could be contaminated by an herbicide. Alder, black ash, aspen, paper birch, willow, red maple, and balsam poplar are the main competitors to be controlled.

To produce timber, thin middle-aged stands initially to a residual basal area of 130 square feet, then thin at 10-year intervals to around 90 square feet, favoring dominant and codominant trees. Thinning below 150 square feet may stimulate advance tree reproduction and shrubs.

Pests and Diseases

White-cedar is relatively free of major insect and disease problems. Wind may cause breakage and uprooting, mainly along stand edges and in stands opened up by partial cutting. White-tailed deer and snowshoe hare commonly browse northern white-cedar so severely that new stands cannot become established. Overbrowsing may be minimized when regenerating stands if large patches (40 acres or more) are completely cleared. Roads, beaver dams, and pipelines that impede the normal movement of soil water will kill northern white-cedar.

Red (Norway) Pine

In the northern Lake States red pine grows in extensive pure stands (Figure 6-14), but more often it is found with jack pine, eastern white pine, or sometimes northern pin oak. On coarser, drier soils, common associates are jack pine, quaking aspen, bigtooth aspen, northern pin oak, and bear oak. On somewhat better soils (fine sands to loamy sands), in addition to the species mentioned earlier, associates may be eastern white pine, red maple, black cherry, northern red oak, white oak, balsam fir, black spruce, and occasional specimens of the better hardwoods. On sandy loam and loam soils, red pine's associates include sugar maple, eastern white pine, American basswood, red maple, balsam fir, paper birch, yellow birch, American beech, northern red oak, eastern hemlock, white spruce, white ash, northern white-cedar, and eastern hop hornbeam.

In the absence of fire or other catastrophes, ecological succession in the Lake States is from jack pine to red pine to white pine, and finally to northern hardwoods or spruce-fir. On coarser, more infertile sands, succession may stop with red pine.

Figure 6-14. Range of red pine.

Products and Uses

Red pine is grown primarily for lumber, pulpwood, piling, poles, cabin logs, railway ties, posts, mine timbers, box boards, and fuel. Red pine stands generally provide poor habitat for game birds and animals, but old-growth trees are used as nesting sites by bald eagles and many songbirds. Open canopy stands with a shrub understory offer better wildlife habitat than closed canopy stands.

Site Conditions

In the Lake States red pine commonly grows on level or gently rolling sand plains or on low ridges adjacent to lakes and swamps, but not in swamps. It occurs mainly on dry, sandy soils low in fertility, but is also found on organic debris over rock outcrops and some red clays where it may be stunted. It grows well on silt loams, but not on heavier soils. It grows especially well on naturally subirrigated soils with well-aerated surface layers and a water table 4 to 9 feet deep. Best plantation development is on soils ranging from moderately drained to moist. It prefers a pH of 4.5 to 6.0. Site index curves are in Appendix B-11.

Regeneration

For wood production the recommended rotation age for red pine is 60 to 90 years. However, red pine is a long-lived species, providing opportunities to grow stands for 200 years and individual trees to even greater ages.

Seed production begins when trees are 15 to 25 years old in open grown trees and 50 to 60 years old in closed stands, but it peaks in trees 50 to 150 years of age. Good seed crops occur at three- to seven-year intervals. Seeds may be disseminated up to 900 feet by wind, but the effective range averages only 40 feet. The heaviest seedfall occurs within a month after cones fully ripen in autumn, but seedfall continues through winter and into the next summer.

Red pine may naturally regenerate where there is a fine sand seedbed, thin layer of moss or litter, a water table within 4 feet of the soil surface, and some shade (25 to 45 percent of full sunlight). A summer fire provides a satisfactory seedbed, kills some competing trees and shrubs, reduces cone insect populations, and produces an open overstory canopy. Other requirements for good natural regeneration include a good red pine seed crop, not too thick a layer of ashes, 4 inches of rainfall from May through July, and subsequent freedom from fire for several decades. If rainfall is deficient, seeds can lie over for one to three years before germinating. Such conditions may occur only once in 75 to 100 years.

After seedlings have grown above the sparse ground cover that favored germination and early survival, the number of seedlings and height growth increases with light up to full daylight. Red pine is shade intolerant.

Because natural regeneration is unreliable, clear-cutting followed by planting is the most common regeneration method. Common spacings are 6 feet by 8 feet and 6 feet by 10 feet. Trees can be planted at wider spacings (up to 10 feet by 10 feet) if high survival is expected. Closer spacing reduces tree taper and branch size, promotes early crown closure, and suppresses competition, but also requires more frequent thinnings. If precommercial thinnings are not feasible, avoid close spacing.

The most common planting stock is 3-0 bareroot seedlings, but 2-0 seedlings sometimes are used. On difficult sites use transplants or the largest seedlings available. To extend the planting season, use containerized seedlings.

Site preparation should reduce competition for light, water, and nutrients without causing any serious soil loss. Full-tree skidding to remove slash may be all that is needed, but most sites require shrub control and mineral soil exposure. Mechanical methods of controlling competition may include disk trenching, roller chopping, brush raking, or scalping. Herbicides are very effective at killing undesirable trees and shrubs in red pine stands. Prescribed burning is less effective than herbicides, but can reduce slash and set back woody competition. Conifer slash can be burned almost immediately after harvest, but hardwood slash needs several weeks to cure. In mature red pine stands, use one or more summer fires to eliminate shrubs and reduce duff before harvesting.

Intermediate Treatments

Cultural practices are needed to keep red pine crop trees free from overhead shade and faster growing competitors. Red pine seedlings may need a complete release from shrubs and other low competition by the second or third growing season. Release plantations overtopped by hardwoods as soon as possible. Herbicides are the most efficient means to control competition. Apply spray after pine leader growth is complete and the terminal bud is set (around mid-July), and before the end of the growing season. Instead of herbicides, consider using a hand-held, motorized brush cutter, recognizing that hardwoods will resprout and may need cutting again in a few years.

In seedling stands (less than 2 inches average DBH) with more than 2,000 trees an acre, at least 100 potential crop trees should be given a minimum growing space of 25 square feet each. Dense sapling stands (2 to 5 inches average DBH) with 160 square feet or more of basal area an acre

should be thinned to give 50 square feet of growing space an tree. For stands averaging 5 inches in diameter, minimum recommended stocking is about 400 trees (60 square feet basal area) an acre while the upper limit is about 1100 trees (150 square feet basal area). The stocking chart for red pine (see Appendix C-6 on pg. 210) provides guidelines for thinning pole and sawtimber stands. Pole stands (5 to 9 inches DBH) with greater than 140 square feet of basal area an acre should be thinned to about 90 square feet of basal area an acre. Small sawtimber stands (9 to 15 inches average DBH) grow well at densities around 120 square feet of basal area an acre. Large sawtimber (15 inches or larger average DBH) can be managed at densities of 150 to 180 square feet of basal area an acre.

As a general rule, remove less than half of the basal area in any one thinning, and during early thinnings, cut trees that are smaller, slower growing, and of poorer quality than the stand average. The remaining trees should have a live crown ratio of 30 to 40 percent. In mixed-species stands, favor red pine crop trees at each thinning or leave other species for greater biodiversity, better wildlife habitat, or more diverse timber products.

To encourage natural pruning, plant red pine seedlings at high densities (about 800 trees an acre). Since red pines may not self-prune until age 40, you can improve tree quality by clear-stem pruning at least 17 feet high. Begin pruning when trees reach 4 to 6 inches DBH. Prune only the best dominant and codominant trees, removing live branches less than 2 inches in diameter and all dead branches. Prune in late fall to early spring.

Pests and Diseases

Red pine may be killed or damaged by fire, ice and sleet storms, very strong winds, de-icing salt spray along highways, and spring flooding lasting 20 days or more.

Several sawflies and jack pine budworm defoliate and may kill seedlings and damage older trees. Control them with insecticides where needed. The

Saratoga spittlebug, which often damages young plantations, may be controlled by removing sweet-fern, its alternate host. White grubs cut seedling roots and may kill trees in dry years. Reduce the grub population by killing sod in plantations. Pine root collar weevils also injure or kill red pine. Reduce their habitat by pruning lower branches and raking up needles near the tree base. Bark beetles are very serious pests of red pine, particularly in dense stands on sandy soils during drought years. Bark beetles breed in recently cut or killed trees, stressed trees, freshly pruned or wounded trees or logging slash greater than 2 inches in diameter. Do not create breeding material from February 1 to September 1 in the northern Lake States or from March 1 to September 1 in the southern Lake States. Any breeding materials created during the breeding period must be removed from the site or destroyed as soon as possible.

Scleroderris canker, red pine shoot blight, diplodia, root rots, butt rots, and needle blights may be important in some areas. The best control measures are to remove infected trees and maintain stand vigor. Do not establish young red pine stands beneath or near infected older red pines.

High populations of snowshoe hares, cottontail rabbits, and mice often kill or reduce height growth of red pine seedlings. Eliminate protective grass to reduce their populations. When preferred foods are lacking, white-tailed deer browse and may destroy red pine seedlings. Manage your deer population or use bud caps or deer repellents. Porcupines girdle red pines from sapling to mature tree stages.

Silver Maple–American Elm

The silver maple-American elm forest type is common in the southern Lake States (Figure 6-15) on well-drained moist sites along river bottoms, floodplains, and lake shores. It often replaces stands that originally held cottonwood, willow, and red-osier dogwood. Other associates may include pin oak, green ash, red maple, basswood, black walnut, black cherry, hackberry, and boxelder. American elm is no longer a major component of mature stands because of Dutch elm disease.

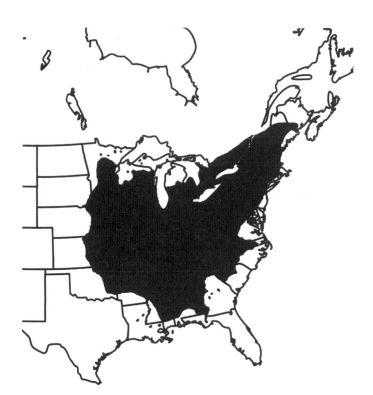

Figure 6-15. Range of silver maple.

Products and Uses

Silver maple, cottonwood, green ash, and associated hardwoods are used primarily for lumber, veneer, and firewood. In some areas cottonwood is used for pulpwood. Green ash is used in specialty items such as tool handles and baseball bats. A high number of wildlife species, especially birds, can be found in a mature bottomland hardwood forest. Mature and overmature stands provide cavities that are essential to many wildlife species, including woodpeckers, wood ducks, barred owls, and raccoons. White-tailed deer, beaver, and other fur-bearers also can be found in this forest type. Silver maple buds are a staple food for squirrels in the spring. Beavers feed on silver maple and cottonwood bark.

Site Conditions

Silver maple commonly is found on the alluvial flood plains of major rivers where there are moist, fine-textured silt and clay soils that are imperfectly drained. Its best growth is in better drained, moist areas. Soil pH should be above 4.0. Silver maple seedlings are intermediate in tolerance to water-saturated soils but can tolerate prolonged periods of inundation.

Green ash grows naturally on a range of sites from clay soils subject to frequent flooding and overflow to sandy or silty soils where the amount of available moisture may be limited. It grows best on fertile, moist, well-drained soils. Green ash commonly is found on alluvial soils along rivers and streams and less frequently in swamps. It can remain healthy when flooded for as long as 40 percent of the time during a growing season. Young green ash can withstand flooding for several months during the dormant and early growing season. It prefers a pH of between 7.5 and 8.0.

Cottonwood survives on deep, infertile sands and clays but makes its best growth on moist, well-drained, fine sandy or silt loams close to streams.

Stands with site indexes below 70 for green ash (see Appendix B-5), eastern cottonwood (see Appendix B-6), or silver maple should be managed for wildlife, aesthetics, or other nontimber uses.

Regeneration

Silver maples begin producing seed at about age 11. Seeds ripen from April through June. Dissemination is mainly by wind and occasionally by water. Natural regeneration is most successful on a seedbed of moist mineral soil with considerable organic matter. Initial seedling growth may be rapid, but because silver maples cannot compete with overtopping vegetation, first-year mortality is high if they are not released. The preferred size of seedlings for plantations is 12 inches in height and 0.25 inches in root-collar diameter. Sprouts appear readily from stumps that are 12 inches or less in diameter.

Green ash starts producing seed when trees are 3 to 4 inches DBH. Seeds drop from late September into the winter. Most seeds are dispersed by wind within short distances of the parent tree. Some dispersal by water also may occur. The best seedbed is in partial shade on moist litter or mineral soil. Stumps of sapling and pole-size green ash sprout readily. Cuttings made from 1-0 seedlings or 1-year-old sprouts root easily under greenhouse and field conditions. Cuttings may be planted horizontally under the soil or vertically with good results.

Cottonwood seed production starts when trees are 5 to 10 years old and good crops occur annually. Seeds disperse from June through mid-July via wind and water. Abundant deposits of seed occur along water courses as spring floodwaters recede. Cottonwood seedlings require very moist, exposed mineral soil, such as fresh silt deposits, and full sunlight for establishment. Artificial propagation normally involves use of cuttings from 1-year stem growth from nursery trees. These may or may not be rooted before planting in fields or forest settings.

To stimulate natural regeneration, clearcut all trees greater than 2 inches DBH. Tree seedlings present in the understory before harvest usually are not abundant, and if present, will probably include elm, maple, and possibly ash. A dormant season harvest encourages more stump sprouts, but should be planned to scarify the soil surface, providing exposed mineral soil for seed germination.

Consider planting within two years after harvest if natural regeneration is not adequate. Since planting is expensive, confine planting to the best sites and avoid locations that frequently flood. Prepare sites as follows:

1. Shear all residual woody vegetation near ground level.
2. Pile debris in windrows and burn it.
3. Rake the entire surface to collect any remaining vegetation.
4. Deeply disk and till the planting bed.

Silver maple and ash generally are established from seedlings. Cottonwood generally is established from cuttings. Plant at a 12-foot by 12-foot spacing as early as possible in the spring using genetically improved stock, if available. Planting with an auger will create better odds for survival than using a planting bar. Mechanical weeding will be necessary for the first two or three years.

Intermediate Treatments

Follow the guidelines below based on the dominant species in your stand.

The shade tolerance of silver maple ranges from tolerant on good sites to very intolerant on poor sites. On upland soils, silver maple grows well but is highly intolerant of competing vegetation. In very dense stands a precommercial thinning and weeding of undesirable trees is recommended to encourage the growth of the most desirable trees. The first commercial thinning should occur when codominant trees average 8 to 10 inches DBH. Two or three more thinnings will be required every 7 to 15 years to sustain fast growth. Remove diseased trees and those of low vigor or poor form. Follow the crop-tree release method described in Chapter 5: Woodland Improvement Practices or the stocking chart for elm-ash-cottonwood in Appendix C-2 to determine when and how much to thin. At final harvest most stands should have 120 to 130 square feet of basal area (roughly 50 high-quality trees) per acre of commercial species.

Green ash varies from intolerant to moderately tolerant of shade. Natural stands may have enough volume to allow commercial thinnings at 25 to 30 years. To ensure reasonable volume production and reduce epicormic branching in the remaining trees in the stand, do not reduce the basal area below 100 to 120 square feet an acre.

Cottonwood is very intolerant of shade. In natural stands, uneven spacing and size permit some trees to become dominant and natural thinning allows production of large trees. Under plantation conditions, and particularly when only clones with similar growth rates are used and all trees get off to a good start, stagnation can occur quickly. Spacing and the timing of thinning become critical under these conditions. Optimum growth of individual trees requires very wide spacing. Start plantations at a 12 foot by 12 foot spacing and thin when crowns begin to close. Thin repeatedly to sustain growth.

Pests and Diseases

Major insect pests in this forest type are the emerald ash borer, forest tent caterpillar and cankerworms. The emerald ash borer continues to move westward across the Lake States. Follow state department of agriculture recommendations about handling stands that are infested with emerald ash borer and about moving ash wood. If there is an emerald ash borer infestation within 10 miles of your stand, harvest your ash trees as soon as possible to salvage their value and remove possible host trees.

Chemical or microbial insecticides may be required to control defoliators. Major diseases include Dutch elm disease, ash yellows, and cytospora canker. Harvest commercial-size elms whenever possible to salvage their value before Dutch elm disease kills them. Retain elms during thinning only when no other desirable tree is available. Reduce canker damage by thinning to promote tree vigor, but be very careful to avoid damaging remaining trees.

Tamarack

Tamarack or eastern larch (Figure 6-16) is found in pure stands, but more commonly appears in mixed stands with black spruce, northern white-cedar, black ash, red maple, eastern white pine, or paper birch. Tamarack stands usually are even-aged.

Figure 6-16. Range of tamarack.

Products and Uses

Tamarack is used for pulp, poles, and lumber, although it has relatively minor economic importance. Red squirrel, snowshoe hare, and porcupine are found in tamarack stands. Tamaracks provide habitat for many songbirds and are critical habitat for the great gray owl and its small mammal prey species.

Site Conditions

Tamarack commonly grows on peatland where the organic soil or peat is more than 12 inches deep. It occurs on a wide range of peatlands, but is most characteristic of poor swamps where soil water is weakly enriched with mineral nutrients. The best sites are moist, well-drained loamy soils along streams, lakes, or swamps, and mineral soils with a shallow surface layer of organic matter. It grows well on upland sites, but is quickly eliminated by competition from more shade-tolerant species. Tamarack will not survive prolonged flooding. Site index curves for tamarack are shown in Appendix B-12.

Regeneration

The regeneration system recommended for tamarack stands is a combination of clearcut and seed-tree with natural seeding. Good seed years occur every 3 to 6 years starting when trees are about 40 years old. The best seedbed is a warm, moist mineral or organic soil with no brush, but a light cover of grass or other herbaceous vegetation. Hummocks of slow-growing sphagnum moss often make good seedbeds. Most seeds fall within 200 feet of the seed tree.

Harvest strips should be oriented perpendicular to the wind and may be up to 200 feet wide. After clearcutting the first strip, wait about 10 years or until the area is well stocked with seedlings, then clearcut a second strip adjacent to the first and on the windward side. Again wait until regeneration is established, then use the seed-tree method to cut the remaining strip. The seed-tree cut should leave about ten well-spaced dominant tamaracks an acre. Once the regeneration is established, harvest or kill the seed trees.

You may need to prepare the site following a harvest to ensure tamarack regeneration. Broadcast burn mixed species stands to remove slash. Since tamarack slash does not burn well, harvest pure tamarack stands by full-tree skidding to remove slash, then treat the brush with herbicides. Alternatively, you could pile and burn the slash or shear or chop the brush.

Tamarack seedlings need abundant light and constant moisture. Seedlings established under a fully stocked stand will not survive beyond about the sixth year. Early seedling losses are caused by damping-off fungus, drought, flooding, inadequate light, and snowshoe hares. Given enough light, tamarack is one of the fastest growing conifers on upland sites.

Intermediate Treatments

Thinning is economically feasible only on good sites when the objective is to produce poles or saw-timber. If a market exists for small products such as posts or pulpwood, make a commercial thinning as soon as the stand produces these products. Additional periodic thinnings are recommended up to 20 years before the end of the rotation. Each thinning should leave a basal area of 80 to 90 square feet an acre.

Pests and Diseases

The larch sawfly is a serious insect pest that can kill tamaracks after several years of defoliation. Chemical control may be required to manage sawfly populations Because there is no effective cultural control. Bark beetles can kill tamaracks that are stressed by defoliation or competition in densely stocked stands. Tamaracks also are susceptible to root and heart rots. Minimize rots by avoiding damage during intermediate cuttings. Porcupines can cause extensive damage by feeding on the bark of the main stem.

White Oak–Black Oak–Northern Red Oak

White oak, black oak, and northern red oak comprise the majority of stocking in this type, but any one of these species may dominate the type depending on site conditions (Figure 6-17). Other common associates are northern pin oak, bitternut hickory, shagbark hickory, pignut hickory (southern Michigan), yellow poplar (southern Michigan), sugar and red maples, white and green ash, American and red elm, and basswood. Occasionally black walnut, black cherry, American beech, and eastern hemlock may be present.

Figure 6-17. Range of northern red oak.

Products and Uses

Oak is valued in the manufacture of furniture, flooring, paneling, ties, and fuelwood. White oak also is used for barrel staves. Red oak usually is the most valuable species in this type for wood products.

Oak woodlands are home to many animals, including white-tailed deer, gray and fox squirrels, raccoon, opossum, red fox, bobcat, skunk, turkey, ruffed grouse, and many songbirds. Acorns are an important food for squirrels, deer, turkey, mice, voles, and other mammals and birds. Wildlife prefer white oak acorns, but will eat acorns from any oak species.

Site Conditions

Oaks grow on a variety of soils with texture varying from clay to loamy sands and on some soils that have a high content of rock fragments. Oaks may occur on all topographic positions from valley floors to narrow ridgetops and on all aspects. Red oak is most common on moist sites. White oak occurs over a range of moist to dry sites. Black oak is most abundant on drier sites. This type tends to be succeeded on moist sites by sugar maple, basswood, white ash, elms, beech, and other moisture demanding species. On drier sites, the type is stable.

Oaks grow best on north- and east-facing, gently sloping, lower slopes; in coves and deep ravines; and on well-drained valley floors where soils are at least 36 inches deep. Medium-quality sites have moderately deep soils (20 to 36 inches) on upper and middle slopes facing north and east. Oaks survive, but grow poorly, on narrow ridgetops or south- and west-facing steep, upper slopes where soil is less than 20 inches deep. Oaks survive better than most other tree species on dry sites, but they do not produce much merchantable timber on such sites. There is fierce competition among tree species on the best sites, so oaks are difficult to regenerate there.

Site index curves for northern red oak are in Appendix B-13.

Regeneration

These recommendations focus on regenerating northern red oak, which typically is the most valuable species in this type. Oaks may live for several hundred years, but for timber production on moderate to good sites, regenerate when the:

- Oaks are 80 to 120 years old and trees average 18 to 24 inches DBH.
- A stand is greatly understocked.
- Most trees are of poor quality or of undesirable species.

Oaks commonly reproduce from acorns. Red oaks produce good acorn crops at 2- to 5-year intervals beginning about age 50. The best seed producers are dominant or codominant trees with large, uncrowded crowns. Acorns drop in the fall. White oak acorns germinate soon after falling, but red oak acorns germinate the following spring. Insects, mammals and birds can eat or damage more than 80 percent of the acorn crop in most years and nearly all of the crop in very poor seed years. Gravity and the caching activities of squirrels and mice disperse seeds only short distances. Birds distribute acorns over longer distances, but such dispersal is not reliable for regeneration. The best germination occurs when acorns are in contact with or buried in mineral soil under a light covering of leaves.

Northern red, black, and white oaks are intermediate in shade tolerance, although white oaks are more tolerant than the other two. In stands with a dense understory or overstory, there will be few oaks in the understory.

Natural oak regeneration is most reliable where there is plenty of advance regeneration. The number of oak seedlings needed to successfully stock the next stand depends on seedling size before the harvest. The larger the seedlings, the more likely they are to survive to harvestable size.

Table 6-3. Recommended seedlings per acre based on seedling height.

Seedling Height in Feet	Recommended Seedlings per Acre
<1	15,435
1 – 2	3,087
2 – 4	1,029
>4	514

Stands that are well-stocked with advance regeneration and that have relatively little competition from undesirable understory trees, shrubs, or other vegetation may be clearcut. Such conditions are more likely to occur on moderately dry sites. Clearcut at least one-half acre and preferably at least two acres; otherwise, shade from the surrounding timber will suppress oak seedlings. For regeneration purposes there is no maximum size for clearcuts, so long as there is good advance regeneration.

If there is a seed source present, but few oak seedlings, the problem often is too much shade. Acorns may germinate and the seedlings may survive for several years beneath heavy shade, but advance oak regeneration will not accumulate over a long period. Northern red oak reaches maximum photosynthesis at about 30 percent of full sunlight.

To reduce shade produced by an understory of shade-tolerant hardwood trees, shrubs, or ferns, cut or treat vegetation with herbicide, depending on the species to be controlled. If dense shade is produced by a high canopy, also conduct a shelterwood

harvest, leaving 75 to 85 percent crown cover in species and individual trees that you want to have provide seed for the next generation. Harvest carefully to avoid damaging the remaining timber.

Following a shelterwood harvest and understory removal, wait several years to be sure that a satisfactory number of oak seedlings are present, then clearcut. If the oaks take more than five years to regenerate, apply additional understory control as needed. To protect advance reproduction and encourage stump sprouting, clearcut when the ground is frozen. If you need to harvest in other seasons, restrict log skidding to narrow corridors to reduce the soil disturbance that favors germination of undesirable species.

An alternative to the shelterwood harvest is to wait until there is a good acorn crop, then clearcut and disturb the soil after the acorns drop but before the ground freezes. Soil disturbance helps to bury the acorns and uproot competing vegetation.

Because of the risk and possible delay involved when relying on natural regeneration, you may want to plant seedlings after a shelterwood or clearcut. Planting also enables you to supplement natural regeneration, to use genetically superior stock when it is available, and to choose the species. Control undesirable trees and shrubs by cutting, bulldozing, or treating with herbicide in the fall. Harvest by shelterwood or clearcut, then plant oak seedlings the next spring. On forest sites, plant oaks 20 to 25 feet apart, allowing other trees to provide the necessary stand density. In open fields, plant trees 5 to 8 feet apart within rows and 10 to 12 feet apart between rows.

The best oak seedlings have a fibrous root system and a stem at least 3/8-inch in diameter. If large seedlings are difficult to handle during the planting operation, just before planting clip the tops of the seedlings—and the roots, if necessary—leaving each about 8 inches long. Plant 200 to 800 seedlings an acre, depending on their size and the amount of advance reproduction already in the stand. Control weeds around the oak seedlings for up to three years. Herbicides are often effective and economical for weed control.

▲

Oaks also reproduce from stump sprouts following a harvest. Sprouting frequency declines as tree diameter and age increase. Northern red oaks sprout more frequently than white and black oaks. New sprouts grow rapidly and are usually straight and well formed, especially if they arise close to ground level.

Intermediate Treatments

Control undesirable tree species that compete with crop trees when the stand height averages at least 25 feet (when the trees are 10 to 20 years old). When growing trees for timber production, thin stump sprouts when they are about 10 years old (but no more than 3 inches in diameter). Leave one or two dominant sprouts that have good form and arise within 6 inches of the ground. When managing oaks for timber, keep stands fairly dense until the bottom 20 to 25 feet of the stems are essentially free of live branches. This generally will occur when trees are 40 to 50 feet tall (30 to 45 years). At this stage, thin stands to stimulate the stem diameter growth of crop trees. Select 75 to 100 croptrees per acre and release them from crown competition. Select crop trees that are 20 to 25 feet apart. Provide at least 5 feet of clear space around three sides of the crop tree crowns. As an alternative, follow the stocking charts for upland central hardwoods in Appendix C-7. Repeat thinning every 15 to 20 years, but stop thinning when stands reach about 60 years. Pruning will improve wood quality and may be needed if the stand density is not high enough to cause natural pruning.

Pests and Diseases

The most destructive defoliating insect attacking oaks is the invasive gypsy moth. It repeatedly defoliates trees and has killed oaks throughout the northeastern United States. It is present in Michigan and Wisconsin and is moving westward. Northern red oak can recover from a single defoliation but may be weakened enough for some disease or other insects to kill them. Several other defoliators occasionally cause serious damage or weaken trees. To reduce damage from defoliators, maintain stand vigor, consider spraying high value stands with an insecticide if repeated defoliations occur, and manage stands for species diversity.

Minimize chestnut borer damage by maintaining vigorous stands. Specifically, in upland stands with site indexes of less than 65 (see Appendix B-13), maintain basal areas at less than 120 square feet an acre in stands with trees averaging 7 to 15 inches DBH, and at less than 100 square feet an acre in stands averaging more than 15 inches DBH. Avoid thinning for five years after a serious drought or defoliation.

Oak wilt is the most serious disease that affects oak trees. To minimize infections, do not thin or prune oaks from mid-April through mid-July, when fungal spores are present and can be transported by picnic beetles to fresh wounds. Dormant season operations are best because spores are not present and the trees are not susceptible to infection. Since oak wilt commonly spreads through root grafts between neighboring oaks, surround valuable oak stands in areas with a high oak wilt hazard with a 100-foot buffer of an alternate species. If trees become infected, harvest them before the following spring. Use a trenching machine or vibratory plow to break the root grafts through which the disease spreads. Trench placement and depth are critical. Consult a forester for advice before trenching. Left untreated, oak wilt will spread through the stand until it kills all the red oaks. White and bur oaks are not commonly affected by oak wilt.

Minimize damage from shoestring root rot by maintaining vigorous, well-stocked stands.

References

Baughman, M. J. and R. D. Jacobs. 1992. *Woodland Owners' Guide to Oak Management*. University of Minnesota Extension. 8 p.

Chapter 46 Swamp Hardwood Type. 1990. *In Silviculture and Forest Aesthetics Handbook*. Wisconsin Department of Natural Resources. http://dnr.wi.gov/forestry/publications/Handbooks/24315/46.pdf.

Erdmann, G. G., T. R. Crow, R. M. Peterson, Jr., and C. D. Wilson. 1987. *Managing Black Ash in the Lake States*. Gen. Tech. Report NC-115. USDA Forest Service, North Central Forest Experiment Station. 10 p.

Kotar, J. 1997. *Approaches to Ecologically Based Forest Management on Private Lands*. St. Paul, MN: University of Minnesota Extension. 18 p.

Michigan Technological University. (2006-07). *Ash Reduction Model*. http://www.ashmodel.org. Houghton: Michigan Technological University, School of Forest Resources and Environmental Science.

Red Pine Management Guide. USDA Forest Service, North Central Research Station. http://www. ncrs.fs.fed.us/fmg/nfmg/rp/index.html.

U.S. Department of Agriculture, Forest Service. 1990. *Silvics of North America*. Agriculture Handbook 654. http://www.na.fs.fed.us/spfo/pubs/ silvics_manual/table_of_contents.htm.

▲

Chapter 7:

Forest Health

Melvin J. Baughman, Extension Forester, University of Minnesota

During its long life, a tree may be subject to damage by animals, weather and other environmental conditions, insects, diseases, and fire. Inspect your woodland at the beginning and end of each growing season and whenever a fire, windstorm, ice storm, flooding, prolonged drought, or other such event may have caused damage.

It can be very costly to control damaging agents once they become established so it is wise to prevent damage before it occurs. To minimize damage:

- Match the tree species to the sites and conditions where they are likely to grow best.

- Maintain tree species diversity by either mixing tree species within a stand or growing several different species in pure stands.

- Regulate stand density to encourage fast growth while maintaining relatively full stocking.

- Use pest-resistant planting stock when available.

- Prune or thin during the winter rather than during the growing season.

- Avoid wounding trees when operating heavy equipment or logging in the woodland.

- Clear firebreaks around conifer stands.

Descriptions of common sources of tree damage follow, along with information about various types of damage, and their potential severity. Chapter 6: Managing Important Forest Types briefly describes the most common pests and diseases associated with different forest types and how to prevent or control them. Contact a forester to help you identify problems, assess damage, and design a control strategy for any serious problem. A forester also can help you plan stand management practices that will reduce future problems.

Animal Damage

Animals that frequently damage trees include birds, deer, small mammals, and livestock.

Birds

Woodpeckers cause the most noticeable tree damage as they probe beneath loose bark or peck holes into sapwood in search of insects. Such feeding activity is concentrated on dead, dying, or damaged trees so the bird's feeding is a sign of poor tree health, but not its cause.

One exception to this is the yellow-bellied sapsucker which feeds not only on insects, but also on sweet sap. Sapsuckers bore 1/4-inch diameter holes in closely spaced, parallel rows that may completely encircle a tree. These birds are known to feed on more than 250 species of woody plants. Birch, maple, and hemlock are their preferred food sources in the Lake States.

Sapsucker holes lead to wood stain and may become points of entry for wood decay. If you leave their favorite feeding trees untreated, sapsuckers will concentrate their feeding activities on those trees, which helps protect nearby trees from serious injury. Sapsuckers are especially attracted to aspen with heartwood decay, which they can excavate for nesting cavities. To protect a valuable aspen timber stand, eliminate trees that show signs of decay when you are thinning the stand. This may help discourage sapsuckers from using the area.

Figure 7-1. Sapsucker damage on a tree.

Some bird species, including pine grosbeaks and ruffed grouse, eat buds, causing minor damage.

Bird damage usually is limited, so no bird control measures are needed in woodlands. Most bird species (except English sparrows, European starlings, and pigeons) are protected by federal law. A federal permit is needed to destroy protected birds, even if they are pests. Check with the U.S. Fish and Wildlife Service before attempting any control method that may harm birds.

Deer

Deer browse on branch tips, especially on young trees and stump sprouts. Browsing stunts tree growth and disfigures trees by causing them to develop crooked stems. Browsing may seriously damage regeneration where there is a high deer density and relatively little natural browse or few agricultural crops available. Browsing damage occurs mainly in winter. Bucks also rub small tree stems and branches with their antlers to remove velvet. Antler rubbing may kill small trees (usually those that are less than 3 inches DBH), but few trees are damaged in this manner so control is not warranted.

In most cases the deer population can be controlled by hunting following state regulations. High fences are effective deterrents, but are prohibitively expensive for forestry purposes. Electrical fences with high voltage and low impedance are more economical and in some cases may be justified to protect young, high-value plantations. Contact a forester or wildlife damage control expert for advice on fencing. Commercial chemical repellents sometimes are effective, but may need to be reapplied after a rain or wet snow. Bud caps are sometimes placed on white pine seedlings to protect them from deer browsing (Figure 6-9, pg. 71).

You also can minimize forest openings and brushy habitat, making your forest less attractive to deer, or make cutting blocks and regeneration areas as large as possible, thus providing more browse than the deer can consume.

Small Mammals

Rabbits, snowshoe hares, mice and other small rodents can girdle or cut off young trees near the ground. Reduce damage by eliminating tall grass and brush piles that provide cover for these animals, especially in or near new tree plantations. Do not place organic mulch (such as straw or wood chips) within 4 inches of a seedling tree stem, because the mulch may provide cover for small mammals.

Figure 7-2. Rabbits and hares eat tree bark in the winter.

Pocket gophers feed on roots and bark around the base of young trees and other plants, especially in sandy soils. They are pests in agricultural fields that are being converted to woodland. The best control is to reduce their food sources by eliminating as much vegetation as possible in a tree plantation. In small areas gophers can be trapped. Where the population is high and the plantation is large, control them using a device that creates an artificial tunnel and drops poisoned grain into it. When using poisoned grain, take great care to prevent spills and accidental poisoning of nontarget animals.

Beavers commonly dam small streams, which can flood woodlands and kill trees in the area. They also fell trees (especially aspen and willow) near streams and lakes and either feed on the bark and small branches or use the wood for building dams and huts. The best way to solve a beaver problem is to trap and remove the animals. Contact a wildlife conservation officer for information on trappers in your area.

Porcupines eat bark and may girdle and kill some trees, especially white and red pines. If damage is serious, they can be live-trapped or killed.

Livestock

High concentrations of cattle, horses, sheep, goats, or other livestock pastured in a woodland compact the soil, trample young seedlings and sprouts, damage roots, rub bark from stems, and eat or defoliate small trees. Heavy grazing and forest management are not compatible on the same site. In general you should fence livestock out of woodlands if you expect to grow high-quality trees in it.

Figure 7-3. Fence livestock out of woodlands to protect small trees.

Grazing may be acceptable for a short period (a few months to a couple of years) when you want to suppress understory vegetation in preparation for a shelterwood harvest that will be followed by natural regeneration or planting trees. Grazing also may be appropriate in a silvo-pasture where trees and pasture are intentionally managed together. You must give appropriate attention to tree selection, spacing, pruning and other cultural practices to develop widely spaced, high quality trees. Likewise the pasture grass must be intensively managed with fertilizer, rotational grazing, and other practices as needed.

Environmental Damage

Trees may be damaged by airborne chemicals, machinery, soil-related problems, too much or too little water, and severe weather.

Airborne Chemicals

Airborne pollutants from industry, automobiles, fires, and other chemical sources can harm trees. Symptoms include defoliation; browning or yellowing leaf margins, tips, or tissue between leaf veins; and stunted foliage growth. Herbicides may cause distortion, curling, and browning margins, or leaf drop in deciduous trees and may cause conifer needles to turn yellow or brown, and succulent shoots to curl and deform. If trees survive such damage, their growth may be stunted or their shape deformed. Where air pollution could be a problem, plant resistant species and maintain well-thinned stands. When applying pesticides, follow label directions and standard application guidelines to minimize chemical injuries. Some pesticides may need to be applied by a licensed pesticide applicator. While most pesticide damage is caused by herbicides, insecticides and fungicides also can damage trees if the tank mix is too strong. Herbicide drift often originates on neighboring properties, so be sure to let your neighbors know the value you place on your woodland. Ask them to take special care when applying chemicals on their own properties to avoid damaging drift to your property.

Machinery

Damage from logging equipment is a concern in any stand where some trees will be left after the harvest. Logging equipment can knock over small trees, break branches, tear bark, and destroy roots near the surface. Careful and experienced equipment operators can avoid much of this damage. Creating a physical barrier between the trees that will be left to grow and the equipment also helps.

Heavy equipment used in plantations (such as cultivators, mowers, and pesticide applicators) can sever small trees, break branches, or tear bark. Reduce damage by planting trees in rows that are 2 to 4 feet wider than the equipment, plant trees in straight rows, and maintain even spacing between rows. Set cultivation equipment to run as shallowly as possible to avoid cutting tree roots. Consider using an herbicide rather than cultivation or mowing equipment.

Figure 7-4. Heavy equipment can easily damage young trees in plantations.

Soil

Soil compaction cuts off water and carbon dioxide to tree roots. Compaction slows tree growth and interferes with root suckering in aspen stands that are clearcut. Compaction may be indicated by dying leaves on mature trees and dying branches on younger trees, but most often reduced growth is the only sign of it.

Soil compaction is a problem mainly on wet clay or silt soils. It occurs where heavy equipment has been driven across a site. Old farm fields may have a compacted plow pan a foot or two below the soil surface. Wooded sites may be compacted on the surface. Compacted soil takes decades to loosen up through freezing and thawing cycles. Reduce compaction in the first place by operating heavy equipment only when the soil is dry or frozen. On farm fields with a plow pan, deep chisel the site to break up the compacted layer, then plant trees.

Changes in the soil level around a tree also affect its growth and odds of survival. Excavating soil and severing roots may lead to windthrow or

root diseases that kill trees. Adding soil decreases air movement to the roots and may kill the tree. Therefore, avoid removing or adding soil near trees.

Mineral deficiency causes a range of symptoms from foliage discoloration to reduced foliage size. A soil analysis will indicate which minerals are deficient. Soil types vary considerably in their natural nutrient content. Always try to match the tree species to sites that meet their nutrient needs. See Chapter 6: Managing Important Forest Types for more information on the soil requirements of various forest types and species. While timber harvesting removes some nutrients from a site, most nutrients are stored in the branches and bark of trees, so leaving those materials on the site after harvest will recycle the nutrients. Nutrients also enter a site from precipitation and air exchange.

Lake States woodlands rarely have significant nutrient deficiencies in stands that are managed over normal rotation lengths. Nutrient deficiencies may occur with repeated short rotations, especially when all woody material is removed from the site (called biomass harvesting). Ask your forester about best management practices for biomass harvesting.

Water

Drought damage occurs when water loss through the leaves exceeds water uptake by the roots. It is most common on sandy and gravelly soils, which do not retain much water. It also occurs if the water table drops suddenly and remains low, depriving trees of the moisture they need. Drought symptoms include leaves wilting or turning brown—beginning with tissue between leaf veins, off-color foliage, and a general decline in vigor. Newly planted trees are especially vulnerable to drought because their root systems are not well developed. Crowns of larger, drought-stricken trees usually die from the top down. Insect attacks often are triggered by drought. For example, wood boring insects may invade drought-weakened trees. Trees already stressed by disease or physical damage may die in a drought.

Figure 7-5. Red oak leaves damaged by drought.

To minimize drought damage, match tree species to the sites where they grow best. Some species are more drought resistant than others, so manage drought-tolerant species on dry sites. Plant new trees in the spring or fall when soil moisture is high. When soil moisture is low, plant seedlings with soil around their roots, such as containerized stock. Do not plant shallow-rooted species in areas of low rainfall or on sandy soils. Thin stands before they become overstocked, but do not thin during a drought.

Table 7-1. Flood tolerance during the growing season of seedlings of selected tree species.

High	Moderate	Low
American elm	Balsam fir	Bigtooth aspen
Black ash	Basswood	Bitternut hickory
Eastern cottonwood	Black spruce	Butternut
Green ash	Black walnut	Northern red oak
Silver maple	Bur oak	Red pine
Willow	Eastern white pine	Sugar maple
	Jack pine	White ash
	Northern white-cedar	White birch
	Quaking aspen	White oak
	Shagbark hickory	White spruce
	Swam white oak	
	Tamarack	
	Yellow birch	

Extended flooding can suffocate roots and kill trees. The extent of the damage typically depends on the tree species (Table 7-1), time of year, tree size, and tree vigor. Flooding for short periods in winter or early spring is seldom a serious problem, but flooding during the growing season can kill seedlings in just a few days. Completely submerged seedlings will be killed more quickly than trees with their crowns above water. In flood-prone areas such as river flats, plant only tree species that tolerate flooding.

Weather

High temperatures and drying winds cause rapid water loss from tree leaves. Water loss causes leaf margins to turn brown and leaves to fall prematurely. Do not plant susceptible trees (such as sugar maple) in locations that are exposed to strong sunlight or wind.

Early fall frosts or extremely cold weather shortly after leaf fall can injure succulent twigs and buds. Late spring frosts can kill buds that have begun growing. Trees usually survive these frosts, but their growth, stem quality, and vigor can be dramatically reduced. To avoid freeze damage, plant trees from seed sources that originate no more than 200 miles south of the planting site. (Near the northern edge of a tree species' range, do not plant trees from seed sources more than 50 miles south of the planting site.) If your planting site is in a low-lying, frost-prone area, select a species that breaks bud relatively late in the spring to avoid frost damage. For example, black spruce buds break dormancy about ten days after white spruce.

Winter sunscald occurs in early spring when the sun heats and activates tissue during the day and then freezing temperatures kill the active cells at night. The injury appears as peeling bark over an elongated canker on the south to southwest side of the tree stem. Thin-barked trees such as young maples are most susceptible. The tree rarely is killed, but diameter growth is reduced, decay-causing organisms often enter the tree, and logs become degraded or ruined. In hardwood stands, avoid overthinning or pruning that might expose tree stems to too much direct sun, especially if the trees are growing near the northern limits of their range. Winterburn and winter drying are caused by warm spring winds that dry the foliage while the roots are still frozen in the ground and cannot replace the lost moisture. This damage is common on most conifer species and may be recognized by the reddening and browning of needles in the spring. Trees usually survive this, but massive defoliation may occur on trees located along exposed plantation borders or on trees that grow along highways, where road salt exacerbates the problem.

Strong winds can topple trees or break their branches. To prevent wind damage, leave a dense row of trees with intact lower branches around the perimeter of woodlands. When thinning old, dense tree stands, progress slowly over a period of years to minimize windthrow.

Figure 7-6. Strong winds can uproot trees.

Hail can break off buds and branches and shred tree foliage. There is no way to prevent or control this type of damage.

Lightning can split trees, cause spiral cracks in their trunks, shatter limbs, and start fires. Trees with crowns high above the general canopy level are most subject to lightning strikes. There is no control for lightning other than to remove high-risk trees before damage occurs. Once a conifer is struck by lightning, remove it quickly before bark beetles attack it and build up a population that can spread to other trees.

Insect Damage

Each type of insect affects very specific tree parts. Insect damage is categorized here by the tree part affected by the insects. Strategies for minimizing insect damage are discussed in Chapter 6: Managing Important Forest Types for the more serious pests.

Defoliating Insects

Defoliating insects remove all or part of a tree's foliage. They weaken the tree by lowering its capacity to respire and to produce starch and sugars. Foliage damage takes many forms. Insects that remove only soft leaf tissue and leave the network of veins are called skeletonizers. Leaf miners bore into and eat the tissue between the upper and lower surfaces of the leaf. Window feeders eat one leaf surface, leaving the other intact. Case bearers and bag makers construct and live inside individual movable cases that are made of webbing and foliage parts. Needle tiers and leaf rollers encase, fold, roll, or tie adjacent leaves and needles together with webbing. Webworms or tent caterpillars make and live in conspicuous webbed tents. Other insects are free-feeders that eat the entire leaf or needle.

Free-feeders are the most destructive defoliating insects. Populations go through boom and bust cycles. When these insects are abundant and defoliate trees in two or more consecutive years, they can kill trees.

Figure 7-7. Red oak defoliated by Gypsy moth in June.

Sapsucking Insects

Sapsucking insects injure trees by removing tree fluids. They usually are not serious pests in woodlands. However, heavy attacks lower a tree's energy reserves and may lead to a secondary pest problem. The general symptoms of sapsucking injury are loss of vigor, deformed leaves or plant parts, yellowed leaves, or dead branches. Galls (abnormal tissue growths) also may form.

The destructive stage of the insect usually is required for precise identification, but sometimes the presence of feeding punctures, sooty mold, eggs, fine webbing, and other signs suffice. The Saratoga spittlebug has been a serious pest in red pine plantations. Several scale insects, such as the pine tortoise scale and the pine needle scale, are important in Midwestern forests. Aphids and mites are other sapsucking organisms that may affect your trees.

Bud, Twig, and Seedling Damaging Insects

Most of these insects deform but do not kill trees. The white pine weevil is one of the most damaging insects in conifer plantations in the Lake States. White pine is their favorite host; they also attack other pines and spruces. The weevil larvae feed just below the terminal bud and cause forking and crooking, especially in open-grown trees from 2 to 20 feet tall. Open-grown trees are widely spaced with no crown competition between trees. The new growth elongates slightly before dying because of the larval borings. Weevils usually do not attack the current year's shoot, but it commonly wilts into a "shepherd's crook." Another damaging weevil, the pales weevil, eats the bark on young seedlings.

Bark Beetles

The succulent and nutritious inner bark on tree stems and large branches attracts many insects, most notably the bark beetles. Adult bark beetles deposit eggs beneath the bark. The emerging larvae feed on the cambium and phloem, preventing stem growth and the normal movement of sugar and water. They hasten the death of weakened trees, attack apparently healthy trees during population explo-

sions and drought, and lower lumber value. They also can introduce disease organisms such as Dutch elm disease fungus and blue stain fungus.

The pine engraver is the most common bark beetle in Lake States pine stands. It attacks healthy trees en masse during drought. Flat-headed inner bark borers such as the bronze birch borer, two-lined chestnut borer, some weevils, and roundheaded borers feed on the inner bark. They rarely kill or damage more than a few trees unless the trees are severely stressed by drought or defoliation. Bark borers are difficult to control with contact insecticides because they are sheltered beneath the bark. Systemic insecticides also have little effect because these insects disrupt water movement in the tree. Cultural practices such as thinning that maintain tree vigor provide good protection.

Figure 7-8. Wood-boring insects destroyed most of this oak log's value.

Wood-Boring Insects

Wood-boring insects attack very low vigor or recently killed trees and rarely are a problem in vigorous stands. While common, they rarely cause tree death. They feed for several weeks in the bark before boring into the wood. Flat-headed wood-borers, round-headed borers, horntails, powderpost beetles, ambrosia beetles, and ants are wood-boring insects of common concern. Problems with chemical controls are the same as with bark borers.

Root-Feeding Insects

Root-feeding insects are mostly a problem in nurseries or in young plantations where sod is well established. They disrupt the absorption and movement of water and nutrients. Root maggots, cutworms, root bark beetles, white grubs, and root-collar weevils are examples of root-feeding insects. In plantations, kill or remove the sod *before* planting trees. Killing sod after planting may cause these insects to concentrate their attacks on tree roots.

Cone and Seed Destroying Insects

Beetles, weevils, moths, and wasps may destroy cones and seeds. Usually they deposit eggs in a seed or cone. The developing larvae then eat and destroy the seed. The red pine and white pine cone beetles, red pine cone worm, spruce cone worm, acorn weevil, and walnut weevil are some of the common seed-destroying insects. Insecticides can help control these insects; however, their use is justified only in woodlands used as seed production areas. Few insecticides are registered for this use. Most are very toxic and require application by a licensed commercial applicator.

Disease Damage

Diseases are categorized here by the tree part they most commonly affect. Strategies for minimizing damage from the more serious diseases are discussed in Chapter 6: Managing Important Forest Types.

Foliage Diseases

Foliage diseases may cause conifer needles to turn yellow or brown or drop prematurely. Hardwood leaves may develop yellow, brown, or black spots. These diseases weaken trees by reducing the ability of their leaves to produce plant food. Brown spot disease affects only red and Scotch pines and is typically confined to the lower half of the tree. Some other typical foliage diseases are rhizosphera needle-cast in spruce, pine needle rust in conifers, and anthracnose and leaf spot in hardwoods.

When the leaves of a hardwood turn yellow or brown and droop, suspect a wilt disease. These symptoms commonly occur when a fungus blocks a tree's water-carrying vessels. Oak wilt and Dutch elm disease, verticillium, dothiorella, and phloem necrosis are typical wilt diseases. Oak wilt and Dutch elm disease are serious problems in woodlands and often spread to adjacent trees through root grafts. Adjoining trees of the same species will sometimes form grafts between their root systems, allowing not only water and nutrient flow between trees, but also disease transmission.

Sooty mold is a black powdery fungus that lives on the honeydew exuded by aphids or scale insects. Powdery mildew is a white fungus that covers leaf surfaces. Both damage trees and shrubs by blocking the sunlight needed for photosynthesis. Their damage is a minor problem in woodlands, but may be serious on some ornamental trees and shrubs.

Abnormal growth, including leaf curling; gall formation on leaves, twigs, and fruits; and witches' brooms (excessively dense branch and twig growth) are the result of high concentrations of plant growth-regulating compounds caused by insects, herbicides, or disease organisms. These conditions are rarely serious by themselves, though they may reduce wood value for some uses.

Stem and Branch Diseases

Cankers are dead areas on stems that are symptoms of diseases such as nectria canker in maple, hypoxylon canker in aspen, and scleroderris canker in pines. Affected areas may be irregular, sunken, flattened, or swollen. They may crack open and enlarge each year until they completely girdle the stem, killing the tree above the canker.

Rust diseases in pines may cause stem cankers and turn the foliage yellow before killing the tree. White pine blister rust is the most prevalent rust in the Lake States. This stem disease requires gooseberry (currant) as an alternate host.

Dwarf-mistletoe is a parasitic plant that is causing a problem in the Lake States. It grows on limbs and small branches and may stunt, deform, or kill conifers. Its visible growth is less than one inch long and may be either single-stemmed or branched and yellow, brown, or olive green in color. Black spruce stands are the most common host for dwarf-mistletoe in the Lake States. Control methods include destroying all trees in a cutting area and any infected trees within 60 feet, then burning the slash.

Figure 7-10. Canker disease causes serious damage to tree stems.

All trees are susceptible to wood rot. The most obvious signs are fruiting bodies (such as conks and mushrooms) that appear after the rot has been active for several years. Decayed wood may either be water-soaked and spongy or dry and crumbly. It usually is discolored. Many decay organisms enter through wounds in a tree's stem or roots. These rots do not kill trees, but they can destroy the commercial value of the wood. Tree stems with rot are more easily broken by the wind and so can be hazardous.

Root Diseases

Root rot causes decline in tree vigor over weeks, months, or years. Twigs and branches die back and leaves appear small and yellowed and may drop or wilt in hot weather. Since the root system is damaged, infected trees do not respond normally to water or fertilizer and are susceptible to windthrow. Root rot also may cause stem decay.

Fire Damage

Wildfires can cause great damage to woodlands. Even in stands where the trees are not killed outright, fires may weaken and eventually kill trees, cause wounds where insects and diseases can enter, increase soil erosion, and reduce soil fertility, wildlife habitat, and recreational quality of a stand. Fire also can be used constructively to manage forest vegetation.

Forest fires are classified as surface, crown, or ground fires based on the way they spread. Most forest fires in the Lake States are surface fires. They burn only the litter and other small fuels on the forest floor. They may scar the bases of large trees and kill small trees.

Crown fires usually start as surface fires that reach into the canopy with the help of dry winds and fuel ladders. A fuel ladder is combustible vegetation that bridges the space between the ground and a tree crown, allowing a fire to climb to a tree crown. They occur most often in conifer stands and are very damaging and difficult to control. Intense crown fires will produce showers of sparks and glowing embers that easily jump firebreaks and set additional fires well in advance of the leading edge. Although conifer crowns frequently catch fire, true crown fires that spread through the air from one crown to the next are much less common than ground fires in the Lake States.

Ground fires burn and smolder below the surface, sometimes going undetected for days or weeks. They consume soil that is high in organic matter, including dried peat and thick litter. Ground fires produce enough heat to kill most of the trees in their path by cooking their root systems. Such a fire may cross firebreaks through roots and dry organic matter. Ground fires are very difficult to control, but are likely to occur only in dry years.

Figure 7-11. Fires that reach tree crowns will kill trees.

Few woodland owners can afford their own fire suppression equipment. Instead, most rely on state and local agencies to control fires. While these organizations respond quickly, there may be some delay before a fire is reported and crews arrive on the scene. For this reason you need to maintain your land so wildfires cause minimal damage before they are suppressed. The following practices will help:

- Maintain a cleared firebreak around conifer stands. A firebreak might consist of a rough bulldozed road with a bare mineral soil surface that can be driven by a four-wheel drive fire truck. Although such a firebreak may stop a surface fire, it is more likely to be a good starting place for a fire suppression crew to build a fire line.

- Consider establishing a trail or road system within a woodland that is larger than 20 acres to provide access to all areas and break it into smaller, more defensible units. The road system also may provide access for other management activities or recreation.

- Provide access for fire suppression vehicles to a stream or lake or create a pond if you have no natural water source.

- Thin and prune pine and spruce-fir stands to keep stands from building fuel ladders that permit a surface fire to climb into the tree crowns.

- Create buffer strips of hardwoods around conifers for added protection. Hardwood stands are less flammable than conifer stands and also may diversify wildlife habitat.

- After timber harvests, lop slash so that it lies close to the ground and decays quickly. You also can pile slash and burn it when there is snow cover.

- Cooperate with adjacent landowners in designing and establishing fire prevention measures.

- Place fire prevention and suppression clauses in logging contracts.

Controlled burns are fires that are set intentionally under specific fuel and weather conditions to:

- Reduce fuel loads that contribute to wildfire hazard.

- Reduce understory vegetation, thus enhancing the growth of overstory trees or benefiting wildlife.

- Kill or set back the growth of undesirable trees and shrubs and to eliminate woody debris that hinders access for planting trees or that may harbor insect and disease pests.

Soil chemistry and physical processes change temporarily after a burn, but eventually will return to normal. However, a poorly planned or improperly controlled burn may kill crop trees and cause other property damage. Consult a forester about firebreak placement, weather requirements, tools needed, legal liabilities, and other important issues. Controlled burns always pose some risk, but they can remain an option if they fit into your management plan.

Chapter 8:

Marketing Timber

Charles R. Blinn, Extension Specialist, University of Minnesota
Angela S. Gupta, Extension Educator, University of Minnesota

This chapter outlines procedures for selecting trees to harvest, obtaining bids, preparing a timber sale contract, and administering a sale. By working with a forester and following the steps recommended here, you can receive a fair price for your timber and better meet your other woodland management objectives.

Why Harvest Timber?

Harvesting is an important timber management tool. You may decide to harvest timber for a variety of reasons, including to:

- Improve the health and vigor of the forest.
- Promote natural regeneration.
- Control stand density.
- Release an established understory from competing overstory trees.
- Develop wildlife habitat.
- Alter the species composition of the forest.
- Establish planting areas.
- Create vistas.
- Clear trails.
- Take advantage of the timber's considerable monetary value to produce periodic or emergency income.
- Salvage its monetary value following damage by ice or snowstorms, high winds, fire, insects, or diseases.
- Clear the land for other purposes.

Steps in Marketing Timber

Follow these steps when marketing timber:

1. Select a forester.
2. Select trees to harvest.
3. Determine seasonal timing of harvest operations.
4. Determine the timber's worth.
5. Determine what method you will use to sell the timber.
6. Create a timber sale prospectus.
7. Advertise your timber sale.
8. Select a buyer.
9. Develop a written contract with the buyer.
10. Inspect the active harvest operation.

Selecting a Forester

As described in Chapter 1: Preparing a Woodland Stewardship Plan, it is important that you identify and select a forester who will work with you during the process of marketing your timber.

That individual should have experience working with many different timber sales and loggers. The forester will help you achieve your ownership goals and make sure that the forestry practices used enhance the future condition and value of your woodland. He or she can take you to previously harvested areas to provide a visual perspective of how a site looks after it is harvested. Using the services of a forester will help ensure that:

- You will receive what your timber is worth.
- You will get a timber sale designed to meet your property goals.
- You will sign an appropriate sale contract.
- Your sale will be administered fairly.

Selecting Trees to Harvest

Select the trees to be harvested with advice from a forester to ensure that the harvest satisfies your management objectives and maintains the woodland in a vigorous and productive condition. For example, the harvest could range from a light thinning that stimulates the growth of the remaining trees to a selection cut, clearcut, or shelterwood cut aimed at harvesting mature timber and regenerating a new stand. The type and amount of harvesting depends on your objectives and on stand conditions. For additional guidelines on selecting trees to harvest, refer to Chapter 6: Managing Important Forest Types.

Your forester will clearly mark with spray paint the timber sale boundaries and either the trees to be harvested or those to be retained so the logger can easily identify them, reducing the chance of harvesting beyond the sale boundary. If all trees in an area are to be harvested, as in a clearcut, only the boundary trees will be marked. If most trees will be cut but some will remain to grow longer, provide seed for regeneration, or offer wildlife habitat value, then leave-trees (the trees that will not be harvested) will be marked. If most trees will remain standing and only scattered trees or groups of trees will be cut, then the trees to be cut will be marked. To avoid confusion, your forester will mark leave-trees with a different color of paint than was used on the sale boundary. Because timber sale boundaries are not legally recognized lines between adjoining property owners, discuss the location of property boundary lines with your neighbors before cutting begins.

After selecting the trees to be harvested, estimate the wood volume or number of products that will be cut, by species. Products commonly produced in a timber sale include sawlogs, veneer logs, pulpwood, fuelwood, posts, and poles. Local mills or buyers will determine the specifications for each product they purchase.

Information about measuring wood volumes can be found in Chapter 2: Conducting a Woodland Inventory.

Determining Seasonal Timing of Harvest Operations

Seasonal timing of harvest operations can be critical to maintaining land productivity. These factors can affect the marketability and price you receive. Your goal should be to maintain the productivity of the land and forest in the future.

Will your soils support logging equipment throughout the year, only during dry seasons, or only when the ground is frozen? Some soils are more susceptible to compaction and rutting by operating equipment. These operations occur across the site with the felling and skidding of trees, on the skid trails and landings and on any temporary haul roads needed to get the cut products to main roads for transportation to the mills. Soils maps and Ecological Classification System ratings and on-site visits to your forest will help you and your forester determine the answers to these questions.

There can be disease or insect issues, such as bark beetles, that can be mitigated by seasonal timing of harvests. There can be wildlife issues such as nest trees of protected species that would limit operations during the nesting seasons. The bark on many hardwood trees is easily damaged and knocked off during the spring growing season. This tree dam-

age significantly reduces the future value of the trees to be left after the harvest. All of these issues should be considered in the process of setting up a timber harvest.

Determining Timber Worth

Timber is an unusual commodity in that it has no pre-established price. Instead, the price is whatever the buyer and seller agree to. It is influenced by many factors, including:

- **Tree species.** Wood from some species is more valuable than wood from other species.
- **Tree size.** Large diameter trees have more usable volume and clear wood than small trees and are of greater per unit value.
- **Tree quality.** Trees with fewer butt log (the first log from the stump) defects (such as branch scars, decay, and embedded wire) have higher quality, more valuable wood.
- **Sale volume.** On large sales, fixed logging costs can be spread over larger volumes, so the buyer can pay more per unit volume for the timber.
- **Distance to market.** The closer the woodlot is to the mill, the lower the hauling costs.
- **Site accessibility.** The ease with which the timber tract can be reached affects road construction costs.
- **Logging difficulty.** The steepness of the terrain and soil moisture conditions affect the equipment that can be used and the speed of harvesting.
- **Market conditions.** Poor markets mean lower timber prices.
- **The mill's log inventory.** Buyers often pay more for logs when their inventories are low to ensure continued mill operations.
- **Your restrictions on harvesting and skidding techniques or additional work required.** Restrictions that protect the site and residual trees tend to increase logging costs. Additional work (such as road or trail construction, trail seeding, construction of a bridge or devices to divert water off roads or trails) increases costs.

A forester can estimate the expected value of a particular sale. However, different buyers may offer substantially different prices for the same timber, depending on their own particular costs and markets. To receive the highest value, contact several potential buyers when you offer timber for sale.

Methods of Selling Timber

We generally advise landowners to sell stumpage (standing timber) instead of harvesting it yourself. When you sell your stumpage, the buyer is responsible for harvesting and transporting your timber, employing people, obtaining machinery and equipment, finding markets for the harvested material, and fulfilling all of the legal obligations associated with operating a business.

There are two general types of stumpage sales based on how the timber is priced: the lump sum sale and the sale-by-unit.

Lump Sum Sale

In a lump sum sale, payment is based on an estimate of the timber volume available in the sale area and not on the actual volume harvested. Such sales are easier to administer than sales-by-unit. Lump sum sale values depend heavily on the accuracy of the timber inventory used to estimate the volume and quality of the timber for sale. Lump sum sales may be appropriate if there is no convenient and reliable method for measuring the volume of cut logs.

You normally receive a single payment for the trees designated for sale. Alternatively, you may require a down payment of one-fourth to one-third of the sale price when the contract is signed and payment of the balance before harvesting begins or after it concludes.

Sale-by-Unit

In a sale-by-unit arrangement (also called sale-by-scale), you are paid a certain amount for each unit (such as per thousand board feet, cord, post, or ton) of product cut. A sale-by-unit requires that someone measure the products harvested (a pro-

cess called scaling). Products can be scaled by the landowner, by a professional forester, by the buyer, or by a receiving mill. You and the buyer need to determine who will scale the products based on who can be trusted to provide the most accurate information at a reasonable cost.

Although final payment is based on the actual volume harvested, some landowners ask for a down payment before the harvest of at least one-fourth of the estimated total value. Some landowners also request additional payments during the harvest, with these payments occurring at specified periods during the timber sale contract or equal to the estimated value of the next area to be harvested. Payment is adjusted at the end of the harvest to compensate for overpayment or underpayment.

Creating a Timber Sale Prospectus

In preparation for advertising your sale, create a timber sale prospectus with a detailed overview of what you are offering for sale and your contract requirements. The prospectus should include anything that may result in an additional cost for the buyer (for example, your restrictions on harvesting and skidding techniques or additional work required). Sale prospectus items include:

- Seller's name, address, and telephone number.
- Location of the timber for sale (legal description and directions, GPS coordinates).
- Description of the timber to be sold (volume by species and product; method used to estimate volume; tree species, size, and quality).
- Type of bid you are seeking (lump sum or sale-by-unit) and whether you will choose a buyer using sealed bids or an oral auction.
- Time period and procedure for inspecting the timber. (Allow at least one month for prospective buyers to inspect the timber.)
- Date, time, and place that sealed bids will be opened or an oral auction will be conducted.
- Whether a bid guarantee (usually a few hundred dollars) is required from all bidders and a down payment deposit (usually 10% or

more of the bid price) binding the offer must be paid when the contract is signed. (Bid guarantees are returned to unsuccessful bidders. For the successful bidder, that amount can be applied toward the down payment)

- When payment is to be made. (In a lump sum sale, ask for full payment before the start of harvesting. If this is not possible, negotiate a definite payment schedule that calls for specific percentages at specified dates. In a sale-by-unit situation, negotiate a definite cutting and payment timetable with the buyer.)
- Any major conditions or limitations on the sale, such as a harvesting deadline, forest management guidelines (for example, equipment limitations, method of slash disposal, restrictions on access to the area, conditions when loggers cannot operate), additional work required (such as construction of water diversion devices on roads or trails when the sale is not active for extended periods or at the end of the sale) or who has cutting rights to tops that could be sold as firewood. (Note that excessive restrictions on buyers may result in fewer bidders or reduced bid prices.)
- The requirement of a performance bond. (A performance bond is an amount of money over and above the sale price, usually 10%, posted by the buyer and held in escrow by the seller. Its purpose is to ensure that the buyer abides by and fulfills all terms of the contract. It should be returned to the buyer when all contract conditions have been met.)
- Statement that the logger will be expected to carry workers' compensation insurance and liability insurance of $1 million or more.
- Method recommended for scaling products.
- When the successful bidder will be notified (usually within seven days after bids are opened) and how much time the buyer has to sign the contract and provide the down payment after being notified of an acceptable bid (usually ten days).
- Statement indicating you have the right to reject any or all bids.

Advertising Your Sale

Foresters usually can provide a list of timber buyers. The most effective way to notify potential buyers about your timber sale is to send them your timber sale prospectus. If you are unable to assemble a list of buyers or have special products to sell, place a brief advertisement in the newspaper or on the internet directing interested buyers to contact you for a copy of the timber sale prospectus. Newspaper and internet advertisement may be particularly useful for locating firewood cutters who do not harvest other products and may not appear on any list of local timber buyers.

Selecting a Buyer

You can sell your stumpage through a single offer, an oral auction, or a sealed bid auction. Your forester can offer you advice about the desirability of asking a particular company or individual to bid on the sale and on a buyer who is right for your needs.

Exercise caution in selecting a buyer who has new employees, buyers who have not previously logged in your area or buyers who don't understand your management goals. Most buyers perform satisfactorily when all the trees in an area are to be cut (that is, a clearcut). However, only experienced and careful buyers should be selected for a thinning or selection harvest in which valuable trees will be left standing.

Obviously, profit is important, but a buyer who employs skilled and experienced operators who anticipate and avoid problems is worth a lot. Seek out buyers who attend training courses on safety, good business practices, and practices that protect the environment. Timber buyers should have all necessary insurance.

Before making a final selection, ask the potential buyer for the names of a few woodland owners with timber similar to yours for whom the buyer has recently harvested timber. Call one or more of those owners and ask about the logging job that was done. With their permission you also could visit one of the harvest areas to look at the results.

Single Offer

One option is to negotiate a sale price with a single buyer. This procedure often produces a price that is well below what the timber is worth, because the buyer has no competition and the seller often is uninformed about the timber's market value. However, the single offer may be the best method for you if:

- You have only a small amount of timber or poor quality timber to sell, so only one buyer is interested in the sale.
- Markets for the species and products for sale are so poor that few buyers would be interested.
- You know and want to work with a particular buyer who has a good reputation.

Oral Auction

A second option is to invite several buyers to inspect your timber and, at a given time and place, bid for it at an oral auction. To attract several buyers and create competition, you need to hold the auction at a time and location that are convenient to buyers. Auctions are most appropriate for high-value sales or when several timber tracts can be auctioned at one time, thus attracting several buyers.

Sealed Bids

A third option is to notify several potential buyers about the timber you have for sale, give them time to inspect your timber (usually four to six weeks), and request that they submit written sealed bids. Written sealed bids produce the best results for private woodland owners in most situations.

Open all of the bids at a specified time and place. Select the highest bidder unless you have other information that influences your decision. To be fair to all bidders, no further price negotiations should take place after the bids are opened, and unsuccessful bidders should be notified that the timber has been sold.

Preparing a Contract

Prepare a signed written contract with the buyer that protects both parties to reduce the possibility of misunderstandings and disagreements and to provide each party with legal assurance that the other will abide by the terms of the sale. The contract does not have to be a complicated document, but it should indicate what you and the buyer have agreed to with respect to the sale. The contract contents should be similar to those listed above for the timber sale prospectus. A sample contract is included at the end of this chapter (pg. 109). Your forester also may have a sample contract.

As a note of caution, preparing a contract is where many good transactions begin to break down. Buyers may have their own ideas of how an area should be harvested. They may believe a different layout may be more effective. They may feel that harvesting additional timber helps spread out their fixed costs or they may have a market opportunity. Some operators will offer a higher value to modify your planned forest management guidelines. They may offer their own contract in place of yours. You must evaluate such offers against your reasons for having a harvest in the first place.

While the buyer's suggestions might be reasonable, consult your forester about the effects of any suggested changes. That is why you hired the forester in the first place. Does the buyer's contract address all of your needs, or place unwanted obligations on you? Your contract terms were designed to protect you and your property, you do not have to modify them for the buyer's convenience. You may be able to find other buyers who will meet your terms. The extra money may look good, but you will have to live with any results.

Inspecting the Active Harvest Operation

Before harvesting begins, your forester should visit the site with the buyer to review the terms of the contract, point out the sale boundaries, discuss the location of log landings and roads, and point out any hazards or areas that require special protection during logging. Once harvesting begins, you or your forester should visit the area frequently to make sure the harvest is proceeding according to the terms of the contract and to discuss questions that might arise. Frequent visits will help you become familiar with timber harvesting operations and help you plan future timber sales. Keep in mind, however, that logging is a dangerous activity. Do not endanger yourself or the loggers by getting too close to an active operation. Wear a hard hat and bright colored clothing whenever visiting an active operation, and do not approach equipment without the operator acknowledging you and motioning you forward.

If you observe any problems while checking the harvest operation, simple suggestions to the buyer usually will resolve them, unless you observe a flagrant violation. Deal directly with the buyer or the buyer's designated representative. Do not complain or make suggestions to other individuals on the job unless they are causing immediate problems and the buyer is not on site.

When all provisions of the contract have been fulfilled, all wood and equipment has been removed, and there are no outstanding financial obligations (for example, repairs to roads or gates, or rehabilitation work on the site), write a letter releasing the buyer from the contract and return the performance bond (if one was posted).

Sample Timber Sale Contract

The sample timber sale contract (below) can be a starting point for your own contract, but we encourage you to contact an attorney for help in designing a timber sale contract that meets your specific needs.

This Contract is entered into by and between _____ (Seller), and _____ (Purchaser). This agreement is made and entered into between the parties below hereinafter called the SELLER and the PURCHASER.

The Seller solely owns the timber rights to this land and has no concurrent sales agreement on the parcel described below.

✦ SECTION 1

The Seller agrees to sell and the Purchaser agrees to buy, under the terms and conditions hereinafter stated, all the timber marked or designated by the Seller on certain lands held by the Seller and described as follows: _____ acres in Section _____, Township _____, Range _____, in _____ County, State of _____.

Timber to be harvested is marked or designated as follows: [Describe cutting blocks and how timber is marked].

✦ SECTION II

The Purchaser and Seller hereby agree to the following payment schedule: [Insert Option A or B]

Option A. Lump Sum Sale:

The Purchaser agrees to pay the Seller [10% of sale value] dollars ($_____) when the contract is signed, and [90% of sale value] dollars ($_____) before any timber harvesting activity begins as compensation for timber harvested. The Purchaser also agrees to pay the Seller [10% of total lump sum sale price] dollars ($_____) when the contract is signed as a refundable deposit to guarantee performance of Sections III and IV of this contract.

Option B. Sale-by-Unit:

The Purchaser agrees to pay the Seller an installment in advance of cutting. The first installment of [10% of estimated sale value] dollars ($_____) shall be paid when the contract is signed and subsequent installments shall be paid before harvesting begins in the next designated cutting block and in an amount equal to the estimated value of standing timber in the next designated cutting block. The volume of timber actually harvested will be measured [Location where timber will be measured, who will measure timber, when timber will be measured] (Note: if the consuming mill is designated as the official measurer of the timber volume, all scale receipts shall be provided to the Seller.)

Within thirty (30) days after the total volume of timber harvested is finally determined, the Purchaser agrees to pay or the Seller agrees to refund any difference in value from the original payment based on the actual scale at the unit prices specified below.

SPECIES	PRODUCT	ESTIMATED VOLUME	UNITS	UNIT PRICE	TOTAL ESTIMATED VALUE
			Total estimated value		

The Purchaser also agrees to pay the Seller [10% of total estimated sale price] dollars ($_____) when the contract is signed as a refundable deposit to guarantee performance of Sections III and IV of this contract.

▲ ——

✦ SECTION III

The Purchaser agrees to cut and remove said timber according to the following conditions:

1. Timber harvesting may begin on [date], and may continue until the termination date of [date] unless an extension of time is requested and granted in writing. The Purchaser shall give the Seller three (3) days notice before harvesting begins. After this termination date all products remaining on the Seller's premises, cut or uncut, become the property of the Seller unless an extension is granted. If extensions of this contract are deemed reasonable by the Seller, the stumpage price agreed upon herein shall be adjusted as follows:
    a. First six-month extension: 0% increase
    b. Second six-month extension: 5% increase
    c. Additional six-month extensions: 10% increase
    d. Other applicable charges or fees: _____

2. The Seller may terminate this contract by oral or written notice to the Purchaser upon its breach. The Purchaser shall cease all operations and immediately leave, and not return to, the Seller's property unless otherwise provided by the Seller.

3. Trees cut for pulpwood shall be utilized to a minimum top diameter of 4 inches and those cut for saw logs utilized to a minimum top diameter of 8 inches unless decay, branching, or stem deformity limits merchantability.

4. Stump heights shall be as low as practicable, but shall not exceed one-half stump diameter.

5. Sawtimber and veneer logs shall be scaled by the Scribner Decimal C rule and pulpwood according to 128 cu. ft./cord for 8-foot wood and 133 1/3 cu. ft./cord for 100-inch wood.

6. Reasonable care shall be taken to protect the residual and neighboring stands from damage caused by logging activity.

7. Only timber designated in Section I shall be cut and removed. Whenever any undesignated trees are cut or needlessly damaged, the Purchaser shall pay for them at a rate of three times their scale value. Crown damage is defined as _____ and bole damage as _____.

8. The Purchaser shall repair, at the Purchaser's expense, damage beyond ordinary wear and tear caused by Purchaser or Purchaser's agents to waterways, trails, roads, gates, fences, bridges, or other improvements on the Seller's property.

9. Locations of roads, landings, etc., shall be mutually agreed to by the Purchaser and the Seller or their agents.

10. Only nonmerchantable wood may be used for construction purposes in connection with the logging operation.

11. The Purchaser agrees to comply with appropriate forest management guidelines for the site for the duration of this contract. Particular guidelines of concern are noted below.

_____

_____

_____

_____

12. The Purchaser shall remove all sale-generated debris within twenty (20) days of sale expiration, including machine parts, oil cans, paper, and other trash, and Purchaser's equipment and structures. Items not removed are deemed abandoned, become the property of the Seller, and may be removed or disposed of at the Purchaser's expense, including but not limited to the performance deposit.

13. Care shall be exercised at all times by the Purchaser and the Purchaser's agents against the start and spread of wildfire. The Purchaser agrees to pay for any and all damage and the cost of suppression of any fires caused by the Purchaser or Purchaser's agents.

✦ SECTION IV

It is mutually understood and agreed by and between the parties hereto as follows:

1. The Purchaser agrees to save and hold harmless the Seller from any and all claims, penalties, or expenses of any nature, type, or description whatsoever, arising from the performance of this contract, whether asserted by an individual, organization, or governmental agency or subdivision. In furtherance of this clause, the Purchaser shall carry public liability insurance in the amount of $_____ and property damage insurance in the amount of $_____. The Purchaser shall be responsible for the same insurance requirements on the part of any of its subcontractors.

2. Workers' compensation insurance, as necessary, and to at least the minimum extent required by law, shall be bought and maintained by the Purchaser to fully protect both Purchaser and Seller from any and all claims for injury or death arising from the performance of this contract.

3. This agreement shall not be assigned in whole or in part by either party without the written consent of the other party.

4. All timber included in this contract shall remain the property of the Seller until paid for in full.

5. The Seller guarantees property boundaries which are marked or otherwise designated. The Seller also guarantees that the Seller has full right and title to the timber included in this sale.

6. The Seller shall refund any performance deposit or notify the Purchaser of intent to retain said deposit within thirty (30) days of sale expiration. The Seller may suspend or cancel all operations for violation of any term of this contract by the Purchaser, and for cause may retain all monies deposited.

7. The Purchaser agrees that it is acting solely in the capacity of an independent party in carrying out the terms of this timber sale contract. It is agreed and acknowledged by the parties that the Purchaser is not an employee, partner, associate, agent, or joint venturer in any of the functions that it performs for the Seller. The Purchaser has a separate place of business.

8. The Purchaser agrees that it will furnish all materials, labor, equipment, tools, and other items necessary for the performance of this contract.

9. The Purchaser shall be responsible for filing its own legally required information returns and income tax forms.

10. The Purchaser has inspected the premises and knows and accepts it as being satisfactory to perform this contract without undue risk to person or property.

11. The Seller agrees that the Purchaser shall have sole control of the method, hours worked, time, and manner of any timber cutting to be performed hereunder. The Seller reserves the right only to inspect the job site for the sole purpose of ensuring that the cutting is progressing in compliance with the cutting practices established herein. The Seller takes no responsibility for supervision or direction of the performance of any of the harvesting to be performed by the undersigned Purchaser or of its employees or subcontractors. The Seller further agrees that it will exercise no control over the selection and dismissal of the Purchaser's employees.

▲ _____

12. Neither party shall be liable for defaults or delays due to acts of god or the public enemy, acts or demands of any government or governmental agency, strikes, fires, flood, accidents of other unforeseeable causes beyond its control and not due to its fault or negligence. Each party shall notify the other in writing of the cause of such delay within five (5) days after the beginning thereof. If such uncontrollable circumstances continue for thirty (30) days and prevent either party from complying with the terms of this agreement, either party shall have the option of terminating upon ten (10) days' notice to the other.

13. In case of dispute over the terms of this contract, the final decision shall rest with an arbitration board of three persons, one to be selected by each party to this contract and a third to be selected by the other two members.

14. Special stipulations:_____

_____

_____

_____

✦ SECTION V

In witness whereof, the parties have set their hands on the dates shown below.

(Note: Separate from this form, the Seller and Purchaser are encouraged to provide one another with their Social Security Number or Federal Employer ID Number, needed to file tax returns or other financial documents.)

Seller: **Purchaser:**

Name _____   Name _____

Address: _____   Address: _____

_____   _____

Phone: _____   Phone: _____

Cell Phone: _____   Cell Phone: _____

We have read and understand the entire contract comprised of _____ pages.

SELLER

Date _____ by _____

PURCHASER

Date _____ by _____

References

Blinn, C. R., and L. T. Hendricks. 1991. *Marketing Timber from the Private Woodland* (NR-BU-2723). St. Paul: University of Minnesota, Minnesota Extension Service. Available online at: http://www.extension.umn.edu/distribution/naturalresources/DD2723.html

Martin, J. 1994. *Forestry Facts: Hiring a Consulting Forester* (Forestry Facts No. 75). Madison: University of Wisconsin–Madison, School of Natural Resources, Department of Forest Ecology and Management. Available online at: http://forest.wisc.edu/extension/Publications/75.pdf

Potter-Witter, K. 1993. *You've Been Asked to Sell Your Timber: What Do You Do Next?* (Forestry Fact Sheet 23). East Lansing: Michigan State University Extension. Available online at: http://forestry.msu.edu/extension/extdocs/facts23.pdf

Potter-Witter, K., and R. Kidd. 1996. *Timber Sale Bids* (Forestry Fact Sheet 25). East Lansing: Michigan State University Extension. Available online at: http://forestry.msu.edu/extension/extdocs/facts25.pdf

Szydzik, J., and J. E. Gunter. 1993. *Timber Sale Contracts* (E-1656). East Lansing: Michigan State University Extension. Available online at: http://web2.msue.msu.edu/bulletins/Bulletin/PDF/E1656.pdf

University of Wisconsin Extension. 2002. Forestry Facts: *Understanding the Sample Timber Sale Contract.* (Forestry Facts No. 94). Madison: University of Wisconsin–Madison, School of Natural Resources, Department of Forest Ecology and Management. Available online at: http://forest.wisc.edu/extension/Publications/94.pdf

Chapter 9:

Harvesting Timber

Charles R. Blinn, Extension Specialist, University of Minnesota
Angela S. Gupta, Extension Educator, University of Minnesota

A timber harvest should be designed to help you accomplish your management goals and objectives. Therefore, decisions such as the location of roads and in-woods skid trails, the specific equipment selected, what to do with limbs and tops and where processing occurs all should relate back to those goals.

Most timber harvesting is done by professional loggers who have the equipment, knowledge, and experience necessary to conduct an effective and safe operation. The work and time your forester spends in planning your timber harvest will reward you with higher profits, a better quality residual stand, and protection of the environment.

Select trees to cut based on your management objectives, stand conditions, and the silvicultural principles described in Chapter 6: Managing Important Forest Types. Local or temporary market opportunities may play a role in the timing or design of your sale. This chapter provides basic information on the harvesting process, including safety, forest management guidelines, the infrastructure needed to create access to and within a timber stand, harvesting equipment, and harvesting systems. Your forester will be able to help design the harvest to fit your management objectives.

Safety

Logging is one of the most hazardous occupations in the United States. Professional loggers should follow standard safe logging procedures. Have a conversation about safety with the logger before any cutting begins. When you visit an active logging site, remain visible to the operators, wear a hardhat and an orange vest, stay away from equipment when it is operating, and avoid going near any trees that may be leaning. Do not speak with anyone operating equipment until the person has stopped the machinery and signaled that it is safe to approach.

Timber Harvesting Guidelines

Timber harvesting operations can affect a number of factors within your forest, including:

- Cultural resources such as historic structures, cemeteries, and archaeological sites
- Riparian areas
- Plant and animal species of special concern
- Soil productivity
- Visual quality
- Water quality and wetlands
- Wildlife habitat

To minimize those effects, states have developed best management practices and forest management guidelines. Incorporating appropriate guidelines into your timber sale contract can help facilitate the sustainability of forest resources. Avoid including inappropriate guidelines because they may reduce interest from potential buyers. Your forester will be able to recommend appropriate guidelines for your timber harvest.

Timber Harvesting Systems

Descriptions of three basic timber harvesting systems—whole-tree or full-tree, tree-length, and shortwood or cut-to-length—follow. The systems differ in terms of the amount of processing that occurs at the tree stump and the form in which wood is transported to the landing for further processing or transport to the mill. One harvesting system may be better suited for accomplishing your objectives than others.

1. **Whole-tree or full-tree** – In this system, the entire tree—including the stem, limbs, and top—is brought to the landing with a skidder or horse. This system removes the maximum amount of material from a site. It also facilitates moving tops and limbs to the landing for processing, burning, or firewood production. However, because the entire tree is taken to the landing, residual trees may be damaged and a larger landing is needed to handle the size of material.

2. **Tree-length** – In this system, trees are felled and the top and limbs are removed before the trees are brought to the landing with a skidder or horse. By leaving limbs and tops at the stump, this system retains nutrients at the stump.

3. **Shortwood or cut-to-length** – In this system, the tree is felled, the top and limbs are removed, and the tree stem is bucked (cut) into individual forest products (such as pulpwood and sawtimber) at the stump area. The shorter product lengths allow a forwarder to move in tight areas. The forwarder may drive on slash mats, reducing soil compaction. A smaller landing is required in this system than in the other two.

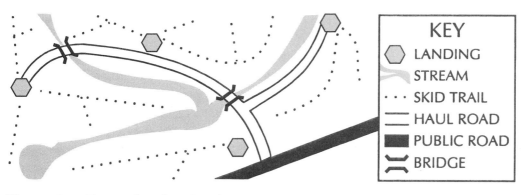

Figure 9-1. Example of a plan for a system of haul roads, skid trails, and log landings.

KEY
⬡ LANDING
STREAM
· · · SKID TRAIL
═ HAUL ROAD
■ PUBLIC ROAD
⋈ BRIDGE

Transportation Infrastructure

Few harvesting decisions have a longer lasting impact than the design and construction of haul roads, skid trails, and landings (Figure 9-1). Haul roads usually are permanent roadways that provide access for trucks to specific points in the woodland for hauling logs or other management purposes. Skid trails generally are temporary, unimproved roadways that enable skidders, forwarders or horses to transport logs from the interior of the woodland to the landing. Landings are areas used for processing (such as sorting products, delimbing, cutting logs to shorter lengths, and debarking) and for loading timber products onto trucks.

The general goal is to minimize the cost and amount of infrastructure and environmental impacts (such as soil erosion) while still achieving your land management goals. While roads, skid trails, and landings are generally constructed by loggers, landowners should understand the basic processes and standards. When planning new infrastructure, locate it in areas that facilitate your long-term ownership goals and plans.

The layout of transportation infrastructure is influenced by property lines, topography, soil conditions, streams and wetlands, economic limits on skidding distances, and other features. Permits may be required for stream and wetland crossings, culvert installations, driveway access, and other road work.

The potential for soil erosion and stream siltation is especially pronounced in areas with steep slopes and erodible soils. To reduce soil erosion avoid building roads and skid trails that run directly uphill or downhill. Use water diversion systems that move water off the exposed surface or away from ditches into the vegetated forest floor. Because water diversion options may impede some recreational uses of roadways, discuss their design with your forester.

Revegetate roads, skid trails, ditches, and landings with grasses and forbs (any herb other than grass) to help prevent erosion. The seed mix and application rate will vary according to your climate and soil. Native seed mixes are recommended to reduce the chance of introducing harmful invasive species. The seed mixture can include food and cover plants that are beneficial to wildlife. Where possible, lightly disk and fertilize the bare roadbed before broadcast seeding.

To protect roads and skid trails after logging:

- Keep ongoing travel to a minimum.
- Use them only when the soil can support the equipment without causing ruts.
- Inspect them periodically to make sure that water diversion structures (such as waterbars, ditches, and culverts) are working correctly.

Skid Trails

Skidding is the process of transporting logs from the stump after trees are felled to a landing where they can be further processed or loaded onto trucks. Logs are usually dragged by a skidder or horse or carried by a forwarder, thus creating skid trails. These trails usually are not graded and need only a minimum amount of clearing. Depending on your management objectives and forest conditions, material may be skidded over a fixed trail network or the logger could use a different skid route for each trip to help knock down undesirable trees and shrubs, thus helping to clear the site for regeneration. Frozen or dry soil conditions are recommended to avoid compacting soils. If soils are not frozen, it is generally advisable to minimize the area affected by skid trails to avoid compacting the soils across a broad area of the forest. Your forester may be able to recommend additional techniques to minimize compaction.

Landings

Landings are busy places during a harvesting operation, producing big impacts on a relatively small area. Carefully select landing locations to provide for efficient timber removal and minimize adverse environmental impacts. Proper construction and maintenance of a landing is similar to that for roads.

Locate landings close to concentrations of timber. Choose locations with a slight slope so that water will drain away. Avoid steep slopes and low, wet areas where trucks cannot maneuver. Locate landings below ridge crests to reduce the need for steep, hazardous roads. The haul road approaching the landing should have a low grade. Landing size and shape will be influenced by the timber length, loading method, type of hauling equipment, and processing to be performed at the landing.

Take special care when storing petroleum products and maintaining equipment in woodlands. Designate a specific place for draining vehicle lubricants so they can be collected and stored until being transported off-site for recycling, reuse, or disposal. Provide receptacles for solid wastes such as grease tubes and oil filters. Locate refueling areas away from water. A landing may be an excellent location for storing these products and maintaining equipment.

Cull logs and other debris may be a hazard to snowmobilers and other recreational users if left on the landing.

Harvesting Equipment

Harvesting equipment is generally designed to perform a limited number of tasks. Those operations (described below), may occur at the tree stump, during in-woods transport from the stump to the landing, or at the landing. While some logging businesses consist of one person who operates different pieces of equipment during the course of the harvest, others have several employees, each operating one piece of equipment. If possible, recommend that the logger power wash all equipment before taking it into the sale area. This may help reduce the spread of invasive or noxious weeds if seed is embedded in dirt or debris that may be clinging to the equipment.

Operations at the Stump

Operations at the stump always include felling the tree. Felling may be done by a chainsaw, feller-buncher, or a processor (Figure 9-2). After felling, the tree may be further processed by removing the limbs and top and by bucking (cutting) it into individual product sections. When material is being transported to a landing, leave the limbs and tops at or near the stump to help avoid scarring remaining trees. This makes even more sense if markets limit the use of this material or if the soil tends to be nutrient deficient. Removing the entire tree may be the preferred option where there are concerns about pest invasions after the harvest, when the whole tree will be processed at the landing, or to make it easier to cut firewood from the residue.

Transporting Material from the Stump to the Landing

Short logs, tree-length material, or whole trees may be transported from the stump to the landing either by skidding (dragging them on the ground) or forwarding (carrying them completely off the ground). Timber can be dragged to the landing using a rubber-tired or tracked skidder, farm tractor, or horse, or carried on a forwarder (Figure 9-2). A rubber-tired skidder is lighter weight, less expensive, faster, and provides better traction over rocks than a tracked skidder. The tracked skidder, on the other hand, may compact the soil less, provide better traction in mud and slippery soils, and be less likely to create deep ruts. Wide tires on a rubber-tired skidder provide similar benefits to a tracked skidder.

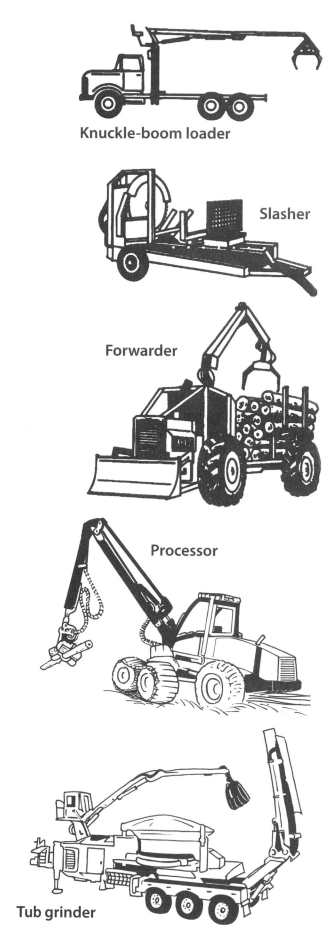

Knuckle-boom loader

Slasher

Forwarder

Processor

Tub grinder

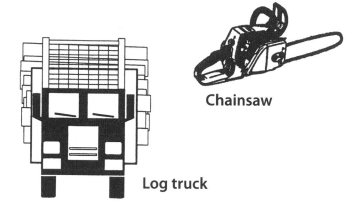

Chainsaw

Log truck

Feller-buncher

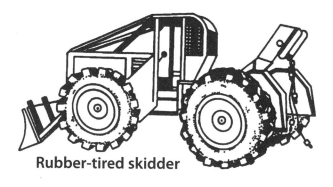

Rubber-tired skidder

Whole-tree chipper and chip van

Figure 9-2. Logging Equipment.

Farm tractors sometimes are used for skidding, but they usually need modifications to become effective, safe skidders. A winch connected to the tractor's power take-off is an important asset. Some also require shields beneath their bodies to protect them from damage by high stumps and rocks.

Forwarding machines are equipped with a hydraulic loading boom and have a bunk for holding a load of logs. Forwarders frequently travel on the debris (slash) from limbs and tops to avoid rutting the soil.

Landing Operations

At the landing, material may be delimbed, topped, bucked or slashed into product lengths; debarked, chipped or ground and blown into a van; or loaded directly onto a trailer before being transported over haul roads to a mill or other site. Landing equipment may include a chainsaw, slasher, chipper, or tub grinder (Figure 9-2).

If bucking, debarking, or other processing occurs on the landing, some limbs, bark, or other woody debris could become piled. That residual wood could be returned to the forest and dispersed by a skidder to redistribute nutrients back to their source. It also could be converted to chips by a chipper or tub grinder, cut for firewood, burned, or left to decay.

Because of the variety of operations that may occur at a landing, it may be as small as the area adjacent to the haul road or a quarter acre in size or larger. Make it large enough to allow the equipment to operate efficiently, to store products that have not been hauled to the market, for trucks to enter and leave, and for safety. Your forester can help determine the most appropriate size for your landing or landings.

Equipment Selection

Your forester should recommend harvesting equipment that is most appropriate to your management goals and desired outcomes. Some of the most important considerations for choosing timber harvesting equipment are described in the following list.

- Tree size affects the size of equipment needed to handle the timber.
- Silvicultural prescriptions (such as clearcutting, shelterwood harvesting, and thinning) influence the choice of felling and skidding equipment as well as where limbs and tops are removed.
- Topography, especially ground slope, affects the type of equipment and method used to skid logs.
- Wood volume to be removed and time constraints influence the preferred mix of equipment.
- Slash cleanup or noncommercial tree removal may require specialized equipment.
- Key site elements, such as unstable soil and proximity to water bodies and wetlands, may limit the size and type of equipment.
- Season of the year.

Forest Certification

Selling forest products that have not been certified is becoming increasingly difficult. Forest certification is a process that verifies whether your forest management, including timber harvesting, is environmentally appropriate, socially beneficial, and economically viable. This process assures consumers that the forest products they are buying were obtained from well-managed forests. The primary certification systems in the United States are those offered by the Forest Stewardship Council, the Sustainable Forestry Initiative, and the American Tree Farm System.

To qualify for forest certification, you typically must:

- Practice sustainable forestry.
- Abide by forestry-related laws.
- Follow best management practices.
- Conserve biodiversity.
- Protect water quality and other important resources.

The process of certifying your woodland requires an independent evaluator (a professional forester) who has no personal stake in your property to review your management plan and inspect your woodland. You pay a fee for this service. If you do not meet all of the certification criteria, you can make changes in your planning, record keeping, and management activities to comply. In some states an association of loggers has trained and certified loggers to harvest timber in a sustainable manner. Under some certification systems, if such a logger harvests timber from your land in compliance with certification standards, the wood harvested from your land will enter the marketplace as certified wood. This is a low-cost means to sell certified timber without the expense of arranging a professional review of your comprehensive plan and inspection of your woodland.

Many public and forest industry lands in the Lake States are certified. Relatively few family forests are certified because of the inspection and compliance costs. These costs can be reduced if you join other landowners in a cooperative to share in the certification process. Since some paper mills, sawmills, and large retail lumber distributors have made commitments to purchase and sell mainly certified wood products, there may be opportunities in the future to earn more for your certified stumpage and, therefore, justify the cost of certification. For timber to enter retail markets as fully certified, all handlers must follow a chain-of-custody process to track the wood from the stump to the retail market.

Certification is a voluntary process for landowners, but demand is growing rapidly for certified wood so certifying your woodland or timber harvest may give you a marketing advantage. Contact a forester for more information about certification opportunities in your state.

References

Garland, J. J. 1983. *Designated Skid Trails Minimize Soil Compaction* (Extension Circular 1110). Corvallis: Oregon State University.

Garland, J. J. 1983. *Felling and Bucking Techniques for Woodland Owners* (Extension Circular 1124). Corvallis: Oregon State University.

Michigan Department of Environmental Quality. 2008. *Sustainable Soil and Water Quality Practices on Forest Land*. East Lansing, MI: Michigan Department of Natural Resources Available online at http://www.michigan.gov/dnr/0,1607, 7-153-30301_31154_31261---,00.html

Minnesota Forest Resources Council. 2005. *Sustaining Minnesota Forest Resources: Voluntary Site-level Forest Management Guidelines for Landowners, Loggers, and Resource Managers*. St. Paul, MN: Minnesota Forest Resources Council. Available online at http://www.frc.state.mn.us/ FMgdline/Guidebook.html

Pope, P. E., B. C. Fischer, and D. L. Cassens. 1980. *Timber Harvesting Practices for Private Woodlands* (FNR-101). West Lafayette, IN: Purdue University, Cooperative Extension Service.

Simmons, F. C. 1979. *Handbook for Eastern Timber Harvesting* (Stock No. 001-001-00443-01). Washington, DC: U.S. Government Printing Office.

Smidt, M. F., and C. R. Blinn. 1995a. *Logging for the 21st Century: Protecting the Forest Environment*. (FO-06518). St. Paul: University of Minnesota Extension Service Available online at: http:// www.extension.umn.edu/distribution/ naturalresources/DD6518.html

Smidt, M. F., and C. R. Blinn. 1995. *Logging for the 21st Century: Forest Ecology and Regeneration* (FO-06517). St. Paul: University of Minnesota Extension Service. Available online at: http://www. extension.umn.edu/distribution/naturalresources/ DD6517.html

Wiest, R. L. 1998. A *Landowner's Guide to Building Forest Access Roads* (NA-TP-06-98). Radnor, PA: USDA Forest Service, Northeastern Area State and Private Forestry. Available online at http://www.na.fs.fed.us/spfo/pubs/stewardship/access-roads/accessroads.htm

Wisconsin Department of Natural Resources. 2003. *Wisconsin Forest Management Guidelines* (Pub-FR-226). Madison, WI: Wisconsin Department of Natural Resources, Division of Forestry. Available online at http://www.dnr.state.wi.us/forestry/Publications/Guidelines/

Wisconsin Department of Natural Resources. 2008. *Maintaining Soil Quality in Woodlands: A Lake States Field Guide* (Pub-FR-409). Madison, WI: Wisconsin Department of Natural Resources, Division of Forestry. Available online at: http://dnr.wi.gov/forestry/publications/pdf/FR-409.pdf

▲ _____

Chapter 10:

Management and Marketing of Nontimber Forest Products

David S. Wilsey, Extension Educator, University of Minnesota
Julie Miedtke, Extension Educator, University of Minnesota

Nontimber forest products (NTFP) include almost everything you find in the woods that is not timber. The term refers to the many products of forest origin that enhance or contribute to our lifestyles and our livelihoods. Collecting and using these products is an integral part of our common regional history and economy and commonly generates strong social and cultural connections.

NTFPs are the various berries, ferns, and mushrooms we pick to eat. They are the game that sustains our families. They are the plants gathered to use in various medicines, the roots and barks collected for basketry and crafts, and the seed cones used to regenerate forests. NTFPs are the balsam boughs and princess pine that, when worked by careful hands, become the wreaths that decorate homes during the holidays. For some people, NTFPs provide affordable outdoor recreation opportunities that strengthen social bonds and ties to the land. For others, they generate a much-needed paycheck.

This chapter introduces the richness of NTFPs. It highlights their value, as well as challenges, and presents some crucial considerations for landowners interested in reaping the rewards from the many goods in their woods. NTFPs may allow you to achieve better forest management and a more stable forest livelihood through the development of complementary forest resource management strategies.

Selected NTFPs

Identifying potential NTFPs and incorporating them into a management plan will help your woodlot achieve its full potential, through utilization of a diverse array of plant and animal resources. A conversation with your neighbor, with friends in town, or with a professional forester may help you identify potential NTFPs on your land and incorporate them into your management objectives. Before harvesting any NTFP, consult with a forester and a buyer to ensure you are following the best management practices and meeting the product standards necessary for commercialization.

Characterizing the varied uses and values of NTFPs is challenging because of the sheer diversity of interesting and useful forest plants and animals, as well as the potential for multiple uses of each resource. Additionally, NTFP use is seasonal, and often practiced on smaller scales than other forest uses such as logging. For these reasons, NTFP value is best considered cumulatively—as a suite of products harvested during a single season or throughout an annual cycle composed of seasonal activities.

Spring

- **Maple Syrup**—Sugar and black maple (*Acer saccharum* and *nigrum*) sap is collected in early spring when mild daytime temperatures contrast with overnight freezes. Other species suitable for tapping include silver and red maple, boxelder, and paper birch. Landowners may sell unprocessed sap but more commonly they reduce and sell it as maple syrup—roughly 40 gallons of sap reduce to 1 gallon of syrup.

- **Morel Mushrooms**—Morel mushrooms (*Morchella spp.*) are a prized and high value specialty forest food. Morels are found in dry or well-drained forest soils and proliferate after burns. Caution: false morels look like morels, but are poisonous. Always consult with a mushroom expert before picking or consuming any mushrooms.

- **Pussy Willows**—Pussy willows (*Salix spp.*) are shrubs with gray-brown bark that are typically associated with wetlands or riparian areas. Willow branches are used by the floral industry when the "cat paws" are bursting.

Summer

- **Berries and Fruits**—Blueberries, blackberries, raspberries, strawberries, juneberries, chokecherries, and wild plums are harvested throughout the summer months for consumption and sale as berries or value-added products such as jams and jellies. Berry producing plants are typically associated with disturbances such as fire or harvest operations.

- **Birch Bark**—The bark of paper birch (*Betula papyifera*) is a traditional material used to construct baskets, decorations, shelters, and canoes. Bark is harvested in the late spring to early summer and, properly done, the harvesting does not harm the tree. Birch is a pioneer species associated with disturbance.

- **Cones**—Cones of various conifer tree species are collected in the summer and fall and sold, unopened, as a source of seed for tree nurseries and public management agencies. Opened cones are sold to the floral and seasonal décor businesses.

Autumn

- **Conifer Boughs**—Boughs of balsam fir, northern white-cedar, and other conifer tree species are picked after the first hard frost for use in the region's wreath industry. Both bough harvest and wreath making provide sources of income.

- **Holiday Decorations**—Club moss or ground pine (*Lycopodium spp.*) is harvested from autumn to early winter and sold for use in holiday decorations such as wreaths and runners. Plants are found most often in pine-hardwood and maple-basswood stands. Care should be taken as the timing of harvest corresponds with reproductive spore dispersal.

- **Ginseng**—Ginseng (*Panax quinquefolius, L.*) is a perennial herb found in the understory of deciduous forests; its root is an important and valuable medicinal product. Caution: Harvesting wild ginseng is regulated by law. Consult with a forester or your state Department of Natural Resources about harvest permits.

- **Dogwood**—Red-osier dogwood (*Cornus stolonifera*) is a shrub with smooth, bright red bark that is used by the floral industry during the holiday season. Harvesting red-osier dogwood will not harm the plant, which responds to cutting with production of coppice sprouts.

Winter

- **Wild Game**—Game animals such as moose, deer, wild turkey, and grouse are much-appreciated components of forest ecosystems. Management interventions can improve habitat and forested areas can be used privately or commercially for recreation or hunting, provided local laws and permitting practices are observed.

- **Furs**—Fur bearing animals found in forest ecosystems, such as weasels and martens, can be trapped for their pelts. Preserved pelts can be sold to fur traders.

Non-seasonal

- **Character and Figure Wood**—The growth of character and figure wood most likely results from insect and bird injury, knots, decay, burls, and irregular grain coloration or patterns. Examples include burls, birds-eye maple, diamond willow, and "spalted" wood. These specimens can be sliced into high-value veneers, turned on a lathe, or carved to accentuate their appearance and increase their value.

- **Small-Diameter Wood**—Sticks, twigs and vines are used as decorative material and in traditional basketry. Some tree species, including alder, aspen, birch, dogwood, ironwood, mountain maple, sumac, and willow are sought after for furniture wood. Birch and other hardwood species are also used to make specialty products such as artificial trees and picture frames. Stems for this use are typically between 2 and 10 feet and less than 3 inches in diameter.

Management and Marketing Considerations

Harvesting NTFPs simultaneously affects the health of individual plants and animals, plant and animal populations and communities, and the broader forest ecosystem. Mild effects may be caused by simply walking around in the forest. At the other end of the spectrum, management for preferred species affects stand structure and species composition. Harvest effects are a function of what is harvested as well as the timing of and technique used in the harvest.

Just as there are forest management guidelines in many states to protect water quality and other natural resource values during forestry operations, the Forest Stewardship Council has produced guidelines for NTFP management that lead to ecologically sustainable forests. The Forest Stewardship Council's generic guidelines for NTFP certification highlight issues to consider:

- Land tenure and access and use rights and responsibilities.
- Forest management planning and monitoring techniques.
- Forest management practices.
- Environmental impacts of harvest, including biodiversity conservation.

126

- Social and cultural impacts of management and harvest.
- Community and worker relations.
- Broader benefits from the forest and economic vitality.
- Chain of custody for NTFPs.

The potential for commercial use of NTFPs depends on:

- The seasonal nature of markets, including the timing of supply and demand.
- The scale of operation that meets both quality and quantity expectations.
- The informality of social and commercial marketing networks.
- Internet opportunities.

Finally, intensive NTFP production, or agroforestry, represents an option for landowners interested in larger scale domestication of certain forest products. The combination of forestry and agricultural techniques is common throughout the world and is gaining recognition throughout the Lake States. Agroforestry enterprises associated with woodlands have focused on:

- Decorative woody perennial crops (such as red-osier dogwood and curly willow) that easily regenerate through coppice sprouts.
- Food crops such as hazelnuts, chestnuts, and berries.
- Wood fiber crops for renewable energy.

All of these enterprises have the potential to provide income to landowners.

Learning More

Utilizing NTFPs has the potential to enhance your livelihood and complement your lifestyle, while connecting you to the region's diverse cultures and shared history and economy. The process begins with a step as simple as a conversation with a neighbor or a local friend. Local colleges, universities, state and federal agencies, private enterprises and the Internet are all potential sources of information and support for NTFP activities and enterprises.

References

Cocksedge, W. (compiler). 2006. *Incorporating Non-timber Forest Products into Sustainable Forest Management: An Overview for Forest Managers*. Victoria, British Columbia, Canada: Royal Roads University, Centre for Non-Timber Resources. Available online at http://cntr.royalroads.ca/files-cntr/Incorporating%20NTFPs.pdf

Jones, E. T., R. J. McLain, and J. Weigand (eds). 2002. *Nontimber Forest Products in the United States*. Lawrence: University Press of Kansas. Meeker, J. E., J. E. Elias, and J. A. Heim. 1993. Plants Used by the Great Lakes Ojibwe. Odanah, WI: Great Lakes Indian Fish and Wildlife Commission.

Reichenbach, M., J. Krantz, and K. Preece. *Non-Timber Forest Products and Implications for Forest Managers*. St. Paul: University of Minnesota Extension Service. Available online: http://www.extension.umn.edu/specializations/environment/ntfp.html

Shanley, P., A. R. Pierce, S. A. Laird, and A. Guillén (eds). 2002. *Tapping the Green Market: Certification and Management of Non-timber Forest Products*. London, UK: Earthscan Publications.

Wilsey, D. S., and K. C. Nelson. 2008. *Conceptualizing Multiple Non-timber Forest Product Harvest and Harvesting Motivations Among Balsam Bough Pickers in Northern Minnesota*. Society and Natural Resources 21(9):812–827.

Chapter 11:

Wildlife and Forest Management

David Drake, Extension Wildlife Specialist, University of Wisconsin–Madison
Scott Craven, Extension Wildlife Specialist, University of Wisconsin–Madison

One of the most common reasons families offer for owning a woodland is to enjoy the wildlife it supports, whether by hunting, bird watching, photography or some other activity. When discussing management of forest-dwelling wildlife, it is impossible to separate wildlife management from woodland management, because the forest type and management activities directly affect the wildlife species that live within the forested habitat. In fact, management of some popular species, like ruffed grouse and woodcock, depends on timber harvesting. Woodland management for these species, and for forest products, affects many other species; some for the better—some for the worse. In some cases wildlife can affect woodland management. For example, high densities of deer can prevent regeneration of oak forests.

128

This chapter will first discuss harvest types related to wildlife management and wildlife species that tend to favor young (also referred to as early-successional) forests. The discussion will then shift to species that prefer older, more mature stands or that occupy and travel freely between stands of diverse types and ages. The chapter ends with an overview of common challenges facing woodland owners.

Figure 11-1. Forests provide aesthetics, recreational opportunities, wood products, and wildlife habitat. Photo courtesy of Mel Baughman

The Midwest has an abundance of terrestrial vertebrate wildlife. Bird species are the most numerous, followed by mammals, reptiles, and amphibians. Many bird species are migratory, as are some of the mammals, namely bats. Other birds and mammals, and all of the reptile and amphibian species, are considered resident species. Individuals of these species typically stay relatively close to the area in which they were born. Whether a species is migratory or residential, or a bird, mammal, reptile, or amphibian, all species require suitable habitat to survive. A good wildlife identification field guide will provide at least a general understanding of species-specific habitat requirements.

To attract wildlife to your property, you must provide suitable habitat. Habitat consists of food, water, shelter, and space.

- **Food:** Most often, wildlife select food sources that provide the best nutrition while also being the most abundant and easiest to find. Seasonal variations in diet occur based on food availability (such as insects or fruits and berries), so the more food you provide on your property in all four seasons, the more wildlife the land will support year-round.

- **Water:** Nearly all wildlife species in the Midwest satisfy their water requirements by drinking from standing water or through their diet. The drier the food an animal eats, the more water from external sources it needs. For example, birds that eat seeds need proportionately more water than do carnivores (meat-eaters). Providing an available and open water source, especially in times of drought or extended periods of below-freezing temperatures, will ensure that wildlife have enough water.

- **Shelter:** All wildlife species require shelter, sometimes to escape from predators, sometimes to stay warm and dry during winter storms. Shelter comes in many forms, and may consist of a hole in the ground, a cavity in a tree, the space under an evergreen tree's drooping branches, or your attic.

- **Space:** Consider not only the size and shape of your property, but also the food, water, and shelter that are contained within your property's boundaries. To manage for species such as wolves and bears that require large areas of habitat (that is, 50 to 150 square miles), you may need to cooperatively manage your forest property with neighboring landowners to create a larger block of habitat than you or a neighbor alone could provide.

As a general rule, the more diverse the habitat that is available, the more diverse the wildlife that habitat has the potential to attract and maintain. The increased plant and animal diversity of mature forests has a price, however. Abundance of any particular species often declines as diversity increases, resulting in a lower potential yield to humans, whether they are hunters, berry pickers, or loggers.

Figure 11-2. Wildlife find food, water, shelter, and space in forests.
Photo courtesy of Mel Baughman

If your management objective is to increase biodiversity (maximize the number of species on your property to the extent possible), you will need to maximize habitat diversity on your property. This could entail managing for mixed species forests (for example, a variety of hardwood or softwood species, or a mixed hardwood and pine habitat), different aged stands, or stands that are both mixed species and mixed age. Alternatively, you may want to manage for one or a few wildlife species and indirectly benefit many other species that share the habitat. Be aware, however, that while some species may benefit from a particular set of management actions, the same wildlife management practices may not benefit—and may actually harm—other wildlife species.

Timber Harvests and Wildlife

Timber harvests provide forest products and economic return, but are also necessary to maintain healthy woodlands. No matter what type of harvest you plan for your woodland, all harvest types will have direct consequences for wildlife.

Clearcutting

Clearcutting results in even-aged stands of shade-intolerant trees. You can achieve a mix of age classes by clearcutting adjoining stands at different times. Clearcut areas provide large amounts of edge habitat, which is beneficial to wildlife that thrive where forest edges meet nonforested areas (such as white-tailed deer). Edges tend to be abundant food sources. Clearcuts also increase stem density, thereby increasing the amount of cover for both prey and predator species. Clearcuts do not benefit wildlife species that require large and unbroken forest interiors (such as interior forest birds like the northern goshawk).

Shelterwood Harvests

Shelterwood harvests also result in even-aged stands and allow sunlight penetration to the ground over the entire harvest area. Shelterwood harvests typically remove up to 70 percent of the trees in a stand, and then a second cut occurring 3 to 15 years later removes the remaining mature trees. Shelterwood harvests are commonly used to regenerate oak species. Acorns from red and white oaks are a staple food for many species of wildlife (such as squirrels, deer and turkeys), so shelterwood harvests often provide abundant food sources for these species.

Figure 11-3. Timber management improves forest health and wildlife habitat.
Photo courtesy of Scott Craven

Timber Stand Improvement (Selective Harvests)

The most common form of timber stand improvement, or selective harvest, is thinning a stand to improve growing conditions for the remaining trees. Thinning allows more sunlight to penetrate to the forest floor. Additional sunlight will increase plant growth of wildlife cover and forage. Thinning also can open up the understory, allowing easier movement for wildlife.

Early Successional (Young) Forests and Associated Wildlife

In the upper Lake States, ruffed grouse are often the primary, or featured, species being managed for in an early-successional, or young, forest. Grouse are very popular as game birds and for their drumming behavior, explosive flushes, and beauty. Forest management for grouse affects an entire suite of species; therefore, we will use grouse management as an example to illustrate how forest and wildlife management go hand-in-hand. We will discuss how managing for one species often benefits many other species, and introduce some additional wildlife and forestry concepts.

Prime grouse habitat requires horizontal and vertical structure that is accomplished by managing a mix of three age classes of forest. Grouse reach their highest populations in aspen forest types. Aspen is the most common grouse habitat and the easiest in which to carry out the multiple age class management in which the birds thrive. Other forest types in the northern Lake States can provide grouse habitat, including conifers mixed with birch, red maple, alder, and hazel. In the southern half of many Lake States, dogwood, alder, hazel, prickly-ash, wild grape, oak, or red maple may provide habitat.

Aspen stands that are less than 5 years old are important brood habitat for hens and young chicks, and may also attract drumming males. Aspen stands that are 6 to 25 years old are most productive for grouse because they provide excellent

cover for drumming males, nesting hens, and wintering adults. Stands older than 25 years provide the buds and catkins necessary for winter food and can include attractive nesting and brood-rearing cover.

Figure 11-4. Ruffed grouse are commonly found in aspen forests. Photo: www.pgc.state.pa.us

Oaks are widely adaptable, but grow best in well-drained, upland soils. Oaks are usually lumped into two groups: the white oaks (white, swamp white, chinquapin, and bur oak) and the red oaks (northern red, black, and northern pin oak,). Oaks, especially young black and northern pin oaks, retain many leaves throughout the winter, providing insulation for grouse and other wildlife. Oak-hickory woodlands are a valuable asset to wildlife in the Lake States. In addition to producing acorns and nuts (hard mast), they provide excellent sites for wildlife dens, nests, and roosts. The value of this forest type for grouse is directly related to the quantity and quality of understory vegetation. Oak and hickory are attractive to drumming males, nesting hens, and broods when mixed with low conifers, tall shrubs, and herbaceous food or cover plants.

Regardless of stand age or forest type, two crucial components of grouse habitat appear to be stem density and food production. Stands with a high density of vertical stems (sapling to pole-sized aspen, hazel, and other brush) protect male grouse

▲ ————————————————————————

when they are vulnerable to predators on their drumming logs. Avian predators cannot easily fly through the dense stands. Management prescriptions for grouse often specify desirable stem densities of 2,000 or more stems an acre.

For wildlife that require large areas to range across, you may provide only part of their required habitat on your land, while your neighbors provide the remainder. For example, at least 40 acres of good grouse habitat should be provided in a contiguous area. However, in areas where grouse habitat is abundant and in close proximity, you may provide only 20 acres on your property because other suitable grouse habitat surrounds your property. This is true with most wildlife— the better the quality of habitat, the less acreage is required to satisfy a particular species' habitat requirements.

Always keep in mind a species' home range requirements. Home range is the area necessary for a species to satisfy its habitat requirements. For species such as timber wolves or black bears that may need as much as 150 square miles to satisfy all of their habitat requirements, you are very unlikely to have the space necessary to hold them on your property 24 hours a day every day of the year. Instead, they may use your property, plus many other properties, to satisfy all their habitat needs. Cooperatively working with your neighbors to provide large blocks of contiguous habitat will benefit species that use large home ranges.

Late Successional (Mature) Forests and Associated Wildlife

Mature forests (also referred to as late successional forests) with large, full-grown, older trees are among the most structurally diverse ecological communities in the world. They provide three-dimensional habitat (forest floor, understory and mid-story layers, and canopy) in contrast to the one-dimensional habitat in early successional stands. Mature forests are home to more bird species, for example, than a field or young forest of comparable size. The more vertical layering a mature woods develops, the more places wildlife

can live and forage for food. Remember, habitat diversity equals wildlife diversity. Do not overlook the value of snags (dead standing trees) and fallen logs when developing the layered structure of your woods. To illustrate some management techniques beneficial to mature forest communities, we have selected several popular wildlife species found in this habitat.

Turkeys

In the upper Midwest turkeys have proven to be adaptable to a variety of habitat types. They have also extended their range further into northern forests than expected. Mixed hardwood stands managed for mature timber provide good turkey habitat. Flocks prefer woodlots of at least 100 acres, although smaller woodlots connected by wooded corridors may be acceptable to them. If you have a smaller woodlot, be content to harbor turkeys for part of their annual cycle. You will not hold a flock year-round on 40 acres. To improve spring hunting success, provide nesting habitat to attract hens, and consequently, gobblers.

Figure 11-5. Turkeys are one of many wildlife species that require forests for survival.
Photo: www.nwtf.org

Turkeys prefer to roost in scattered tall trees with horizontal limbs, including conifers, that rise above the surrounding canopy. A variety of oaks, hickories, cherries, beech, and ash supply a steady source of mast. Selective cuts made in these stands to remove overstory trees will encourage dogwood, viburnum, hawthorn, grape, and other food-producing shrubs. Planting these and other species, such as apples, also may help attract turkeys to your property.

Woodpeckers, Wood Ducks, and Other Cavity Users

In addition to squirrels, raccoons, and other mammals, about 85 North American bird species (including woodpeckers and wood ducks) feed, nest, or roost in dead or decaying trees. To manage for these species, preserve snags and potential snags. Use uneven-aged timber harvest and regeneration systems, leaving some trees to grow beyond their usual rotation age. These old trees will eventually degrade and form snags. A one-fifth acre clump of uncut trees within each five-acre harvest area will provide many wildlife species with snags of proper size (generally greater than nine inches DBH and six feet tall). Alternatively, you can create snags by girdling selected trees and spraying an herbicide into the girdled area to kill the trees. Cavity nesters also will use appropriately sized nest boxes.

The wood duck is one of the most popular woodland cavity nesters. Encourage nesting cavities or place nest boxes within one-half mile of a water source with good brood-rearing potential—generally, a wetland with emergent vegetation.

Songbirds

Most songbirds can handle some habitat change, such as moderate timber harvesting. Notable exceptions are species that require undisturbed forests, including wood thrush, scarlet tanager, pileated woodpecker, vireos, and many species of warblers and raptors.

Birds that breed in undisturbed forests share several important characteristics. They require an undisturbed, interior portion of a woodland for breeding and will not reproduce if a sufficient amount of undisturbed, interior woodland is not available. For example, opening the woodland interior through timber harvesting exposes these species to predators and nest parasitism from cowbirds. In addition,

invasive plant species are more likely to invade a disturbed forest where the canopy is open and sunlight penetrates to the forest floor.

Figure 11-6. Interior forest songbirds, like the ovenbird, migrate into the Midwest to nest.
Photo: www.fws.gov

If you have a stand of mature northern hardwoods, aspen-birch, oaks, or mixed conifers and hardwoods, preserve as much uncut woodland and undergrowth as possible. Work with your neighbors to protect large blocks of mature, undisturbed woodlands. If you do harvest:

- Extend the rotation period where economically feasible.
- Cut a single, large tract, preferably along an existing edge or corner, rather than several small tracts in the interior.
- Preserve snags on the cut edge.
- Build brush piles with the slash to harbor insects on which songbirds feed and to provide shelter for a variety of wildlife.

Mammals

Woodlands with well-developed understories provide habitat for many mammals. Small mammals, such as chipmunks and white-footed mice, may spend their entire lives within an acre of woodland. In contrast, many furbearing predators (such as mink, skunk, raccoon, and fox) travel widely in search of food. Brushy stream borders, ravines, fence lines, and hedgerows connecting woodlots, fields, and wetlands provide these animals with travel corridors and hunting territory.

When logging or cutting firewood, leave hollow logs on the ground. You cannot sell them as sawtimber and their value as firewood is small compared to their value as dens or shelter for ground-dwelling mammals. Depending on their diameter, these logs may be used by anything from the smallest shrew to the largest black bear.

A subset of mammals known as furbearers includes otters, mink, muskrats, beavers, and bobcats. Any mammal bearing fur is a furbearer, but the group of mammals traditionally known as furbearers are those that are trapped or hunted for their pelts. Two furbearers unique to mature coniferous and conifer-hardwood forests are pine martens and fishers, both members of the weasel family.

American pine martens are roughly the size of a house cat, with thick fur ranging in color from blond to reddish or dark brown. The fur color on the head of a marten can be lighter than the fur on the rest of the body, and all martens have a throat patch that can range in color from blond to bright orange or red. Martens eat small mammals and are arboreal (that is, they live and forage primarily in trees). They require mature forests (that is, with a closed canopy) that have abundant vertical structure containing trees of at least 22 inches DBH and large volumes of dead and downed woody debris on the forest floor for resting and foraging sites and maternal dens. Tree cavities measuring about 3 inches in diameter provide spring and summer shelter and den sites.

Adult male fishers are larger than martens, but female fishers can be of equivalent size to martens. Fishers are solidly dark brown to black in color. They have long, bushy tails that are usually a bit darker than the rest of their bodies. Like the marten, fishers are arboreal and eat a range of mammals from mice to rabbits to martens. Fishers are well known for being able to kill and eat porcupines. Fishers use habitats similar to those occupied by martens. Maternal den sites are typically found in large, hollow hardwood trees measuring at least 20 inches DBH. Fishers require a suitable amount of dead and downed woody debris on the forest floor for foraging, and closed canopies to provide protection from avian predators.

Reptiles and Amphibians

Forest-dwelling herptiles (reptiles and amphibians; often shortened to "herps") live in forest wetlands, under leaf litter or loose bark, and in holes and crevices. Most woodland herp species depend on the moist, humid conditions found under the closed canopy of mature forests. Preserving or creating shallow ponds is one way to attract or hold herps on your property.

Figure 11-7. Look under downed logs to find many woodland reptiles and amphibians, like this spotted salamander. Photo: www.itsnature.org

Many woodland amphibians breed in temporary, or vernal, ponds. Shallow ponds are best, but make sure they are deep enough to retain water until mid-August to allow larvae to develop completely. Permanent ponds will attract wetland species, such as bullfrogs and green frogs, which live in or near water year-round. Having both temporary and permanent ponds on your property will reduce competition between the larvae of woodland and wetland species and increase herp diversity.

If you have no permanent ponds on your property, create small ponds by digging out springs or potholes or by building weirs (small dikes or dams) in woodland ravines. On sandy soils, you will have to line the basin of an artificial pond with clay or plastic sheeting to enable it to hold water.

Before creating, modifying, or enhancing any wetland, you must become aware of all wetland laws, regulations, and permitting issues that may affect your plans. For more information, contact your local soil and water conservation district or Natural Resources Conservation Service office for guidance and regulations. Check with your county Extension office for helpful publications about ponds and herp habitat management. Amphibians, deer, turkey, and waterfowl will all use ponds, especially if they are built in or near wooded cover. However, if beaver are common in your area, don't build an impoundment (manmade body of water) near any timber that you can't afford to lose. What they don't cut down, beavers might flood as they try to improve on your engineering.

Leaving unmerchantable logs to rot away on the forest floor benefits herps. They live in or under logs and feed on the invertebrates that are supported by the decaying wood. Rotting logs also provide a moist seedbed for mosses, fungi, ferns, and trees such as cedar and hemlock. Mortarless stone walls set off road or fence corners nicely, and will provide homes for many herps and small mammals. Any little hiding place located near water is particularly good.

Wildlife Challenges

Wildlife management is more than just trying to increase the populations of animals a landowner wants to observe, photograph, hunt, or otherwise enjoy. In some cases, rare or endangered species may be present on a property, and you as a landowner may face legal or stewardship responsibilities for ensuring the well-being of such species and their habitats.

The mere presence of some species in a given area may be controversial such as a wolf pack that is known to have attacked livestock or hunting dogs, or a deer population that has tested positive for chronic wasting disease. You may be faced with making decisions for the common good that might conflict with your own wishes.

Figure 11-8. Managing your forested property for rare species like this wood turtle can provide a unique opportunity. Photo: www.epa.gov

Sometimes wildlife abundance is actually a problem, rather than a blessing. Many species can and do cause significant damage to forest ecology, agriculture, and even buildings and other property. Thus management may need to be undertaken to reduce populations, rather than enhance them.

Wildlife Damage Management

The joys and satisfaction of successful wildlife attraction come with a price. Many wild animals cause damage and nuisance problems ranging from trivial to severe. When facing any damage or nuisance problem that involves wildlife, several general considerations will improve your chances of successful problem resolution, keep you out of trouble with your neighbors or the law, and save you some effort and money.

- **Know your enemy.** Your first priority in effectively resolving wildlife damage is correctly identifying the wildlife species causing the problem. Occasionally you may observe the animal causing the damage. Most often, however, you'll only discover the problem after the damage has occurred—a hole, missing produce, damaged landscape plants—and there is no animal present. In such cases you must do a little wildlife detective work to examine tooth marks, tracks, hairs, droppings and other signs to determine the culprit. If you incorrectly identify the animal causing the problem, you risk applying a control technique that is inappropriate or ineffective for the situation or animal, ultimately wasting both time and money. Many good field guides can help you interpret signs. Please see the "References" section at the end of this chapter for more information.

Figure 11-9. Gray wolves are a native species associated with forested areas. Photo: www.fws.gov

- **Understand wildlife laws!** You must find out what you can and cannot do legally with regard to harassing, relocating, or killing any wild animal, no matter what kinds of problems or damage it may be causing. (See the "References" section at the end of this chapter for the names and contact information for several agencies that can help you learn about the legal issues related to wildlife management.)

It is legal to resolve most wildlife damage issues at any time of year using nonlethal techniques, so long as the animal causing the

damage is not an endangered or threatened species. The vast majority of wildlife, especially birds, is protected by state or federal law, or both! Permits, licenses, or other forms of permission may be required and even then, some actions—such as the use of toxicants on some species—will never be allowed. Laws also vary from state to state and even within some municipalities. If you have any doubt as to the legality of your planned actions, check first with a local department of natural resources conservation officer.

- **Be proactive and persistent.** Problems are often easier and cheaper to prevent than to stop once they occur. Animal problems become increasingly difficult to solve once animals have established a strong behavioral pattern in using a food source, nest site, or shelter. When it comes to wildlife damage, the adage "an ounce of prevention is worth a pound of cure" is certainly true.

- **Spend your money wisely.** The cost for different types of wildlife management practices to reduce or eliminate wildlife damage can range from almost nothing to thousands of dollars. The more expensive management practices do not always translate into increased effectiveness in solving damage problems. Before spending money on any management practice—especially the more expensive ones—estimate your annual economic loss from wildlife damage. Then you will be prepared to make educated decisions about how much money you might want to spend to reduce or eliminate the damage.

- **Understand the basic tools and techniques of wildlife damage control.** Wildlife control is very different from weed or insect control. Few chemical pesticides are registered (or available) for animal control, and "cookbook solutions"—apply X to Y for three days and then the problem is solved—are rare for wildlife problems. Animals often are highly mobile, wary and unpredictable. Resolving a problem may require some trial and error and the use of an integrated control program involving a combination of nonlethal practices (such as exclusion, repellents, harassment, habitat modification, and increased tolerance) and lethal management practices. Success should be measured in terms of whether you have reduced a problem to tolerable levels. Complete elimination of an animal population is rarely achieved and generally not desirable.

Deer Management

Deer are arguably the most important wild animal over the entire Lake States region. As "keystone herbivores," deer have the capacity to affect their own habitat and the habitat of other species. In many areas, especially in the southern part of the region, deer populations are well above wildlife management goals, creating problems for farmers, foresters, and motorists. In fact in many areas, the emphasis on deer management has shifted from habitat management to deer harvest management. However, deer are by far the number one big game animal in the region, providing hundreds of millions of dollars in positive economic impact. Therefore many woodlands are still valued and managed on the basis of their deer hunting potential.

Deer are very adaptable and can be found in any forest type, from suburban parkland to remnant old-growth stands. Their highest population levels tend to occur in areas with a mosaic of agriculture and woodlands, especially younger forests and mast-producing stands. In many cases landowners need to do little to ensure huntable deer numbers on their property.

In the northern part of the Lake States region, providing forest openings, seeded trails, and food plots, along with protecting historic deer yards, may help increase deer numbers.

Harvest management is used to:

- Reduce damage to forest regeneration, plantations, or nearby agricultural operations.
- Reduce deer densities as a disease management technique.
- Manipulate the sex and age structure of the herd to achieve hunting objectives such as older, "trophy" bucks.

The concept of manipulating herd structure and health is the basis for the growing popularity of Quality Deer Management (QDM). Participants keep detailed records, manage habitat, and use hunting to achieve desired sex and age ratios in the herd. Landowners and hunters seem increasingly willing to avoid harvesting buck fawns and yearling bucks to increase future opportunities to harvest mature bucks.

Figure 11-10. White-tailed deer are very popular wildlife, but can negatively impact forest regeneration. Photo: www.dnr.state.oh.us

Landowners may choose their own goals and objectives for deer management, but must operate within the regulations set by their state wildlife agencies. Many helpful sources of detailed information (such as state agencies, deer management associations, and the Internet) and of supplies (such as food plot seed and equipment, hunting equipment, and more) exist. Deer management is a passion for some landowners!

Keep in mind several current aspects of deer management:

- **Deer feeding and baiting:** These practices are very contentious. While nonhunters and hunters alike may enthusiastically feed deer for their own enjoyment or because they feel they are helping the herd, hunters bait deer in hopes of improving harvest opportunities. Most wildlife managers would like to see both practices eliminated, or at least tightly regulated, but hunters are split. The trend does seem to be away from both practices but both are still widespread. There is ample evidence to suggest that feeding changes deer movement patterns, affects deer nutrition, concentrates ecological impacts, facilitates disease transmission, and causes other management problems. Baiting is also questioned by some who think it gives the hunter an unfair advantage because it makes the game species more predictable. Changes in the culture of deer feeding and baiting are likely to be slow.

- **Infectious disease:** Another serious challenge to deer and deer management is the spread of infectious disease. Bovine tuberculosis (TB) has been a problem in Michigan for many years. In 2002 the discovery of chronic wasting disease (CWD) in Wisconsin set off a massive and costly management response throughout the region. These and other disease concerns mean that woodland owners should consider themselves part of the management team that is working to contain or eliminate disease in the deer herd.

Endangered and Threatened Species Management

The U.S. Fish and Wildlife Service defines a federally endangered species as a plant or animal that is in danger of going extinct throughout all or part of its range. A federally threatened species is a plant or animal that is in danger of becoming endangered throughout all or part of its range. In addition to federally endangered and threatened species, every state natural resources agency maintains a state endangered and threatened species list.

Species become endangered or threatened for a variety of reasons. Habitat destruction and over exploitation are historically two of the greatest causes of species becoming endangered or threatened. Introduction of exotic species, disease, and pollution are examples of other factors that can limit a species' population. As a landowner, your ability to control some factors—such as disease and pollution—may be limited, but you can certainly control

invasive species and habitat destruction on your property and help sustain rare populations. Check your state's natural resources agency web site for a list of both federal and state endangered and threatened species in your area. Technical and cost-share assistance is usually available for landowners interested in managing for endangered and threatened species. Many landowners take great pride in knowing they are successfully managing for a rare species on their property, and that they may be the only property in the area where the rare species is found.

Figure 11-11. Wildlife damage management practices like fencing can help protect your forests. Photo courtesy of John Grande

A species typically remains on the federal list or a state's list for a long time. However, there have been a few species delisted due to protections afforded under the Endangered Species Act. The American alligator and bald eagle are two examples of successful delistings.

One recent success story specific to the Lakes States region was the 2007 delisting of the region's population of the gray wolf. The gray wolf was deemed extinct in Wisconsin by 1960, and declining in numbers in Minnesota and Michigan as a result of habitat loss, bounties, and a decrease in the prey base. In 1974 the timber wolf was listed as endangered under the federal Endangered Species Act and it became illegal to kill gray wolves. Habitat management was required to provide suitable habitat and space for the wolf to exist.

Due to these protections, excellent management by state and federal wildlife agencies working cooperatively, research efforts by agencies and universities, and private landowner cooperation and education, the gray wolf population grew to the point where wolves began to move into states such as Wisconsin (where no wolves existed) from states like Minnesota (which had a growing wolf population). Currently, the wolf population is large enough that state wildlife agencies in the Lake States region are contemplating a future harvest season to control population growth.

References

Lake States Cooperative Extension Service web sites

Michigan State University Extension: http://www.msue.msu.edu

University of Minnesota Cooperative Extension Service: http://www.extension.umn.edu

University of Wisconsin Cooperative Extension Service: http://www.uwex.edu

Wildlife Agency web sites

Michigan Department of Natural Resources: http://www.michigan.gov/dnr

Minnesota Department of Natural Resources: http://www.dnr.state.mn.us

Wisconsin Department of Natural Resources: http://www.dnr.state.wi.us

U.S. Fish and Wildlife Service: http://www.fws.gov

U.S. Department of Agriculture – Wildlife Services: http://www.aphis.usda.gov/wildlife_damage/

Wildlife Damage Management Resources

Internet Center for Wildlife Damage Management: http://www.icwdm.org

Elbroch, M. 2003. *Mammal Tracks and Signs: A Guide to North American Species.* Mechanicsburg, PA: Stackpole Books.

Elbroch, M., and E. Marks. 2001. *Bird Tracks and Signs: A Guide to North American Species.* Mechanicsburg, PA: Stackpole Books.

Hygnstrom, S. E., R. M. Timm, and G. E. Larson (eds.). 1994. *Prevention and Control of Wildlife Damage* (2 vols.). Lincoln: University of Nebraska-Lincoln. Available online at http://icwdm.org/handbook/index.asp

Wildlife Management and Identification Resources

Demarais, S., and P. R. Krausman. 2000. *Ecology and Management of Large Mammals in North America.* Upper Saddle River, NJ: Prentice Hall.

Harding, J. H. 1997. *Amphibians and Reptiles of the Great Lakes Region.* Ann Arbor, MI: University of Michigan Press.

Kurta, A. 1995. *Mammals of the Great Lakes Region* (rev. ed.). Ann Arbor, MI: University of Michigan Press.

Partners in Amphibian and Reptile Conservation. 2002. *Habitat Management Guidelines for Amphibians and Reptiles of the Midwest.* Partners in Amphibian and Reptile Conservation. Available online at http://herpcenter. ipfw.edu/index.htm?http://herpcenter.ipfw.edu/outreach/ MWHabitatGuide/index.htm&2

Pearson, C. 1998. *Planning for the Birds: Things to Consider When Managing Your Forest.* St. Paul, MN: Minnesota Department of Natural Resources.

Stokes, D. W., and L. Q. Stokes. 1996. *Field Guide to Birds: Eastern Region.* New York: Little, Brown.

Woodland Habitat Management Resources

Deal, C., J. Edwards, N. Pellmann, R. W. Tuttle, and D. Woodward. 1997. *Ponds: Planning, Design, Construction* (Agriculture Handbook 590). Washington, DC: U.S. Department of Agriculture, Natural Resources Conservation Service.

Gullion, G. W. 1984. *Managing Northern Forests for Wildlife.* Coraopolis, PA: The Ruffed Grouse Society.

Minnesota Department of Natural Resources. 2001. *Beyond the Suburbs: A Landowner's Guide to Conservation Management.* St. Paul, MN: Minnesota Department of Natural Resources.

Sargent, M. S., and K. S. Carter (eds.). 1999. *Managing Michigan Wildlife: A Landowners Guide.* Lansing, MI: Michigan United Conservation Clubs.

Wisconsin Department of Natural Resources. 1996. *Wildlife and Your Land: A Series about Managing Your Land for Wildlife.* Madison, WI: Wisconsin Department of Natural Resources.

Chapter 12:

Noise and Visual Quality

Melvin J. Baughman, Extension Forester, University of Minnesota

Landowners and neighbors as well as visitors spending recreation time near forested areas all appreciate the visual quality of forests and the silence and solitude they offer. Some viewers may not recognize the biological or economic factors that influence your decisions to harvest or regenerate trees, but they will judge your land stewardship by the physical appearance of your woodland and sounds coming from it. The future of some management practices may be influenced, possibly even regulated, as a consequence of public pressure to maintain attractive woodlands. Many management practices affect the appearance of a woodland. Whether the resulting appearance is pleasing or not depends on the observer.

Figure 12-1. People choose to live and recreate in woodlands because of their scenic quality and tranquility.

Visual quality and noise are of high public concern where woodlands are noticeable from adjoining land, and from nearby public roads, trails and waterways that receive heavy public use. Concern for visual quality and noise diminishes as public use declines on such sites and where your forestry activities are less noticeable.

Following are management practices that will affect the public perception of your woodland. Choose those that fit your management goals and are likely to satisfy public opinion. As a general guideline, where the public is likely to see your activities, mimic nature with natural appearing tree stands of mixed species and sizes at random spacings. Avoid straight lines of trees or straight edges on tree stands. Keep noise to a minimum.

Noise Management

Noise from chainsaws and heavy equipment disrupts the peacefulness of a woodland and may irritate neighbors or the passing public. When operating noisy equipment within hearing distance of neighbors and public areas, reduce noise in early morning, late evening, and other inappropriate times whenever possible. Use noisy equipment during days of the week or periods of the year when the public is less likely to be close by. A 100-foot wide dense band of trees and shrubs is a reasonably effective sound barrier for ordinary vehicle noise, but may not be adequate for heavy equipment noise.

Landscape Management

Portions of your woodland that are visible from public roads, trails or waterways require special attention. Try to maintain a natural appearing landscape in those areas. Begin by considering the part that your land plays in the overall landscape of the area.

Where there are large expanses of unbroken forest, trees may become monotonous to travelers. You can provide a visual break and a more interesting landscape along public travelways by creating a mixture of stands with different tree sizes and species. Permanent openings create more diverse habitat that offers opportunities for wildlife viewing and attract a greater diversity of wildlife.

Create or enhance a scenic vista by felling trees in the foreground or by thinning the stand or pruning lower limbs to permit a view of the broader landscape beyond. On a smaller scale you can clear sight lines through heavy undergrowth to draw attention to picturesque trees, rock formations, streams, lakes, and other scenic attractions. Local regulations may restrict land management options, such as tree cutting, near public water bodies.

Manage the tree species composition of your woodland to encourage trees with special visual appeal because of their trunk shape, blossoms, bark color, fall foliage color, or other characteristics. For example, white birch and aspen have white bark that is especially attractive when contrasted with green foliage on spruce and fir trees. In the fall, sugar maple leaves may turn brilliant red while aspen leaves turn golden. Just as gardeners plan flower gardens to bloom all summer, you can manage your woodland to create visual appeal throughout the year.

Some people prefer woodlands with a high canopy but little understory vegetation. Encourage these open, park-like conditions by maintaining a dense overstory that shades the ground and discourages understory vegetation. Dense conifer stands (such as pine, spruce, fir) block sunlight more effectively than deciduous trees. Deciduous trees such as sugar maple and oak have dense crowns that block sunlight more effectively than aspen and birch.

Figure 12-2. A dense overstory, especially conifers, discourages understory vegetation, leaving an open, park-like stand.

To block sightlines into a woodland and screen an objectionable view or create privacy, encourage shrubs and ground vegetation by lightly thinning a dense canopy. Try leaving 60 to 80 percent crown cover. For better year-round screening, establish spruce, fir, or pine along the woodland edge.

Figure 12-3. A broken canopy allows sunlight to sustain small trees and shrubs in the understory.

Roads and Trails

Plan systems of recreational trails, roads, skid trails, and log landings to minimize their visual impact. Locate roads and trails to:

- Minimize the total mileage required to accomplish their purposes.
- Reduce their visibility from nearby vantage points, such as scenic overlooks, streams, and lakes.
- Minimize the need for visible structures (such as bridges, culverts, ditches).
- Minimize the number of stream crossings.
- Utilize the best soils, considering potential for compaction, displacement, and erosion.

Reduce sightlines into clearcuts or landings by using small road openings through a band of trees or by designing curves in road alignment so the road visually disappears into the opening.

Locate borrow pits, rock crushing sites, and log landings out of public view behind vegetation screens or hills.

When clearing roadways, utilize merchantable timber. Avoid large debris piles that will require many years to decay. Disperse cleared debris away from the travel right-of-way so it is less visible. Push stumps off to the side so they remain upright—a more natural appearance.

Soil disturbance is unattractive and a potential source of erosion and subsequent water pollution. Compacted areas also may not regenerate with trees or other vegetation as readily as less disturbed areas. Erosion is most likely to occur soon after construction so shape and stabilize disturbed areas (such as ditches, cut-and-fill sites) as quickly as possible. Install temporary erosion control devices, such as straw bales, mulch or woody debris, to help stabilize soils before vegetation becomes established. Avoid planting grass for soil stabilization in woodlands, if possible since seeding usually introduces nonnative species.

When the road is especially susceptible to damage (such as in spring after the ground thaws and after heavy rain), stop forestry activities and close the roads. To keep mud off public roads,

- Harvest when the ground is dry or frozen, or
- Maintain a hard surface on the haul road, or
- Provide clean fill (gravel or wood chips) on the haul road for about 200 feet before the highway entrance.

Close a road after its primary use has ceased. Remove culverts, temporary bridges, signs, or other structures no longer needed. Fill in ruts and stabilize eroding areas by re-shaping, seeding, and fertilizing as appropriate. Rehabilitate borrow pits when their use has ended. Re-shape the pit to fit natural landscape contours, spread good soil over the surface, and reseed.

Timber Harvesting

In most areas less than 3 percent of the whole forest is subject to harvesting in a single year, so the visual impact of timber harvesting on a large landscape is relatively minor until the effects accumulate over a long period of time. However, in the small areas where timber harvesting does occur, it can dramatically alter the appearance of a woodland. To minimize visual impacts of harvesting, plan harvest and regeneration systems that quickly regenerate trees. Each harvest and regeneration system described in Chapter 4 has a different visual effect.

Determine the preferred operating season for a specific site to help avoid unwanted impacts. Soils are most susceptible to compaction, rutting, and puddling immediately after the spring thaw and following heavy rain. On low-strength soils (such as those with high organic content), use low ground pressure equipment or drive on slash mats to avoid soil damage.

Harvest stands by the single-tree or group selection method to produce an uneven-aged woodland and avoid the temporary barren appearance of clearcuts. Keep in mind, however, that the selection method regenerates mainly shade-tolerant tree species.

The difference between group selection and clearcutting is a matter of scale. Clearcuts often are described as larger than two acres whereas group selection cuts are smaller.

Soften the visual affect of clearcuts by making them appear to be less than 10 acres in size:

- Cut them in narrow, irregular shapes.
- Shape them so only a small portion is visible from a travelway.
- Leave tree islands or corridors of uncut trees across clearcuts.
- Position them to follow major land contours rather than cutting across contours (Figure 12-4).
- Leave bands of uncut trees between the clearcut and public roads, trails, or waterways.
- Feather the borders where they adjoin stands of older trees (Figure 12-5).

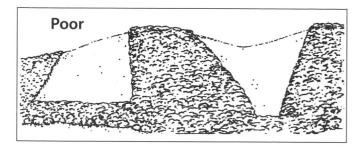

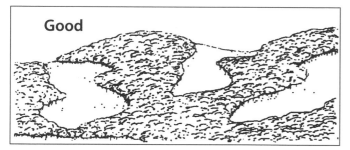

Figure 12-4. In rolling topography, design clearcuts to blend into the landscape.

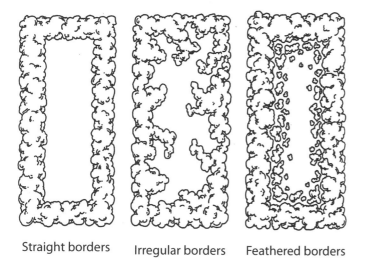

Straight borders   Irregular borders   Feathered borders

Figure 12-5. Irregular or feathered borders appear more natural than straight borders around clearcuts.

Some people prefer the appearance of complete clearcuts where no trees are left standing, whereas others prefer clearcuts that retain scattered live trees. Scattered live trees break up the monotony of large clearcuts and provide vertical habitat for birds. Some songbirds and raptors benefit from the residual trees.

Dead standing trees, called snags, may have little visual appeal, but there are many wildlife species that depend on them for nesting, denning, feeding,

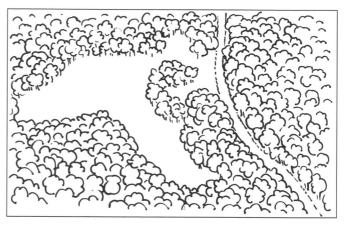

Figure 12-6. Reduce the apparent size of clearcuts by leaving vegetative screens with narrow road openings or tree islands.

and roosting sites as well as escape areas. Near travelways, do not leave snags in the foreground and hide scattered snags with vegetative islands or locate snags around the edge of an opening to allow for camouflage by background trees.

During selection harvests, control the direction of fall to minimize damage to residual trees and position the fallen tree for skidding. Leave bumper trees standing along roads and skid trails to protect nearby trees of better quality that will be left standing. Fell bumper trees last.

Woody debris left in a woodland after harvest can be unsightly. Remove as much wood as possible for products. Cut stumps low and lop slash so that it is no more than two to four feet above ground level. Woody debris near the ground decays more quickly because of higher humidity and is concealed more quickly by new tree growth. Near heavily traveled public roads, avoid piles of woody debris and eliminate or minimize slash within 50 feet of travelways. Slash visible beyond 50 feet should be cut to a maximum height of two feet.

To reduce the amount of unusable logs, limbs, and bark at log landings, trim as much unusable wood from the trees as possible before logs are skidded to a landing. When logging has been completed, burn, bury, or disperse residual woody debris and reseed landings.

Be sure to clean up refuse and discarded equipment from the harvest area.

Regeneration

Plan timber harvests to quickly encourage natural regeneration or to prepare sites for artificial regeneration. Choose a harvest system (see Chapter 4) that is compatible with the tree species you want to regenerate (see Chapter 6). Rapidly growing young trees quickly conceal logging debris and enhance visual quality.

Site preparation may be necessary to control competing vegetation or prepare a seedbed. Controlled burning, mechanical scarification, or herbicides may be recommended. Practices that can be conducted in the spring just before green-up, in the fall just before leaves turn color, or during the dormant season are less visually obtrusive than summer treatments because they do not result in unsightly dead leaves on vegetation. Avoid or screen slash piles that are visible from public travelways. Use low-impact site preparation methods such as patch or row scarification. Where herbicides are needed, use spot or strip treatments rather than broadcast treatments.

Do not plant tree rows perpendicular to travel routes. Instead, plant trees at irregular spacing or in offset rows parallel to the road to encourage natural-appearing stands. Use wider initial spacing to minimize the number of re-entries to the site for thinning and to encourage establishment of other species. Promote a mixture of species, both naturally occurring and planted. Favor long-lived species where appropriate to minimize frequency of management activities.

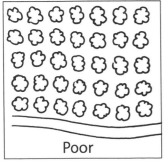 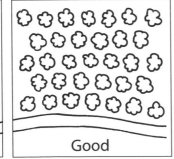

| Poor | Good |

Figure 12-7. Do not plant tree rows perpendicular to roads. Instead plant outside rows of trees parallel to roads, at random spacing or offset rows.

Woodland Improvement Practices

Thinning, culling, weed-tree removal, and pruning are common management practices aimed at changing tree species composition, improving tree quality, and increasing tree growth rates (see Chapter 5). During these activities, harvest and use as much wood as economically feasible to minimize the amount of woody debris left on the forest floor. Near travelways, keep slash height below two feet by removing, lopping, crushing or burning whenever possible. When thinning trees in rows, use selective harvesting hear travelways to break up the row affect.

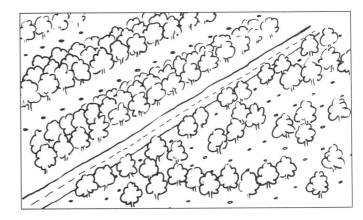

Figure 12-8. To make plantations appear more natural, selectively thin or cut rows parallel to a road.

When the need arises to kill invading broadleaved hardwoods in conifer stands, favor nonherbicide treatments when possible. If herbicides are applied, leave untreated or selectively treated areas adjacent to travel routes. Favor band treatment or spot treatment over broadcast treatment. Choose late-season or dormant-season herbicides.

If you need to deaden unusable trees, kill them standing so they fall down over a period of years. In contrast, a large number of trees felled at one time will form an impenetrable mass of debris. Deaden deciduous trees during the dormant season. When such trees are killed during the growing season, they retain unsightly dead, brown leaves for several months.

▲

Woodland Protection

As described in Chapter 7, woodlands need protection from fire, insects, and disease. Large numbers of trees damaged or killed by these agents are unsightly. Protect your woodland against these pests by following the recommendations in Chapters 6 and 7.

References

Jones, G. T. 1993. *A Guide to Logging Aesthetics: Practical Tips for Loggers, Foresters, and Landowners* (NRAES-60). Northeast Regional Agricultural Engineering Service, Cooperative Extension, 152 Riley-Robb Hall, Ithaca, NY 14853-5701. 30 pp.

Minnesota Forest Resources Council. 2005. *Sustaining Minnesota Forest Resources: Voluntary Site-level Forest management Guidelines for Landowners, Loggers and Resource Managers.* 2003 Upper Buford Circle, St. Paul, MN 55108.

Chapter 13:

Recreational Trail Design

Melvin J. Baughman, Extension Forester, University of Minnesota
Terry Serres, Graduate Research Assistant, University of Minnesota

This chapter provides simple, inexpensive solutions for designing, building, and maintaining sustainable trails for hiking, horseback riding, bicycling, cross-country skiing, snowmobiling, all terrain vehicles (ATVs), and off-highway motorcycles (OHMs). Sustainable trails hold up to intensive recreational use and severe weather conditions, and require minimal maintenance.

Determine Trail Uses

The first step in trail design is to determine how the trail will be used, how much it will be used, and what quality of user experience you want to offer.

Multi-use trails work if:

- There are many primary users but only a few secondary users.
- The trail is used in different seasons by different users.
- The trail is designed and maintained to accommodate all users or the corridor contains parallel treads.
- Clear rules are posted about how to behave (pass, regulate speed, etc.) when encountering other types of trail users.

Consider a single-use trail if:

- Different types of users have different levels of tolerance for noise, effort in using the trail, speed of travel, or influence on the tread.
- You want to offer a high quality trail experience for one type of user.

How much will the trail be used at any one time, day, season or year? As trail use increases, widen the tread and clearing width, make the tread more durable, and decrease grade. These actions make the trail more durable and easier to use by a wide variety of users.

Design your trail to fit the user experience that you want to offer. Consider:

- Physical ability of trail users. For example, reduce trail grade and smooth the trail surface to accommodate people with a range of physical abilities.
- Exposure to personal risk (such as injury, getting lost) the trail offers.
- Duration of the experience. Is it 30 minutes or 3 hours?
- Purpose for the trail. If the trail simply leads to a destination, choose the shortest and easiest route. If the trail itself is the destination, choose the most interesting route.

Select the Corridor

Perhaps the most enjoyable step in trail design is exploring the corridor to determine where to place the trail. A trail corridor is a wide swath through the landscape that will encompass the trail. Analyze the entire area, refining the trail location as you gather more information.

Use Photos and Maps

Aerial photographs help you identify land uses on your property and neighboring properties (such as cropland, pasture, forest, river, lake), roads, trails, buildings, and utility rights of way. Look for photos in a scale of at least 4 inches to 1 mile, but preferably 8 inches to 1 mile.

Topographic maps (1:50,000 scale or larger) are helpful in hilly and mountainous terrain, especially if your trail covers a large geographic area. They show elevation changes, forest and open areas, rivers, lakes, wetlands, buildings, roads, trails, cemeteries, and other features.

Soil maps and accompanying data tables describe soil physical characteristics such as depth, texture, erosion potential, and flood frequency as well as soil suitability for roads, structures, farming, forestry, etc.

When evaluating large sites, other maps or geographic information system (GIS) data may provide information on water resources, rights of way, utilities, land uses, roads, land ownership, vegetation cover types, wildlife habitat, flood zones, etc.

Scout the Trail Corridor

Scout the corridor in the trail's primary season of use. To clearly see landscape features, scout when deciduous trees have lost their leaves. If possible, scout in all seasons to reveal attractive features and hazards that may affect trail location, construction or maintenance. Look for:

- Spring: high water, ephemeral ponds, flowers
- Summer: dense foliage, normal water level
- Fall: foliage color
- Winter: icicles, snow scenes, frozen water

▲

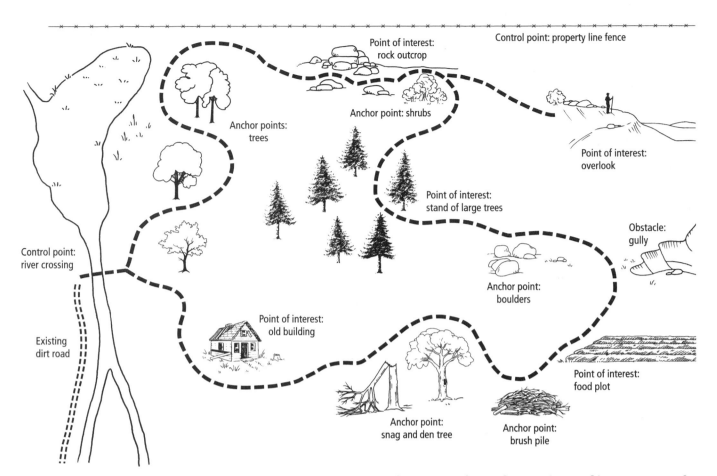

Figure 13-1. Consider existing roads and trails, control points, obstacles, points of interest, and anchor points in trail layout.

Note existing trails and roads, control points, obstacles, points of interest and anchor points (Figure 13-1). Take notes and mark locations on a map or record GIS coordinates.

Existing trails and roads may be good links to new trails. Also look for natural pathways that require little clearing or construction (such as a ridge top, hillside bench, or river bank terrace).

Control points are physical or legal constraints on a trail's location. Ownership or management unit boundaries, a steep slope forcing a trail through a narrow section of hillside, a cliff that forces a trail around one end, a wetland forcing the trail along a narrow upland ridge, or a stream that can be crossed easily in only a few places are examples of control points.

Obstacles can include a steep slope, rocky soil, boulder field, rock slide, sand dune, cliff, rock ledge, eroding bank, steep-sided gully, gorge sub-ject to flash floods, water body, wetland, habitat for rare species, historic and cultural sites, fence, highway, sources of objectionable sound, and objectionable views. Obstacles often require expensive crossing structures.

Run your trail past significant points of interest, such as unusual landforms (sink hole, esker, sand dune, hill, valley, gorge); different forest types or ages; forest opening; grassland; farm land, especially if it attracts feeding wildlife; scenic vista; boulders; rock outcrop; wetland; ephemeral pond; lake; river, creek, waterfall; historic site (may also be an obstacle); archeological site (may also be an obstacle); and wildlife habitats (den trees, rock piles, dense thickets, layers of forest vegetation, water sources, sand banks, cliffs, caves, crevices). Attract wildlife to the trail corridor with nesting boxes, breeding sites, food plots, feeding stations, roost poles, watering devices and other constructed habitats.

Figure 13-2. Recommended Trail Design Standards.

Trail Use	Configuration	Length	Tread Surface	Tread Width	Clearing Width	Clearing Height	Grade
Hiking	Loop or multiple loops for day hikes; variety in landscape; frequent curves and grade changes; spur trails to points of interest	5–15 mi	Mineral soil, embedded rocks, bedrock, asphalt, or concrete	2–3 ft light use or 1-way, 4–6 ft heavy use or 2-way	4–6 ft light use or 1-way; 6–10 ft heavy use or 2-way	8 ft	1–7% preferred, 10% maximum sustained, 40% for short distances
Horse	Loop or multiple loops with variety of scenery and terrain, and open parade area; 1-way traffic; avoid water and road crossings; avoid wet areas and steep slopes where it is difficult to maintain tread	5–25 mi	Mineral soil; crushed, compacted gravel	2–4 ft light use or 1-way, 6–8 ft heavy use or 2-way	8 ft light use or 1-way; 12 ft heavy use or 2-way	10 ft minimum, 12 ft preferred	1–10% preferred, 10% maximum sustained, 20% for short distances
Touring Bike	Loop and linear trails; 1-way traffic	5-50 mi	Limestone fines; other crushed stone 3/8" or less; 2" asphalt over 3"–4" base of compacted gravel	3–6 ft light use or 1-way, 8–10 ft heavy use or 2-way	8 ft light use or 1-way; 10–14 ft heavy use or 2-way	8–10 ft	0–3% preferred, 5–10% maximum sustained, 15% for short distances
Mountain Bike		5-20 mi	Mineral soil, bedrock	2–3 ft	6–8 ft		
Cross-Country Ski	Loop or multiple loops (always); 1-way traffic best; 2-way okay on access trail, but provide separate uphill and down-hill segments on slopes over 8%; north- and east-facing slopes retain snow longer	4–10 mi	Remove rocks, logs, stumps from tread; maintain vegetation to hold snow; groom when snow 6–12" deep	5–6 ft light use or 1-way, 8–10 ft heavy use or 2-way	8 ft light use or 1-way, 12–14 ft heavy use or 2-way	8 ft above expected snow depth	(Varies by skill level): 0–5% preferred, 10% maximum sustained, 25–40% max. for short distances and experts; break steep climbs with short, level resting places; make end of downhill slopes straight and level or gently rising
Snowmobile	Cross steep contours at right angles; avoid steep hillsides with rollover risk; 1-way traffic except on access trails; if 2-way, provide separate uphill and downhill segments on slopes over 8%	5–50 mi	Remove rocks, logs, stumps from tread; maintain vegetation to hold snow; hard surfaces promote melting but asphalt or concrete okay where snowfall is sufficient; groom heavily used trails	8–10 ft light use or 1-way, 10–14 ft heavy use or 2-way	8–12 ft light use or 1-way, 14–16 ft heavy use or 2-way	8 ft above expected snow depth	0–25% preferred, 25% maximum sustained, 40% for < 50 yards
All-Terrain Vehicle (ATV)	Trail system with loops of varying difficulty, easy trails provide access to more difficult trails; two-way trails; occasional obstacles	5–20 mi.	Mineral soil; bedrock; loose rocks less than 6" diameter	5–7 ft light use or 1-way, 8–12 ft heavy use or 2-way	6-10 ft	8 ft	0–25% preferred, 25% maximum sustained, 45% for < 100 yards
Off-Highway Motorcycle (OHM)		5–50 mi.	Mineral soil; bedrock; rocks firmly embedded in tread surface	1.5–2 ft light use or 1-way, 3–6 ft heavy use or 2-way	6-8 ft	8 ft	0–30% preferred, 30% maximum sustained, 50% for < 100 yards

Turn Radius	Sight Distance	Water Crossing	Other Uses	Unique Facilities
Not critical, but 6 ft preferred	Not critical, but 50 ft recommended, especially at road crossings	Stepping-stone ford if water less than 2 ft deep; culvert or bridge, 3–4 ft wide for light use, 5–6 ft for heavy use; at least one handrail if bridge is high-use, more than 12 ft long, or more than 4 ft over water	Low-use horseback riding, snowshoe, cross-country ski, snowmobile	Resting benches
6 ft	50 ft minimum, 100 ft preferred and at road crossings	Ford slow-moving water less than 3 ft deep – select site w/ stable sand or gravel base; soil-covered culvert is better than bridge; bridge only if water is deep and swift, must be well-designed	Hiking; if no winter riding: snowmobile, cross-country ski, snowshoe	Parking with trailer space, tether line; campsites with tether lines or corrals, water, manure dump
radius in feet = (1.25 x velocity in mph) + 1.5 4 ft minimum, 8 ft preferred	50 ft minimum, 100 ft at road and water crossings and on 2-way trails	Culvert, bridge or boardwalk w/ handrails; orient deck boards 45–90º to direction of travel; width 4–8 ft for light use or 1-way, 10 ft for heavy use or 2-way	Hiking, off-season cross-country ski, snowshoe, snowmobile	Bike rack
50 ft minimum, 100 ft preferred; avoid curves at foot of downhill slopes, or provide warning 100 ft before entering curve and runout zone, widened trail, or wider turning radius	50 ft minimum on steep downhill runs or when crossing roads, waterways, or hazards	Straight, 0–5% grade on approaches; culvert, bridge or boardwalk w/ handrails; width 6–10 ft, bridge and boardwalk decks flush with tread surface, boards spaced 3/8" or less to hold snow; frozen water crossings only on narrow, shallow (< 12"), early-freezing streams and wetlands	Snowshoe; off-season hiking, OHM, ATV, mountain bike, horse	Resting benches at regular intervals, shelter every 8–12 miles
50 ft minimum, 100 ft preferred (depends on speed)	50 ft min., 100+ ft preferred (depends on speed)	Straight, 0–5% grade on approaches; culvert, bridge, or boardwalk; width 8–10 ft, bridge and boardwalk decks flush with tread surface, boards spaced 3/8" or less to hold snow; reflective markers on corner posts at bridge ends; frozen water crossings only on narrow, shallow (< 12"), early-freezing streams and wetlands	Off-season horse riding, hiking, mountain bike, OHM, ATV	Parking with trailer space, open area near entrance to warm up snowmobiles; rest stops or shelters after 15 miles
10 ft minimum, 25 ft maximum	50 ft minimum, 100 ft preferred	Culvert, bridge w/ handrails, or boardwalk w/ curbs; orient deck boards 45–90º to direction of travel; width 4–8 ft for light use or 1-way, 10 ft for heavy use or 2-way	Mountain bike, snowmobile; OHM	
4 ft minimum, 10 ft maximum	50 ft minimum, 100 ft preferred	Culvert, bridge w/ handrails, or boardwalk w/ curbs; orient deck boards 90º to direction of travel; width 4–6 ft for light use or 1 way, 10 ft for heavy use or 2 way	Mountain bike, ATV, snowmobile	Parking with trailer space, warm-up loop; rest stops or shelters after 15 miles

At frequent intervals, take the trail past subtle anchor points (such as large or unusual tree, rock, patch of shrubs) that add interest and draw attention to landscape features.

Additional Points to Consider

Avoid placing your trail in areas with threatened or endangered flora, fauna, geology, and natural plant communities. Ask your state's department of natural resources whether these resources exist or are likely to be found on or near the trail location.

Protect cultural resources such as historic structures (buildings, dams, bridges, fire towers, etc.), archaeological sites (above and below ground), cemeteries (including unplatted historic cemeteries, burial mounds, and other ancient burials), and traditional use areas where natural resources are gathered for food, medicine, or ceremonial uses. Cultural resources can be damaged by soil disturbance, soil compaction, rutting, change in public access, and change in vegetation and other features. Whenever a government permit, license, or funding is needed for a project, a cultural resources management review may be required. To learn about locations of cultural sites, contact a state archaeologist.

Discuss your trail project with neighbors to learn about the impact on their properties and potential linkages to other trail systems.

Consider your budget for land and right-of-way acquisition, trail construction, and maintenance. This will put a reality check on your design plans.

Establish Design Standards

After exploring the trail corridor, but before flagging the exact trail location, set your design standards. Base the standards on the trail uses; the quality of experience you want to offer, including the level of risk; and your construction resources, including budget and expertise. Use the Recommended Trail Design Standards in Figure 13-2, pg. 150 as a starting point. Modify them to fit your needs.

Consider these aspects of trail design: trail configuration, trail length, tread surface, tread width, clearing width, clearing height, grade, turning radius, sight distance, water crossings, and special requirements.

Trail configuration is the overall shape of the trail (Figure 13-3).

- Linear trails are appropriate for long distance travel (several miles) or where the land ownership (right-of-way) is too narrow to permit development of a loop trail.
- Spur trails are short linear trails that take users to points of interest or connect different loop trails.
- Loop trails permit the user to begin and end at the same location without repeating any part of the trail.
- Stacked loop trails (a series of interconnected loops) permit users options for different distances, routes, or destinations.

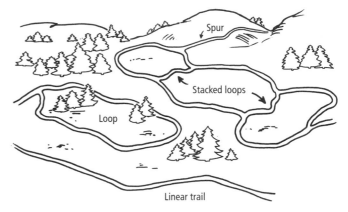

Figure 13-3. Trail configuration is the overall shape of a trail.

Trail length is the distance that users could travel in one day.

Tread surface refers to the material (such as soil, gravel, rock) on the usable part of the trail, and its condition (such as smooth, rolling, rough). High-use trails require more durable materials and smoother surfaces than light-use trails.

Tread width is the width of the usable trail surface. In general, the tread width that is suitable for light use or one-way travel should be doubled for heavy use or two-way travel.

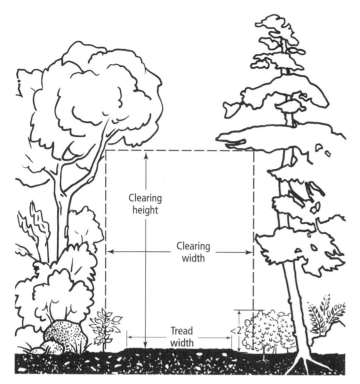

Figure 13-4. Tread width, clearing width, and clearing height.

Clearing width is the total width to which rocks, trees, tree limbs, and other obstacles should be removed. As a general rule, clear at least two feet on each side of the tread. Where a trail passes through dense vegetation, vary the clearing width to avoid an unnatural tunnel effect. In general maintain clearing width from the ground up to the clearing height, except you may leave vegetation, rocks, and other objects less than two feet tall near the tread edge. Center the tread within the clearing width, except on hillside trails where clearance may be less on the downhill side.

Clearing height is the height above the tread surface to which overhanging rocks, tree limbs, and other obstructions must be removed. As a general rule, clear two feet above the user's head. Keep in mind that leaves will bend deciduous tree branches one to two feet lower in summer than in winter while snow will bend evergreen tree branches and raise the tread surface.

Grade is the slope angle (expressed in degrees or percent) along the trail's centerline.

% grade = (degrees of angle) x (tangent)

It is easy for trail users to travel long distances on low grades. High grades require more work and should extend for shorter distances. Measure grade with a commercial or homemade clinometer (Figure 13-5).

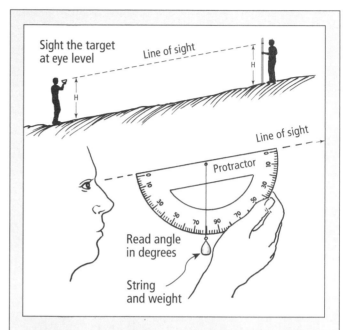

Make a clinometer with a protractor, short string, and small weight.

To measure grade:

1. Sight along the protractor's flat edge and read the degree aligned with the string.

2. Determine the slope angle:

   90° - (angle read on protractor) = slope angle in degrees

   Example: 90° - 80° = 10° slope

To convert degrees of slope to percent slope:

1. Look up the tangent of the slope angle in degrees on a scientific calculator or in a tangent table in a book.

2. Determine the percent of slope: Tangent (of slope angle in degrees) x 100% = % slope

   Example: Tangent (10°) x 100% = 0.176 x 100% = 17.6 or 18% slope

Figure 13-5. Making and Using a Clinometer.

Turning radius is the radius of an arc drawn through the centerline of the tread where the trail curves. As travel speed increases, lengthen the turning radius, bank the trail higher on the outside edge, widen the trail, or clear a runout zone.

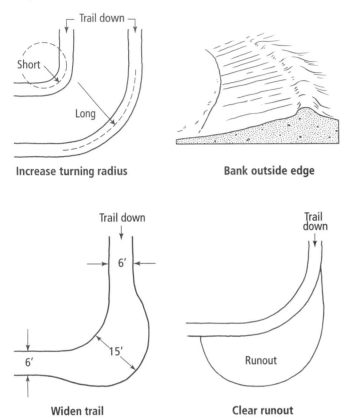

Figure 13-6. Design options for safer turns, especially on steep slopes.

Sight distance is the distance that a trail user can see down the trail from any point on the trail. Adhere to the recommended minimum sight distance, but vary sight distances to add interest, lengthen sight distance to allow faster travel, and reduce sight distance to slow travel.

Water crossings refer to the type of structures recommended for crossing bodies of water. A ford, stepping stones, culvert, boardwalk, or bridge may be appropriate. Your choices will be affected by the type of user, type of experience you want to offer, type of water body, length of crossing, legal status of the water body, your ingenuity, and your budget.

Mark Trail Location

As you mark the trail, keep your design standards in mind.

Mark the centerline of the trail using one of these materials:

- Rolls of plastic flagging (tie 15-inch strips to branches).
- Wire flags (stiff wire, 2 feet or longer, with plastic flag).
- Wooden stakes (12 to 18 inches or longer) topped with brightly colored flagging or paint.

Space the markers approximately 20 feet apart in dense vegetation and up to 100 yards in open fields. Write cumulative distances on markers every 100 feet to make it easy to match markers with trail maps and notes.

Map the route. Use a global positioning device or a compass to develop a trail map. Mark structures and special instructions on the map. Make special note of places that require deviations from trail standards. Photograph sites where trail structures are needed to assist in planning materials and equipment or show potential contractors what these sites look like.

Obtain permits for crossing streams, wetlands, railroads, highways, rights-of-way, etc.

Begin constructing the trail soon after flagging, before markers are moved or damaged.

Clear the Trail

Clear the trail in these stages:
1. Remove small trees, shrubs, and limbs from large trees.
2. Cut large trees.
3. Remove stumps and boulders.
4. Move soil to level the tread.

The extent of clearing needed depends on the clearing height and width of the trail, the quality of the user experience (such as a rough, challenging trail or a smooth, easy trail), and the primary season of use (such as snow will cover some obstacles in winter).

Construct the Tread

Create a tread surface that is smooth and durable enough for intended users. Save effort by placing the trail on soils that withstand trail use.

Factors Affecting Tread Choice

Consider how tread materials will react to compaction, displacement, and erosion.

- Compaction comes from downward force from feet, hooves, wheels, etc. When a tread is fully compacted, it holds its shape and resists displacement and erosion. Compact the tread as much as possible during initial construction. Some materials have better compaction properties than others. Tread materials that do not compact (such as sand, organic soil, water-saturated soil) or that compact too much (such as peat) will not retain a desired shape. Excessive compaction tends to lower the tread and encourages water to collect in depressions.

- Displacement is sideways force that moves tread material off the trail, raising trail edges over time. Displacement also lowers the tread, enabling water to collect in depressions.

- Water and wind erosion remove tread material, destroying the tread. The potential for erosion from running water increases as the slope and/or volume of water increases.

If possible, use materials for the tread from the immediate surroundings. Natural materials are inexpensive and blend well with the landscape.

Consider hardening the tread with rock pavers, or other materials as a last resort when:

- Drainage is poor and mud is a problem.
- Flowing water causes unacceptable erosion.
- Tread material compacts or displaces too much to retain the desired tread shape over the long term.
- Tread must be narrow and clearly delineated to protect the surrounding area.

Tread Materials

Bedrock
If available, smooth bedrock makes a very durable tread. It can be slippery for horses, especially on slopes. Avoid using bedrock where snow retention is desirable. Sites with vegetation retain snow longer.

Soil
Mineral soil is composed primarily of sand—(coarse texture), silt—(medium texture), and clay—(fine texture). Soil with a high percentage of silt, moderate percentage of sand, and small percentage of clay makes a very durable tread. Such a soil resists excessive compaction and erosion while allowing internal drainage.

Soil composed mainly of sand will not erode with water or become muddy but, because sand does not compact, it is subject to displacement and wind erosion. Soil with a high clay and silt content is subject to water erosion and mud. Soil composed mainly of clay retains water and can be muddy and slippery when wet and, unless it is highly compacted, it is also subject to water erosion.

Organic soil (humus) is composed of decomposing plant materials that compact and erode, and can become water saturated and muddy. It is not desirable for trails and likely will need artificial hardening (such as boardwalk) unless the trail receives light, low-impact use only when dry or frozen. Soil composed mainly of undecomposed organic material, such as peat, compacts too much to be suitable tread material.

Vegetation
Try to maintain natural vegetation (primarily grass) for hikers and horses, and for snow retention for skiing, snowmobiling, or snowshoeing. Vegetation survives best on a lightly used trail in full sunlight. Vegetation is difficult to sustain in sandy soil (which is dry and nutrient poor), on steep slopes (where there is more abrasion from trail users and erosion), and in deep shade.

Duff is undecomposed organic matter (such as leaves, twigs, moss, pieces of bark and wood) that litters a forest floor. Duff does not compact well and is easily displaced. During construction, remove duff to expose the ground surface for shaping the tread. However, a light duff layer can help soak up moisture and break the erosive force of rainfall. If a natural surface is desired, you may allow duff to accumulate on a finished trail.

Wood Chips

Use wood chips to define the tread on newly constructed foot trails, to suppress vegetation growth, and to raise the tread in muddy areas. Apply a 3- to 4-inch layer of large wood chips that do not contain leaves or small diameter twigs (which decay rapidly). Hauling and spreading wood chips requires extensive labor, and wood chips need to be replaced every three years as they decay or are displaced. In most situations, wood chips should be a temporary tread material.

Rock

Rocky material includes gravel (from sand to 3-inch diameter), cobbles (3- to 10-inch), stones (10- to 24-inch), or boulders (greater than 24-inch).

Rocks are useful on trails that receive heavy use, especially by horses or heavy motorized vehicles, or where a very firm, smooth tread is needed such as for touring bicycles or wheelchairs. Rocky material resists excessive compaction and displacement and provides a very strong tread. If protruding rocks are hazardous or too bumpy for your quality standards, excavate rocks or chip off the protruding piece.

Crushed rocks compact and resist displacement better than rounded rocks (such as from beaches, river beds, and glacial till). Crushed rock made from hard rock is more durable than from soft rock. A tread composed entirely of rounded cobbles is prone to displacement, but when embedded in clay, cobbles add durability to the tread. If used in a mixture of sizes including plenty of small particles to fill voids, rocks interlock well. To achieve a smooth, firm surface, mix small gravel with rock dust from a commercial-scale rock crusher.

For small jobs, haul a portable rock crusher to the work site. To produce a small quantity of gravel for chinking crevices, crush rocks with a sledgehammer or the rounded end of a steel pry bar.

Paving Stones/Bricks

Concrete paving stones and bricks are available in many sizes and shapes. Interlocking pavers may be most useful. These manufactured materials are uniform in size, easy to handle, and easy to acquire. Pore spaces between pavers may be filled with soil then seeded with vegetation. Pavers are heavy to transport and their uniform geometric shapes and colors may not match native materials.

Porous Pavement Grids

Sectional grids made from plastic or steel are laid directly on the ground to provide traction while protecting underlying soil from erosion. Vegetation can grow through the grid. Consider grids for ATV trails on moderately steep slopes that are prone to erosion.

Solid Pavement Panels

Easy to install plastic panels (approximately 4 feet square and 2 inches thick) that lock end-to-end can provide a firm walkway over sand or gravel.

Asphalt

Asphalt is a good choice where a hard surface is needed, such as for wheelchairs, touring bicycles, in-line skaters, or heavy hiking use. Asphalt is expensive compared to natural surfaces and crushed rock, and the site must be accessible to the equipment needed to apply and roll it. Tree roots may uplift and fracture asphalt laid on shallow soil over bedrock. Asphalt applied with heavy equipment is most durable, but tread width is limited by the equipment, typically eight feet or wider. Where a narrow tread is desired, asphalt may be laid by hand but it will be less durable. Use a hot mix for new construction or large repairs. Use a cold mix for small repairs, less than one cubic yard. Asphalt can be colored to some extent by the gravel used in the mix.

Concrete

Use concrete in the same situations mentioned under asphalt. Concrete is more durable than asphalt, but also more expensive. Haul large quantities to the site by truck; mix small quantities on-site. You can color concrete to blend with the surrounding site. For better traction on steep slopes, broom the surface, trowel grooves across the tread, or leave the surface unfinished.

Tread Edging

Tread edging (such as rocks, logs, timbers) that creates a visual/psychological barrier helps to:

- Prevent trail users from getting lost when the tread is not distinct from the surrounding ground surface.
- Encourage users to stay within the tread, protecting surrounding natural resources.

If tread edging is intended to hold tread fill material in place (such as sand, gravel, asphalt), install hard, continuous edging (such as preservative-treated 2" x 4" lumber, 4- to 8-inch diameter round logs or sawn timbers) along both sides of the tread. Where the trail curves, cut shorter pieces or use edging material that can be bent. Also see references to curbs under Boardwalks, page 164 and Curbs and Railings, page 168.

Install Structures

The structures you need to cross obstacles on a trail depend upon the conditions you encounter, the type of user experience you want to offer, the amount of use, and your budget.

Crossing Flat Land

Flat land may seem like an easy place to build a trail, but if the soil is mainly clay or silt, or the water table is high, poor drainage may lead to muddy puddles. Solutions include relocating the trail where there is side-hill drainage (see Crossing a Hillside below) or raising the tread above the surrounding flat ground (see Crossing Wet Soil, page 162).

Crossing a Hillside

A hillside trail must quickly drain surface water off the tread while maintaining its shape and a grade that is comfortable for trail users. Options for

crossing a hillside include full-bench and cut-and-fill trails, retaining walls, diverting water across the tread, and diverting water flowing down the tread.

Full-Bench and Cut-and-Fill Trail

A flat trail bed cut from a hillside provides a safe and comfortable crossing for users. In a full-bench trail, the full width of the tread is cut from the hillside. A full-bench trail usually has a well-compacted base because the underlying material has been in place for thousands of years.

If part of the tread is built upon fill material that was cut from the hillside, it is a cut-and-fill trail. Fill material may be difficult to compact, especially with hand tools. If fill material is not well compacted, horses and vehicles may destroy the tread. If fill material must be used for part of the trail bed, use large rocks to form the trail bed and serve as edging, and cover them with tightly compacted soil.

Backslope is the area above a trail where material has been cut from a hillside in the process of leveling the tread. The backslope grade necessary to prevent soil erosion depends on the material. A backslope of 1.5:1 (horizontal run: vertical rise) is adequate for stable materials whereas a backslope of 4:1 may be needed on erodible materials.

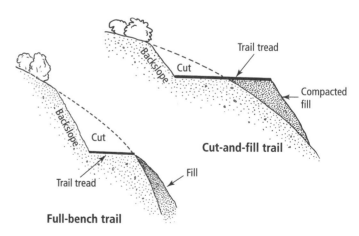

Figure 13-7. Full-bench and cut-and-fill trails provide safe travel across steep slopes.

158

Retaining Wall

Where a trail cuts across a slope and vegetation does not stabilize exposed soil above or below the tread, a retaining wall will prevent soil erosion. A retaining wall below the tread may be more durable than one along the backslope (perhaps because trail crews are more careful in building walls that support the tread). Building a retaining wall to support the tread may negate the need for cutting into the backslope, thus preserving natural vegetation that holds the soil. Tie walls into the embankment with a deadman (such as geotextile fabric, logs, or large rocks). Build walls without mortar, or install drain pipes, to allow water to seep through a wall.

Stone retaining wall

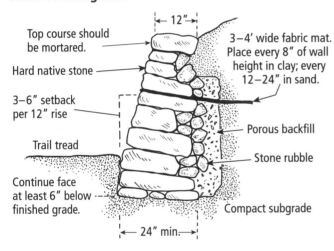

Wood retaining wall

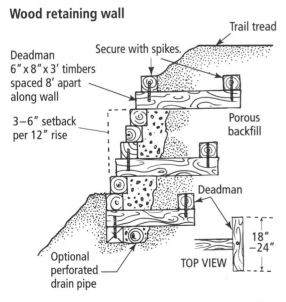

Figure 13-8. On steep slopes use walls to support the backslope or the tread.

Outslopes and Inslopes

Where a trail crosses a hillside with medium- to coarse-textured soil, outslope the tread to quickly drain off surface water. A 2 to 5 percent outslope is quite common and suitable for most trail users. In heavy rainfall areas, outslope up to 10 percent, provided trail users can safely negotiate this slope without slipping or rolling off the trail.

Some trail designers recommend no outslope on horse trails. Horses tend to walk on the outside edge of a tread and will crumble the edge over time. A sloped tread also increases the likelihood that horses will slip when the surface is wet. If you build a flat-cross-section trail, divert water from the tread using rolling grade and water bars (described below.) On flat-cross-section trails that traverse steep slopes, you may wish to create an edge berm (raised shoulder), except at grade dips, to protect the outside edge of the tread from erosion and to create a safer trail for users. Strengthen an edge berm with vegetation or rocks.

Where a trail crosses a hillside that has fine-textured, erodible soil, inslope the tread to a ditch, then divert water in the ditch across the trail and downhill through grade dips or culverts.

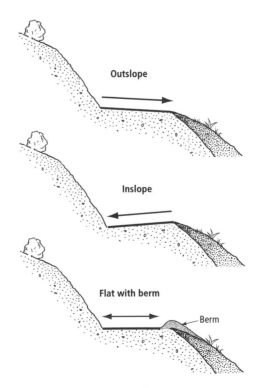

Figure 13-9. Outslope, inslope, and berm.

Divert Water Flowing Down the Tread

Where the tread has a relatively flat or concave cross-section, some water will run down the length of the trail. To prevent soil erosion, divert water off the tread with rolling grade or waterbars.

Rolling Grade

A rolling grade divides the trail into narrow watersheds with undulating crests and dips like a gentle roller coaster. Water drains off at the dips. Ideally, no part of the tread is completely level. Outslope the bottom of each dip and make the outlet wide enough to drain off water without clogging. Place tread dips at natural drainage ways and at other locations as needed. Rolling grade is most appropriate when traversing hill slopes (fall lines) of 20 to 70 percent. On hill slopes less than 20 percent, water does not drain well at the dips.

Drainage dips can deposit sediment into waterways. To reduce sedimentation, consider these alternatives: maintain a low tread grade on the approach to the drainage; design a small tread watershed with a short slope toward the waterway; harden the tread; or maintain a nearly level tread and install a boardwalk, bridge or culvert over the waterway.

Also use rolling grade to ascend/descend hillsides. In those situations, rolling grade is most effective when the tread grade is less than 1/4 to 1/3 of the hill slope. For example, if the hill slope is 45 percent, the tread grade should not exceed 15 percent, and 10 percent is preferred. As the trail climbs, periodically reverse the grade downhill for a few steps to create a dip that allows water to drain off.

Even when a trail is outsloped, insloped, or center-crowned, a rolling grade is desirable. These cross-sectional shapes are difficult to sustain over long periods without substantial maintenance.

Adjust the size of each tread watershed based on these factors:

- When the watershed above the tread is large, increasing the potential for runoff, make tread watersheds small.
- If the water infiltration rate of the upslope soil is slow, resulting in more potential runoff, make tread watersheds small.
- If the potential for erosion is high, make tread watersheds small. Hardening the tread, placing the trail beneath a tree canopy that will intercept precipitation and reduce splash erosion, or reducing tread width to minimize exposed soil will also reduce risk of erosion.
- Where trail grade is steep, make tread watersheds small or reduce the trail grade by lengthening the trail or adding switchbacks or turns. Tread erosion risk is relatively low when tread grade is less than 5 percent, moderate when tread grade is 5 to 10 percent, and higher when tread grade is greater than 10 percent.
- When hill grade is steep, make tread watersheds small. Tread dips drain best when there is a substantial difference between the tread grade and hill grade.

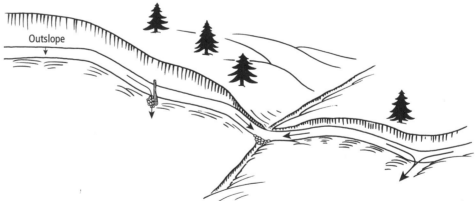

Figure 13-10. A rolling grade uses undulating crests and dips to divert water off the tread.

Waterbars

A waterbar is an obstruction placed across a trail tread to divert surface water off the tread. Waterbars may be needed on a sloping trail with a flat cross-section (no outslope) or where rolling grade

160

is not adequate to divert water at tread dips. Because most waterbars create a significant bump in the trail, they are not desirable on trails used for bicycling, skiing, or snowmobiling. A rubber waterbar (Figure 13-11) can be used for bicycle trails. When waterbars are placed on horse trails, horses tend to compact the soil immediately above and below the water bar leading to depressions that collect water and mud. Horses also can damage waterbars because of their weight and strength. When used on horse trails, anchor waterbars well.

Place waterbars at a 30 to 45 degree angle across a trail. Where heavy runoff is expected, place stones at the outflow to disperse water without causing soil erosion.

If a waterbar diverts water into a ditch, make sure the bar does not protrude into the ditch where it might catch debris and block the ditch.

Use judgment and experimentation in spacing waterbars. Closer spacing is needed where the trail grade is steep, the soil is erodible, or you want a high quality tread without the expense of hardening materials.

Earthen waterbar

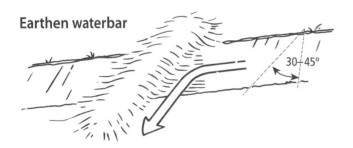

Rubber waterbar

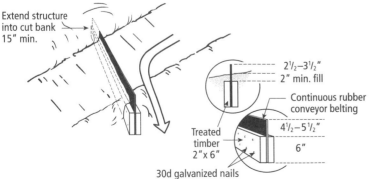

Figure 13-11. Waterbars are another way to divert water off the tread.

Climbing and Descending Steep Slopes and Cliffs

Switchbacks

A switchback reduces trail grade by lengthening the trail in a zigzag pattern. Design each trail segment to conform to the desired grade as much as possible. Place a switchback where the trail reaches an impassable obstacle or begins to run too far in the wrong direction. Avoid closely spaced switchbacks to discourage trail users from taking shortcuts, leading to erosion. To further reduce shortcuts, locate switchbacks at interesting focal points (such as conspicuous tree, boulder, or rock outcrop) and place barriers (such as boulders, logs, thorny bushes) in the cutoff zone. Build the switchback platform with a 2 to 5 percent grade. On a very steep slope install a treadwall to support the platform, or install steps. If the main trail has a substantially higher grade than the platform, create a transition grade as the trail approaches the switchback platform. Divert surface water off the trail above the switchback by means of inslope to a ditch. The switchback turning radius must work for the intended users. Switchbacks may not be practical for skiers and snowmobilers because of the long turning radius they require.

Log waterbar

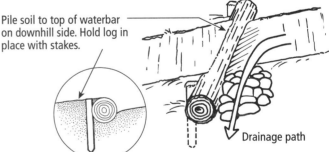

Rock waterbar

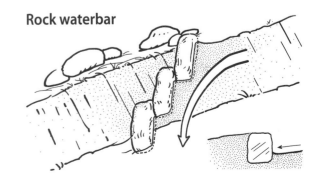

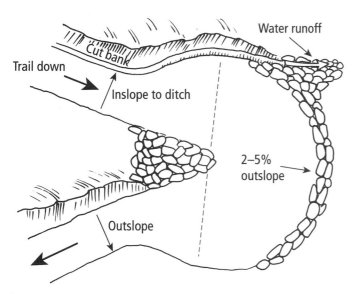

Figure 13-12. Switchbacks help the user climb a steep slope at a comfortable grade.

Fixed Ropes

On a lightly used foot trail with a steep slope and soil that becomes slippery when wet, tie a rope (1/2" or larger diameter) to a firm object at the top of the slope and lay the rope along the tread or tie it to trees along the trail as a handrail.

Climbing Causeways (Turnpike)

When a slope has an uneven surface or is composed of erodible materials, a climbing causeway can build up the tread in short sections. A climbing causeway is useful on hiking and horse trails, but hazardous for skiers, snowmobilers, bicyclists, motorcyclists, and ATVs. Place 6- to 10-inch diameter logs or sawn timbers along each side of the tread to hold fill material in place. Using the same material,

place crossbars at four-foot or longer intervals to prevent fill material from migrating downhill. Fill the spaces between logs with soil or gravel, varying the fill depth to create long steps that provide the desired grade. A climbing causeway is most useful on grades of 10 to 20 percent. For steeper grades, see the section on Steps, below.

Steps

Where trail grade exceeds 20 percent, steps help prevent erosion while aiding hikers and horses. Make step height (rise) 5 to 9 inches (7.5 inches is ideal) and step depth (run) at least 10 inches. You can vary step depth up to several feet to fit the hill slope. Make simple steps by anchoring logs, sawn timbers, or large stones across the tread and backfilling with soil. Make more durable steps from 6- to 8-inch diameter logs or sawn timbers positioned into a three-sided box fastened with steel rods and backfilled with soil or gravel.

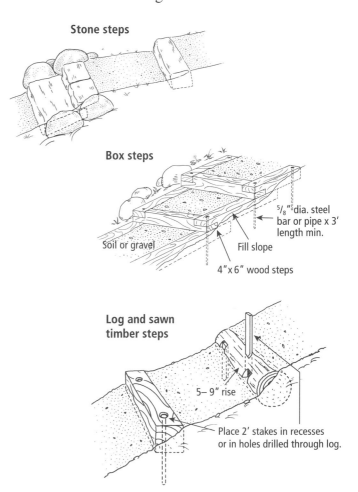

Figure 13-14. Steps help prevent erosion and make it easier to navigate a slope.

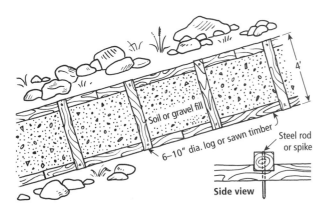

Figure 13-13. A climbing causeway allows you to hold fill material on a steep grade.

162

Ladders

A wooden ladder can be a good solution for helping hikers climb a steep slope or cliff. If you need a ladder longer than 16 feet, butt two long pieces of lumber together and nail an overlapping reinforcement of 2" x 6" lumber across the joint. For longer ladders, build a platform at intervals of about 32 feet that allows users to get off the ladder and rest before ascending/descending another ladder. A platform at the top of a ladder permits users to safely get on and off.

On a primitive trail a flexible cable ladder that conforms to changing land contours can be used to climb a steep, actively eroding slope.

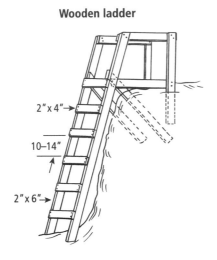

Wooden ladder

2" x 4"
10–14"
2" x 6"

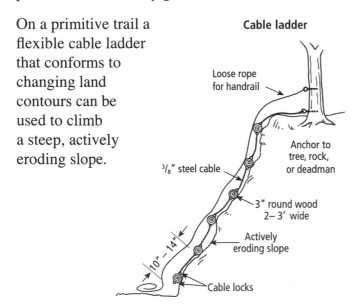

Cable ladder

Loose rope for handrail
Anchor to tree, rock, or deadman
3/8" steel cable
3" round wood 2– 3' wide
Actively eroding slope
10" – 14"
Cable locks

Figure 13-15. A ladder can be a good way to help hikers climb a steep slope.

Crossing Wet Soil

Poorly drained soil on flat land may develop mud or water puddles after snowmelt or rainfall or where groundwater seeps from a hillside and flows across the trail. The solution is to raise the tread.

Corduroy Logs and Tree Cookies

On a primitive trail, corduroy logs, 6- to 10-inch in diameter, placed side by side across the trail will raise the tread and allow surface water to flow naturally between the logs. For added buoyancy in waterlogged soil, place log stringers along trail edges beneath the ends of corduroy logs. A corduroy tread is uneven and somewhat slippery but may be used for short distances by hikers, ATVs, skiers, and snowmobilers.

Tree cookies are cross-sections of tree stems cut at least 4 inches thick and 12 inches wide. On primitive trails, tree cookies may be used as steps for hikers, but they are extremely slippery when wet and often tip downward in soft soil causing the hiker to slip or fall. Corduroy logs or firmly imbedded stepping stones are safer!

Select naturally decay-resistant wood for corduroy logs and tree cookies, although they may still last only a few years. These are primitive, low cost, temporary solutions to crossing muddy areas.

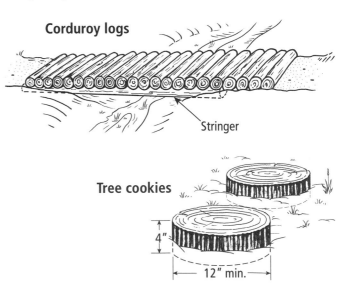

Corduroy logs
Stringer

Tree cookies
4"
12" min.

Figure 13-16. Corduroy logs and tree cookies are inexpensive ways to raise a tread in wet soil but they are slippery to cross.

Drainage Lens

If surface water continually seeps slowly across a section of trail creating a perennial mudhole, a drainage lens that enables water to seep beneath the tread may be required. First excavate several inches of water-saturated soil in the trail bed, then backfill with a layer of large rocks. Add layers of progressively smaller rocks on top of the first layer, leaving large pore spaces between rocks at lower levels. Top this rock fill with soil or gravel to form the tread.

If saturated subsoil is extremely deep or unstable, first lay geotextile fabric on the ground, then add rock layers. Place additional geotextile fabric on top of the rocks and top with soil or gravel. Geotextile fabric separates rock fill from the substrate, preventing soil from clogging pores between the rocks yet allowing water to percolate through the fabric and the fill material.

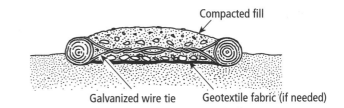

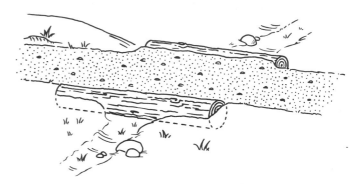

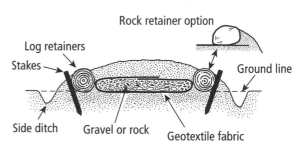

Figure 13-18. A causeway (turnpike) raises the tread above wet soil.

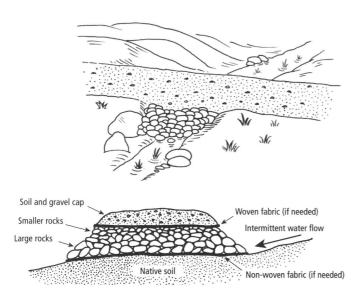

Figure 13-17. A drainage lens allows water to seep beneath the tread.

Causeways (Turnpike)

A causeway produces a raised tread that is suitable for all trail users. Place curbs made from logs, cut timbers, or rocks along both sides of the tread and fill the space between curbs with soil or gravel. If fill material is expected to sink into the substrate, first place geotextile fabric on the ground surface, then install curbs and fill material. If surface water actively flows across the site, place a ditch on one or both sides to divert water to culverts through the raised tread.

Center Crown with Ditches

A center crown is constructed like a highway with a raised tread and ditches on one or both sides. Use material from the ditches to raise the center tread if it is the appropriate texture. On very wet soils, place geotextile fabric on the ground surface before adding fill.

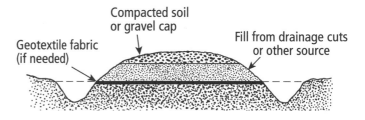

Figure 13-19. Center crown with ditches.

Boardwalks

A boardwalk enables trail users to cross over wetlands, fragile vegetation, or unstable soil.

On hiking trails make the boardwalk deck (tread) from 2" x 6" lumber. Use thicker lumber on boardwalks intended for heavier users, such as ATVs or horses. Full-sized boards are stiffer and last longer than typical 2" x 6" lumber that really is 1.5" x 5.5".

Boardwalks are slippery when wet. To increase traction, orient deck boards at a 90-degree angle to the direction of travel and consider using rough-surfaced lumber (unplaned or split rather than sawn) or cover boards with a roughening product. Leave gaps between planks to further increase traction and to facilitate air movement that dries wood more quickly, lengthening its useful life. A 3/8" to 1/2" gap works well for most users. Closer spacing helps retain snow for skiing and snowmobiling. Wider spacing may be acceptable on primitive trails and for OHVs. Build the deck as level as possible for safety. Install steps on sloping ground, if compatible with trail uses.

Support the deck with stringers running beneath the deck. Orient stringers with the direction of travel. For weather protection, inset the stringer from the ends of deck boards. Space the stringers according to the stiffness of the materials—the stiffer the material the further the spacing (typically 18 to 30 inches). For example, wood-plastic composite lumber is not as stiff as sawn lumber, thus requiring closer stringer spacing.

Use one of the following to support stringers:

- Sleepers oriented 90° to the direction of travel and resting on the ground.
- Cribbing made from rocks or logs.
- Vertical posts (such as wooden poles or helical screws) sunk into the ground and spanned by ledgers. Sunken posts are the most stable, but there may be situations where you do not want to dig into the ground (such as rocky ground or organic soil).

On high-use boardwalks or those built more than two feet above ground, add a raised curb along each edge to help prevent users from stumbling off the boardwalk. Install a railing on one or both sides of a boardwalk that is more than four feet above the ground, crosses open water, or is intended for use by persons with mobility impairments. See more information about curbs and railings in the section on Bridges, page 166.

For decay resistance, select preservative-treated lumber, wood-plastic composite lumber, or naturally decay-resistant wood for boardwalk components. Some tropical hardwoods have a durable life of more than 50 years without chemical treatment, but are very expensive.

To cross deep water or connect trail users more closely with water environments, use a floating boardwalk. Make floats from thick styrofoam contained in wood or plastic, or from more durable sealed plastic or steel airtanks. Commercially available floating docks offer easy installation.

Boardwalk with piles and ledgers

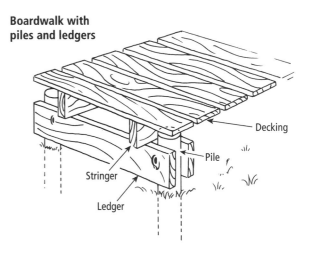

Decking

Pile

Stringer

Ledger

Boardwalk with sleepers

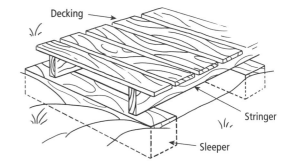

Decking

Stringer

Sleeper

Figure 13-20. Boardwalks allow users to cross over wet or sensitive landscapes.

Crossing Waterways and Gullies

Stepping stones, fords, culverts or bridges help users cross open water in springs, streams, and rivers.

Stepping Stones and Fords

On a primitive trail, hikers might appreciate stepping stones that are firmly imbedded in the stream bottom. They might also wade across a slow-moving stream (less than two feet deep) through a ford. Horses can ford a slow-moving stream (less than three feet deep). Place a ford where the streambed has firm sand or gravel.

On horse trails remove large rocks from the streambed to prevent tripping. If a small dam is installed to stabilize water depth and bottom structure, a government permit may be required.

Stepping stones

Ford

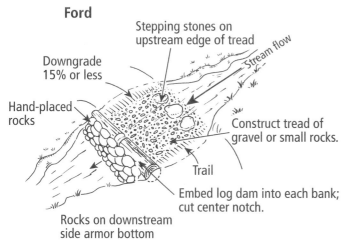

Ford side view

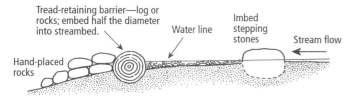

Figure 13-21. Hikers and horses can use stepping stones and fords to cross small bodies of water.

Culverts

Install a culvert to channel water across a trail, allowing trail users to cross a narrow stream. An open-top log or rock culvert is easy to clean when it becomes clogged, but creates a hazard for some trail users. A pipe culvert covered with soil can be used by all trail user. Pipe culverts may be steel (durable, but heavy) or plastic (less durable, but lightweight for transporting into areas with difficult access). To permit fish movement on streams, a culvert should slope no more than 1 precent and its end must be flush with the stream bottom. Place rocks around the culvert's upstream end to armor the bank against erosion.

Seek professional advice from a soil and water expert to gauge the appropriate diameter culvert to install. If the culvert is too small, high water will wash it out or flood land upstream from the culvert.

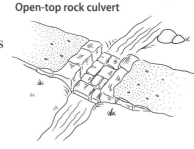

Figure 13-22. A culvert is a good option for crossing a narrow stream.

Bridges

Bridges are expensive to build and require a high level of expertise. Use them where necessary for safety or to protect natural resources. First consider other alternatives, such as trail re-alignment, culverts, causeways, or boardwalks. This section provides only general guidelines; seek engineering assistance for any bridge that is long or high. Because of cost, make bridges as short as possible by installing them where gaps are narrow. Select a location where the approach is relatively level and straight, and where you can build firm abutments at each end above the normal high water level.

Any construction in waters and wetlands that drain into or are connected to a navigable stream requires a U.S. Army Corp of Engineers 404 Permit. Bridges that span navigable waters must have a 3-foot minimum clearance above the ordinary high water level. Temporary bridges must have a 3-foot minimum clearance between the lowest portion of the bridge and normal summer stream flow.

Abutments

Abutments support the ends of the bridge and provide intermediate support for long bridges. If the terrain is subject to flooding, raise end abutments to elevate the bridge above flood level. On a primitive, lightly used trail, a very small bridge may be anchored with a cable on one end with the expectation that it will break loose during a flood, but can be retrieved and repositioned. Construct abutments from durable materials since they are in contact with ground moisture, and may deteriorate more quickly than stringers, decks, and railings. A sill is a simple abutment made from a single structure, such as log, sawn timber, gabion, or concrete. Sills require little excavation, but should be used only for small bridges that can move with frost heaving. A crib is a box-like structure made from logs or sawn timbers and filled with rocks. A retaining wall is an earth-retaining structure tied into the banks with a deadman. A retaining wall may be made from logs, sawn timbers, gabion, or concrete. Piles are wood or steel posts that are pounded or screwed down to a firm footing and cross-braced to prevent sway. To estimate the depth required to obtain a firm footing, drive a small diameter steel rod into the substrate.

Log sill

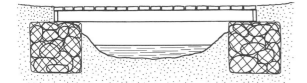

Timber crib filled with rocks

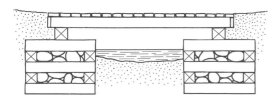

Wire gabion filled with rocks

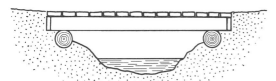

Retaining wall with deadman

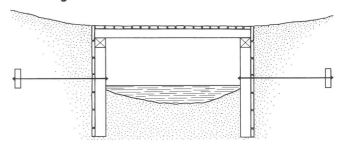

Pilings

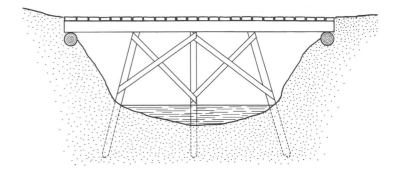

Figure 13-23. The best type of abutments for your bridge depends on the size of the bridge and the surrounding conditions.

Girders and Trusses

Girders and trusses rest on top of the abutments and support the deck (tread). On a simple deck, they also may serve as the deck.

On a deck girder/ truss bridge, the deck is fastened directly to two or more girders or trusses that span the gap. Girders may be logs, timbers, glue-laminated timbers, or steel I-beams. Trusses usually are steel beams with steel cross-braces.

Log girders

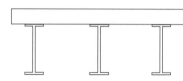

Timber girders

Steel I-beam girders

Steel trusses

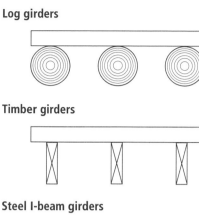

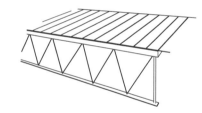

Figure 13-24. Girders and trusses support the bridge deck.

Cable suspension bridge

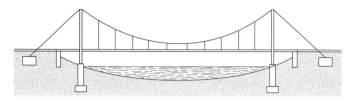

Stayed suspension bridge

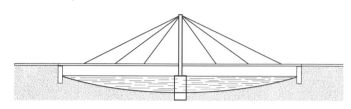

Cable car

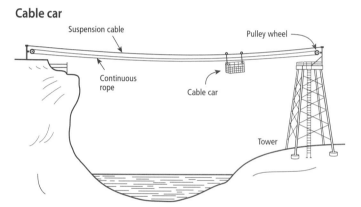

Figure 13-25. Suspension bridges can span wide bodies of water.

Suspension Cables

A suspension bridge is supported by two steel cables, one on each side of the deck, that span the gap. Suspender cables or steel rods hang down from the two support cables to support the deck below.

A stayed suspension bridge has multiple steel cables spread from the top of a tower down to the deck to support it.

A suspension cable car has a cargo box suspended by rollers from a single steel cable that spans the gap. A continuous loop rope, passed through pulleys at both ends of the bridge, can be grasped by the users while sitting in the cable car to pull the car across the gap.

Decks

The tread on a bridge is called a deck. If possible, build the deck to the same width as the tread on other parts of the trail. If railings are used, make the deck two to four feet wider or slant the railing outward at the top to provide more shoulder width. If the bridge deck is a different width from the approaching trail tread, gradually adjust the trail tread width as it approaches the bridge.

To prevent water from flowing down the trail and onto the bridge deck, create a drainage dip in the trail approach or elevate the bridge deck. Hikers can step up to a deck, but for other trail users the ends of the bridge deck must be flush in elevation with the approaching trail tread.

When estimating the strength needed for the deck, consider not only the weight of trail users, but snow loading, wind loading, and the weight of equipment that will cross the bridge. Select materials that will not be slippery when wet. Options for decks materials include split logs, sawn planks, wood-plastic composite lumber, steel grids, or fiberglass sheets bonded to shallow fiberglass structural shapes with coarse sand embedded into the gel coating to increase roughness. For more information on deck materials and placement, see Boardwalks, page 164.

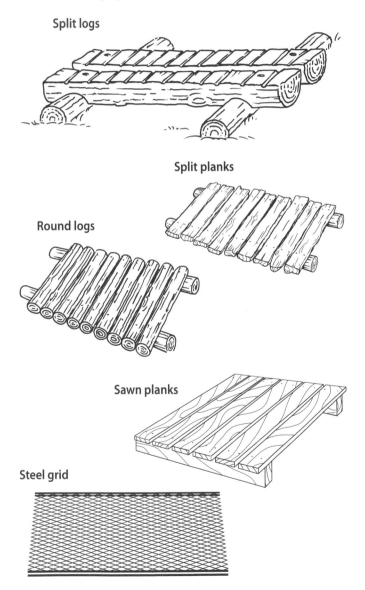

Split logs

Split planks

Round logs

Sawn planks

Steel grid

Figure 13-26. Choose deck materials suitable for your trail users.

Curbs and Railings

Curbs or railings may be needed on boardwalks and bridges to protect users from hazards (such as steep drop-off, hot spring) and/or to protect trail-side resources (such as archeological sites, fragile vegetation, rare species).

On decks built more than two feet above ground, add a raised curb along each edge to help prevent users from stumbling off the edge. Fasten a 4"x 4" timber or round log on each side of the deck held 2 inches above the deck by short sections of 2"x 4" lumber. Gaps beneath the curb allow water and debris to wash off the edge.

In highly accessible areas where a deck is more than four feet above ground, crosses open water, or is used by persons with mobility impairments, install a railing on one or both sides. In more remote areas you might do without rails on decks less than eight feet above ground. If a railing is provided on only one side, place it on the side that exposes trail users to the greatest risk or where users turn to view an interesting scene. If the drop from a bridge or boardwalk is no more hazardous than other unprotected drops along the trail, a railing probably is not needed.

In remote areas design railings to match the level of risk and trail experience that you want to offer. In general make such railings at least 42 inches high for pedestrian traffic and at least 54 inches high for bicycle or horse traffic. Install one or more intermediate rails so the vertical distance between rails does not exceed 15 inches.

Railings attached to buildings, such as visitor centers, and on trail bridges in urban settings that are expected to attract unsupervised children must meet local building codes. The Uniform Building Code (UBC 509) requires a handrail at least 42 inches high that a 4-inch sphere will not pass through.

Railings on trail bridges frequently used by unsupervised children, especially near trailheads, must meet the American Association of State Highway and Transportation Officials (AASHTO) Standard Specifications for Highway Bridges. This code requires a handrail at least 42 inches high for pedestrian traffic and at least 54 inches high for bicycle or horse traffic. A 6-inch sphere must not pass through the railing in the bottom 27 inches and an 8-inch sphere must not pass through the area higher than 27 inches.

On a wheelchair-accessible trail where the grade is steeper than 5 percent, place a rail 30 to 34 inches above the deck so that a person in a wheelchair can grasp it to pull their wheelchair along or rest without rolling downhill, and place a second rail 42 inches above the deck.

Bridges for OHVs and snowmobiles must have reflective hazard markers visible above the snow level at each end of the bridge.

The strongest railings have vertical support posts that are anchored into the ground and fastened to the girders or stringers before extending up to the top railing. Somewhat less sturdy, but still strong railings can be fastened to the girders or supported by outriggers.

Cut vertical support posts lower than the top railing to encourage use of the railing.

Materials for Bridges

Select bridge construction materials for durability, strength, esthetics, economics, and environmental acceptability.

Select wood that is naturally decay resistant or is treated with environmentally safe chemicals. On portions of trail bridges or boardwalks that trail users touch frequently, such as railings, use wood treated with waterborne chemicals or light solvent oilborne chemicals. Wood without a chemical preservative may last 2 to 12 years depending on its natural decay resistance, though some tropical woods resist decay for over 50 years.

Use steel that is painted or galvanized, unless it is a corrosion-resistant weathering steel. Do not use un-coated weathering steel in coastal areas or in areas with high rainfall, high humidity, or persistent fog.

Concrete should have an air entrainment of 4 to 6 percent and a minimum design compressive strength of 3,000 pounds per square inch. Concrete can be texturized, colored, stained, or painted to better match esthetic values.

Fiberglass should have a waterproof, colored surface treatment to protect it from ultraviolet radiation.

Use screws and bolts, not nails. Use non-corrosive fasteners that are hot-dipped galvanized, anodized plated, or stainless steel.

Railing fastened to posts in ground

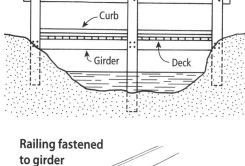

Railing fastened to girder

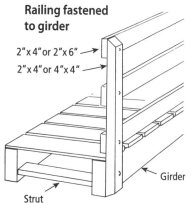

Railing supported by outrigger

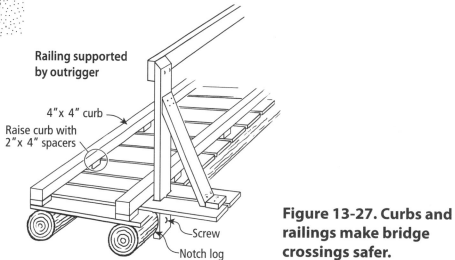

Figure 13-27. Curbs and railings make bridge crossings safer.

Inspection

Inspect bridges at least twice a year. A qualified bridge inspector should evaluate bridges with long spans or complex designs.

Trails that Cross or Utilize Roads

Crossing Roads

As a trail approaches a road crossing, add a tight turn, ridges and dips in the tread, and/or narrow the clearing width to slow down users. On the final approach, the trail must be at a right (90 degree) angle to the road, nearly level, and have a sight distance adequate for trail users to see the oncoming road in time to stop. Expand the clearing width 1 1/2 to 2 times its normal width or thin forest trees to provide good visibility from the trail toward the road.

Install warning signs if trail users include horseback riders, skiers, snowmobilers, bicyclists, motorcyclists, or other motorized vehicle users that may not be able to stop suddenly. Work with the road authority to determine what signs to use and where to place them. If both the trail and road are lightly used and good sight lines are present, install a Yield or Stop sign on the trail at the road intersection. A Stop sign is not required for non-wheeled and pedestrian-speed users. If traffic along the trail or road is moderately heavy, add a Stop Ahead sign on the trail. If traffic along both the trail and road are heavy, add a Trail Crossing Ahead sign along the road to warn vehicle drivers.

If the trail may be entered from a public road, install a barrier (such as posts, a gate, boulders, mound of dirt) to prohibit unauthorized entry. Install a sign visible from the road that indicates which trail uses are prohibited or permitted.

Ditch Trails

Regulations governing trails in public road ditches vary by state. In some states, for example, low-use trails are permitted between the ditch and the outside edge of state and county road rights-of-way. Off-highway vehicles and snowmobiles may not use the inside slope, shoulder, and road surface of state and county roads. Motorized vehicles in a ditch are expected to travel in the direction of road traffic, so ditch trails are needed on both sides of a highway to permit two-way traffic. However, a bi-directional, non-motorized trail can be provided on one side of a highway only. Along designated ditch trails, utility poles, guy wires, and other trailside obstacles must be marked with a hazard marker. For safety purposes, ditch trails that are within 10 to 20 feet of the road edge should be separated from the road by a different elevation, fence, or guard rail. Separation is more critical where the road curves. All ditch trail design and construction is subject to approval by the local road authority.

Modifying Logging Roads

If a logging skid trail or haul road will be used both for logging and recreational use, it must be designed to accommodate logging equipment. If the skid trail or road will not be used for 10 years for logging purposes, then design it more like a recreational trail. When the time comes to use it for logging, make temporary modifications, such as harden the tread, install temporary stream crossing devices for heavy equipment, expand the clearing width, and install more durable culverts or other drainage devices.

Crossing Fences and Gates

Fences may be necessary to restrain trail users from entering an area, to designate a property boundary, or to contain livestock. Hikers can cross a fence at a stile or a gate. A gate is necessary for all other users. Trail users may leave a gate open when it should be closed or closed when it should be left open. To keep a gate open, fasten it so that it cannot be closed. To keep a gate closed, place a spring or counterweight on the gate or tilt it to close automatically from its own weight. Install a latch that locks automatically when the gate closes and place a sign on the gate, Please Close Gate.

Gate width can help regulate the types of users. For example, a 2 1/2-foot-wide gate will admit hikers, skiers, and bicyclists, but exclude snowmobilers, horses, and ATVs. A 6-foot-wide gate will admit all users except full-sized SUVs and pickup trucks.

Some gates are more a visual barrier than a physical barrier, such as a single horizontal bar (log or steel pipe), steel cable, or several vertical posts spaced across the tread. This type of simple gate, along with a sign that defines what types of trail users may enter, will discourage some potential users, but some unauthorized trail users may go around or under the gate. If you are serious about keeping out certain types of users, your gate and adjoining fence must create a physical barrier. Other barriers also may be appropriate, such as an earthen berm, trench, or large boulders.

Install light reflectors on gates—whether you expect people to use the trail at night or not! Reflectors are especially important safety features on gates that may be entered by motorized vehicles when gates are made from a single horizontal pole or cable that is not clearly visible at night.

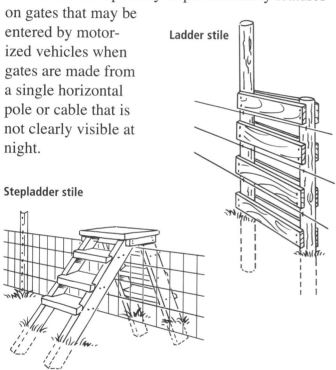

Ladder stile

Stepladder stile

Walk-through stile

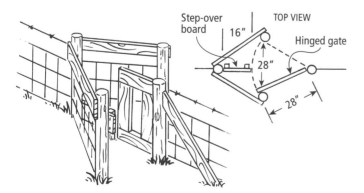

Figure 13-28. Hikers can easily use stiles to cross a fence.

Sign the Trail

Four types of signs may be needed: trailhead sign, confidence markers, directional signs, and warning signs.

Trailhead Sign

A trailhead sign may be needed when you have frequent visitors or allow public use on trails. It may include some or all of the following information:

- Map showing trail route, key features along the trail, a "you are here" mark, north arrow, and map scale or distances along major trail segments.

- Name or number of trail—if there is more than one trail.

- Types of trail uses permitted (such as hiking, skiing, etc.) and uses specifically prohibited.

- How the trail is marked (such as paint marks, signs, rock cairns).

- Rules for trail use (such as stay on the trail, only skiers may use the trail when there is snow cover, pets must be on a leash, hikers get off the trail to let horses pass).

- Warnings, including hazards along the trail (such as poisonous plants, poisonous snakes, dangerous animals, steep cliffs, falling rocks, unsafe drinking water) and environmental features that must be protected (such as fragile vegetation, rare animals, natural spring).

- How to contact the landowner and emergency help (such as sheriff, fire, hospital).

Post trailhead information on a large rectangular board, sized to include all relevant information. To protect signs from weather, build a small roof over the sign board and/or enclose signs in a shallow box with a window.

Lay out the trailhead sign in components that can be changed without remaking the entire sign. Print signs in fade-resistant ink. (Photographs and some inks fade when exposed to sunlight.) Make letters at least 1 inch (72-point typeface) for headers and 1/4 inch (18-point typeface) for body text.

Figure 13-29. A trailhead sign provides essential information about the trail.

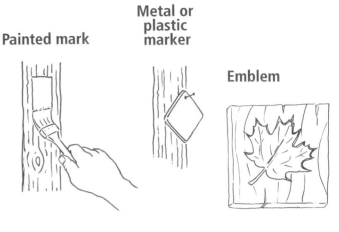

Figure 13-30. Confidence markers help users stay on the trail.

Confidence Markers

Confidence markers placed strategically along the trail reassure users that they are on the trail. Place them at least every 1/4 mile in open country and much closer where the trail could be lost, such as at significant turns, where the trail crosses roads or other trails, or where the tread is indistinct from the surrounding landscape.

- Paint marks on trees or rocks; use a template to create a geometric design, and change colors for different trails in the same area.

- Use aluminum nails to fasten 4"–6" square steel, aluminum, or plastic diamonds to a tree, or preferably a post, so they are visible in both directions along the trail.

- Inscribe a board or order pre-fabricated markers with an emblem, trail number, or name routed, painted, or burned into it.

- Pile rocks to form a cairn. Such markers are easily destroyed by weather and vandals.

Directional Signs

A sign with an arrow may be needed in a parking lot to direct trail users to the trailhead or at a sharp bend, fork or trail crossing. At trail intersections, place a sign that provides information about where each trail leads and how far away the next significant feature can be found. Rounded posts provide the most flexibility in positioning directional signs to point in the correct direction. Fasten a crossbar beneath the soil to prevent vandals from twisting the post.

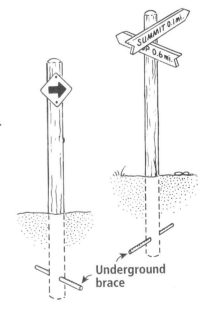

Figure 13-31. Directional signs.

Warning Signs

The trailhead sign should alert trail users about hazards along the trail or environmental resources that require protection. Along moderately to heavily used trails place warning signs where trail users actually encounter hazardous situations or fragile environmental resources. A good warning sign will tell trail users what to do or not do, why, and what the consequences are. Be friendly, but persuasive. Consider using humor through your words or drawings. Drawings are as good as words if their meaning is clear.

The following are poor warning signs because they give no reason for the required action:

- Stay Out!
- Keep Off

Here are better warning signs:

- Be polite, give a reason: "Please stay on the trail. Protect the fragile plants!"
- More forceful: "Stay behind the fence, dangerous water, strong currents!"

It may help to give a warning and explain the consequences: "$100 fine for walking on cryptobiotic soil!"

Trail users appreciate humor and still get the message:

- "Please stay on the trail so you don't disturb the rattlesnakes." (The real purpose is to keep people from trampling fragile vegetation.)
- "Please stay on the trail so you don't trample the poison ivy." (This may be the reason or it may be a way to keep trail users from short-cutting a switchback.)

You also can provide a mixture of signs along a trail, some that are polite and others that are more forceful:

- "Please stay on the trail to protect fragile wetland plants"
- "Walking on the trail is free. Walking on wetland vegetation costs $100"

Figure 13-32. Warning signs help protect trail users and the environment.

Install Facilities

The most popular facilities and structures that support trail users include: access road, parking lot, toilet, box of trail maps, trash container, drinking water, picnic area, campground, and bearproof food storage.

Chapter 14:

Financial Considerations

Melvin J. Baughman, Extension Forester, University of Minnesota
Karen Potter-Witter, Professor and Extension Specialist, Michigan State University
Charles R. Blinn, Extension Specialist, University of Minnesota
Michael R. Reichenbach, Extension Educator, University of Minnesota

This chapter draws your attention to programs that may save money, provide income, or improve investment returns through income taxes, property tax, financial analysis, land protection options, carbon credits, and estate planning.

Federal Income Tax Guidelines

Federal tax regulations change frequently. Consult the Internal Revenue Service (IRS) or your tax advisor for information on specific situations or to learn about recent changes in tax regulations.

Defining Your Operation

How you report woodland management income and expenses for tax purposes depends on your purpose for owning woodland (personal use, investment, or business) and the type of taxpayer (individual or corporation).

Your purpose in owning woodland, whether for personal use, investment, or business, affects how you should report income and expenses. Property not used to produce income is considered to be held for personal use. For example, if you own woodland primarily for a home site or recreation, that is personal use, even if you someday expect to sell the property for more than you paid for it. If you own woodland primarily to produce income, but it is not a major source of income and you have infrequent business activities (especially product sales), that is an investment. If you own woodland with the intent to make a profit and have frequent activities, including production of income, the IRS may classify that operation as a business. In addition, you may have an active or passive role in a woodland business. This distinction affects how and when you may deduct expenses. You actively participate in a timber business if you materially participate on a regular, continuous, and substantial basis. Any rental business is a passive activity whether or not you materially participate. Material participation rules are explained in IRS Publication 925.

There are two basic types of taxpayers: individual and corporate. This chapter focuses on taxpayers as individuals managing timber as an investment or as sole proprietor of a business.

There are tax advantages to operating your woodland as a business.

- An active business may deduct expenses from any source of income.
- Timber sale income is treated as a capital gain which carries a lower tax rate than ordinary income.
- There is no self-employment tax on capital gains.
- You face no reduction of social security benefits when generating timber sale income since capital gains are not considered earned income.

Take the following steps to help prove to the IRS that you are managing your woodland as a business:

- Get a written woodland management plan that includes
  - a goal to make a profit from forest products.
  - information necessary to make business decisions on each management unit, such as timber volume, value, management actions planned, and a timeline.
- Maintain a timber account showing your basis or original value of all timber and additions or subtractions from that basis.
- Keep a journal of forest management activities and their associated costs or income, e.g.
  - Forest related work completed or proposed
  - Why did or will you conduct the work
  - Relation of the work to increased productivity, production of timber, or resource protection
  - Date of activity
  - Hours you, or your family spent on the activity
  - Hours others spent on the activity: Who:
  - Miles traveled: Odometer Start: Finish:
  - Revenue $ generated
  - Expenses incurred
  - Acres affected
  - Comments

- Produce a financial analysis for significant management actions.
- Write a Will legally setting up the transfer of your woodland business to heirs.

Expenses

As a general rule you may deduct expenses from taxable income that are ordinary and necessary to make a profit. How and when deductions may be taken depends on the purpose of your woodland ownership and the type of expense: capital expense, operating expense or carrying charge, and sale-related expense.

Capital Expenses

A capital expense is money spent to acquire or make improvements in real property or equipment. Examples include purchase of land, timber, and buildings; purchase or major repair of machinery and equipment with a useful life of more than one year; costs associated with tree planting; and construction of bridges, permanent roads, and firebreaks.

Capital expenses usually cannot be fully deducted in the year they are incurred. Instead, the original cost (or other basis) should be recorded in a capital account and then be deducted as the property is used up, worn out, or sold. The basis in your capital account may need periodic adjustments to the original value. New capital expenses will increase the basis while deductions claimed for depletion, depreciation or amortization will reduce it. Update your capital account to reflect these capital additions or deductions.

Original Basis: Your original basis for a capital asset depends on whether you acquire it by purchase, inheritance, or gift.

If you buy an asset, your original basis is the acquisition cost which includes the purchase price plus any additional costs such as a land survey, forest inventory, or attorney fees. If funds are expended to create a capital asset, such as tree planting, then your basis includes all establishment costs.

The original basis for an inherited asset is its fair market value (FMV) (or special use value, if elected) on the decedent's date of death (or alternate valuation date, if required by the federal estate tax return). Fair market value is the price at which property would change hands between a buyer and seller, neither being required to buy or sell, and both having reasonable knowledge of all necessary facts.

For assets received by gift, the original basis is the donor's adjusted basis at the time of the gift, plus that portion of the gift tax applicable to the difference between the donor's adjusted basis and the gift's FMV at the time of the gift. If a gift's FMV is less than the donor's basis, then the donee's basis is the gift's FMV.

Allocate Original Basis to Separable Assets: Woodland you acquire may have several assets. (such as land, timber, buildings). By allocating the basis of this total acquisition among the individual assets in proportion to their FMVs, you can deduct the basis of an asset, such as timber, from income at the time of its sale to reduce taxable income (Example 1). If you do not separate timber and land accounts, you can deduct timber acquisition costs only when the land is sold.

Example 1. In Year 1 you bought 80 acres of woodland, including 70 acres of merchantable timber and 10 acres of premerchantable young trees. The total acquisition cost included the property's cost ($160,000), boundary survey ($2,000), title search ($200), land appraisal ($500), and timber inventory ($1,300). Next you obtained appraisals of the FMV of the merchantable timber, young growth and bare land. A consulting forester inventoried and valued the timber, determining there were 1,200 cords of merchantable timber with a FMV of $36,000 and 10 acres of young growth with a FMV of $5,000. A land appraisal determined the bare land's FMV to be $120,000.

Calculate the original cost basis for merchantable timber, young growth, and bare land by determining the proportion of the total FMV represented by each and multiplying this ratio by the total acquisition cost. For example, 1)

divide the merchantable timber's FMV by the total FMV of the property ($36,000 ÷ $161,000 = 0.22), then, 2) multiply that by the total acquisition cost (0.22 x $164,000 = $36,080) to determine the merchantable timber's original cost basis. Repeat for each asset.

Asset	Fair Market Value	Proportion of Total Fair Market Value	Original Cost Basis	Units
Merchantable timber	36,000	0.22	36,080	cords
Young growth	5,000	0.03	4,920	acres
Land	120,000	0.75	123,000	acres
Total	161,000	1.00	164,000	

If you acquired forest land several years ago, it may be possible to determine the timber's FMV at the time the property was first acquired by having a forester inventory and appraise the timber based on prices at the time it was acquired, then deduct the volume and value that grew since you acquired it.

Establishing Capital Accounts and Deducting their Costs: As discussed above, you should record the original basis of each capital asset in a separate account (land, timber, depreciable land improvements, and equipment).

Land Account—In a land account, record costs for land and permanent improvements to the land. This includes earthworks acquired with the property or constructed later (such as permanent roadbed, land leveling, impoundment). You may deduct their costs when the land is sold or otherwise disposed of. The costs of road building or improvement, if done for the purpose of a timber sale, may be deducted as the timber is removed from the land.

Timber Account—A timber account should include, if applicable, subaccounts for merchantable timber, young growth (naturally regenerated trees of premerchantable size), and plantations (planted trees of premerchantable size). Timber subaccounts may be subdivided by species or location.

In each merchantable timber subaccount show the quantity of timber (in cords, 1,000 board feet, or other appropriate unit) and its original basis.

Change the quantity when an updated timber inventory shows the volume has changed due to timber growth, harvest, or casualty. The basis will change when timber is sold or more is purchased (Examples 2 and 3).

In young growth and plantation accounts show the number of acres and original basis. All costs for materials, labor, tools, equipment rent, and depreciation attributable to equipment used to establish natural regeneration or plantations must be capitalized since they are used to establish your woodland asset. Examples of costs that must be capitalized are costs for site preparation; seedlings; planting; and control of weeds, brush, and rodents until the stand is established. You then increase the basis as more costs are incurred to establish new stands. When trees reach merchantable size, transfer values in these accounts to the merchantable timber account (Example 2). Tree planting or reforestation costs also may be eligible for an immediate deduction or amortization over eight tax years (Example 4).

Example 2. In preparation for a timber sale in Year 5, you hired a forester to remeasure the timber you bought in Year 1 (see Example 1). Your timber on 70 acres had grown by 175 cords so you add this quantity to your merchantable timber account. Young growth on 10 acres had reached merchantable size and was estimated to contain 25 cords. Transfer this quantity and its cost basis ($4,920) from the young growth account to the merchantable timber account. In Year 5 you purchased an additional 40 acres of forest land containing 800 cords of timber with a cost basis of $25,000. Add this quantity and basis to your account.

Transactions	Quantity (cords)	Adjusted $ Cost Basis
Merchantable timber in Year 1	1,600	36,080
Addition for growth (Year 1-5)	175	0
Young growth that became merchantable in Year 5	25	4,920
Timber purchased in Year 5	800	25,000
Net quantity and basis in Year 5	2,600	66,000

Depletion Allowance—When you sell timber, you may deduct that portion of the adjusted basis attributable to the quantity of timber sold. This deductible amount is the depletion allowance. If you acquire standing timber and later sell the entire stand in a single transaction, your depletion allowance would be your entire adjusted basis in the timber. If you acquire standing timber, then sell portions of it in several transactions over a period of years, you need to calculate the depletion allowance for each portion of the timber sold. To do so, first divide the timber's adjusted basis by the total pre-sale quantity of timber in the block to get the depletion unit, or cost per unit of timber. Next multiply the depletion unit by the total quantity of timber sold to get the depletion allowance for that timber (Example 3).

Example 3. In Year 5 you sold 1,000 cords of timber from your 120-acre tract (see Example 2). To calculate your depletion allowance, first divide the adjusted cost basis by the total quantity of timber on the property ($66,000 ÷ 2,600 cords) to get the depletion unit ($25.38 per cord). Multiply the depletion unit by the number of units sold ($25.38 × 1,000 cords) to get the depletion allowance that may be deducted ($25,380).

Transactions	Quantity (Cords)	$ Cost Basis
Merchantable timber in Year 5 before harvest	2,600	66,000
Timber sold in Year 5	(1,000)	(25,380)
Adjusted quantity and cost basis at end of 1998	1,600	40,620

Following this sale you still have 1,600 cords of timber remaining on the property with an adjusted cost basis of $40,620. In the future when you prepare to sell more timber, you will again need to remeasure the total quantity of timber on the property and calculate the depletion allowance for the quantity sold.

If you harvest timber for personal use (such as firewood for your home), you may not claim a depletion allowance and subsequently reduce the dollar amount in your merchantable timber account. However, if you cut very much timber, you may need to adjust the quantity of timber in the account to reflect the lower quantity available for commercial sale.

Depreciable Land Improvements Account—Depreciable assets are those held for use in a business or for the production of income that have a determinable useful life of more than one year and wear out, decay, get used up, become obsolete, or lose value from natural causes. Depreciable land improvements include bridges, culverts, temporary roads, gravel for roads, fences, and temporary structures. Establish a separate account for each improvement so you can recover its cost over a period of years according to IRS depreciation schedules.

Equipment Account—Set up subaccounts showing costs for each item or class of items of equipment, such as power saws, tractors, trucks, and tree-planting machines. Add costs to these subaccounts for major repairs or reconstruction that significantly increase value or prolong the life of the equipment. Recover these costs through depreciation.

Depreciation and the Section 179 Deduction—The cost of machinery, equipment, and certain land improvements may be reclaimed through annual depreciation deductions. If you actively participate in a timber business, you may be able to deduct up to a fixed amount of the cost (set annually by the IRS) for tangible personal property (such as machinery, equipment, and single-purpose agricultural and horticultural structures), in addition to the normal depreciation deduction, in the year it was first placed in service. This is an IR Code Section 179 deduction. There are no unique rules for forestry-related equipment; read IRS Publication 946 for rules about depreciation and the Section 179 deduction.

Reforestation Amortization and Investment Tax Credit—Direct expenses incurred to establish a timber stand by planting, seeding, or natural regeneration are capital expenses. There are several ways to deduct these costs, depending on your purpose for tree planting and type of taxpayer.

Under IR Code Section 175, farmers that plant trees under certain conservation programs may annually deduct such tree planting costs up to 25 percent of their gross income from farming during that year. The expenditure must be consistent with a plan approved by the USDA Natural Resources Conservation Service or comparable state agency.

If you plant at least one acre of trees for timber production in the United States, then the first $10,000 of your establishment costs may be deducted in the year trees were planted. Report the cost as an investment or business expense, depending on your type of operation. Amounts over $10,000 may qualify for amortization over an 84-month period under IR Code Section 194I(1). You may deduct or amortize the direct costs of stand establishment, such as site preparation, seed or seedlings, labor, tools, and depreciation of equipment used in planting or seeding. Expenses for planting Christmas trees, shelterbelts, windbreaks, nut trees, or ornamental trees do not qualify for amortization. You may not deduct or amortize costs reimbursed by a government cost-share program.

To amortize reforestation expenses, deduct 1/14 of the expense in the year incurred, 1/7 in each of the next six tax years, and the remaining 1/14 in the eighth tax year (Example 4).

Example 4. It cost you $11,400 to plant 40 acres of trees for timber production and you received no government cost-sharing. You elected to report the first $10,000 as an investment expense and will amortize the remaining $1,400. For the tax year in which you incur planting expenses, deduct 1/14 of $1,400, or $100. In each of the next six tax years, deduct 1/7 of $1,400, or $200. Deduct the remaining 1/14 of $1,400, or $100, in the eighth tax year.

Year	Amortization Deduction ($)
1	100
2-7	200
8	100
Total	1,400

Operating Expenses and Carrying Charges

Operating expenses include costs for tools with a short useful life or low cost (such as axes, hand saws, and tools); equipment operation and maintenance; salaries or other compensation (such as hired labor, consulting forester, lawyer, accountant); travel directly related to your property's income potential; fire, insect, and disease protection; and precommercial thinning and timber stand improvement (such as labor, equipment, materials) after the stand is established. Carrying charges include property taxes, loan interest payments, insurance premiums (such as fire, windstorm, theft, general liability, workers compensation), and certain other expenses related to property development and operation.

Ordinary and necessary expenses for managing, maintaining, and conserving forest land may be deducted if you are growing timber for profit and the expenses are directly related to the property's income potential. An activity is presumed to be managed for profit if there was net income in at least three of the five consecutive years ending with the current year. If this test cannot be met, then other facts and circumstances may be considered in determining whether the activity was engaged in for profit. Fortunately for timber growers, profit includes appreciation in the value of assets which occurs as timber grows in volume and increases in quality over time. If audited, however, you may need to prove by a financial analysis or other means that you expect to make a profit as a result of your timber-related expenses. If your timber management activities do not earn a profit in three out of five years and you cannot show that a profit is likely, based on a financial analysis or appreciation in the value of your timber asset, then you are presumed to manage timber as a hobby.

The extent to which you are permitted to currently deduct operating expenses and carrying charges depends on whether the expenses are for a hobby, an investment, or a business in which you are an active or passive participant.

Hobby: Operating expenses for timber being grown for a hobby may be deducted only from hobby income in years when income is earned. Expenses that exceed hobby income in a year are permanently lost; they may not be capitalized. Report hobby expenses as "miscellaneous itemized deductions" and deduct them only to the extent they exceed two percent of adjusted gross income.

Investment: Corporate taxpayers may deduct operating expenses from any source of income. However, noncorporate taxpayers report operating expenses as "miscellaneous itemized deductions" and may deduct them only to the extent they exceed two percent of adjusted gross income. As an alternative, you may capitalize operating expenses.

Both corporate and noncorporate taxpayers may fully deduct property and other deductible taxes from any source of income or they may be capitalize and deduct taxes from timber sale income.

Corporate taxpayers may deduce unlimited investment interest expense from any source of income. However, noncorporate taxpayers may deduct investment interest expense only up to the total net investment income from all investments. As an alternative, you may elect to capitalize all or part of the interest paid instead of currently deducting it.

Business: The extent to which you may deduct operating expenses, taxes, and interest depends on whether you materially participate in managing the business. To materially participate, you must be engaged on a regular, continuous, and substantial basis. The IRS offers other tests to aid your classification.

If you materially participate in managing a business, you may fully deduct all operating expenses, taxes, and interest from income from any source each year as incurred. If business deductions exceed gross income from all sources for the tax year, the excess net operating loss generally may be carried back to the two preceding tax years and, if necessary, carried forward to the next succeeding 20 tax years. You may instead elect to capitalize these timber-related expenses and recover them when the timber is sold.

If you do not materially participate in managing a business, you are considered to be a passive participant. C corporations (subject to corporate income tax) that are not classified as closely held or as personal service corporations may deduct operating costs and carrying charges from a passive timber business from income from any source without limitation. Closely held C corporations (other than personal service corporations) may deduct costs associated with a passive timber business from income from active businesses (but not against portfolio income). Other types of passive businesses may currently deduct operating expenses, taxes, and interest only to the extent of their income from all passive activities during the tax year. Expenses that cannot be deducted during the year incurred may be carried forward to years in which you either realize passive income or else dispose of the entire property that gave rise to the passive loss. You may instead elect to capitalize expenses and deduct them from income when the property is sold.

Capitalizing Operating Expenses and Carrying Charges

It generally is advantageous to deduct operating expenses and carrying charges in the year they are incurred, but you may need to capitalize them if you do not have sufficient income to offset the expense deduction. Capitalize such expenses by adding them to the timber's basis and deduct them from income when timber is sold. As a general rule only carrying charges may be capitalized, however, there are exceptions that permit capitalization of some operating expenses, and many timber growing expenses fit within the exceptions. You elect to capitalize expenses by describing them on a written statement attached to your tax return for the year they are incurred.

Employee Expenses

If you hire someone to work on your woodland, that person may be your employee. As an employer you must withhold, deposit, report, and pay:

- Income tax withheld from employee's wages.
- Social Security and Medicare taxes (employer and employee portion).
- Federal unemployment tax (paid by employer; not withheld from wages).
- IRS Form W-2 at end of each year.

You are an employer if you have the right to control and direct the individual who performs the services, not only as to the result to be accomplished by the work, but also as to the details and means by which that result is met (see IRS Publication 15-A).

Timber Sale Expenses

Deduct your sale-related expenses from timber sale income to determine net taxable income (or loss). Sale-related expenses may not be deducted from ordinary income that does not result from the sale. Deductible expenses may include advertising, timber cruising, marking, scaling, and fees for a consulting forester or attorney. These expenses are deductible in the year of sale regardless of your purpose for holding timber or the type of taxpayer.

Timber Sale Income

When you sell standing timber or cut logs, you must determine the amount and type of income.

Determining Amount of Income

To determine net income from a timber sale, start with gross income and deduct sale-related expenses (such as advertising, timber cruising, travel, marking, scaling, consulting forester, lawyer). You also may deduct your depletion allowance (Example 3) for the timber sold to reduce your taxable gain (Example 5). If you do not have a timber inventory and valuation from which to calculate your depletion allowance, that allowance may be recovered when you later sell the land.

Example 5. In Year 5 you sold 1,000 cords of timber from your 120-acre tract (see Example 3) for $30,000. A consulting forester charged $1,500 to cruise and mark your timber, prepare a timber sale contract, and supervise the sale. Advertising cost $120. Your depletion allowance for the timber was $25,380. Deduct your sale expenses and depletion allowance from gross timber sale income, to calculate your net timber income of $3,300.

Transactions	$ Amount
Gross timber income	30,000
Consulting forester fee	1,500
Advertising	120
Depletion allowance	25,380
Net timber income	3,000

Determining Type of Gain or Loss

Determining whether your timber sale income is ordinary or capital income is a necessary step in determining how to report the transaction and subsequently the tax rate that applies to it.

There are good reasons to set up your timber sale to qualify for capital gains treatment. Tax rates on ordinary income (including income from the sale of capital assets held less than 12 months) for noncorporate taxpayers vary across five income brackets, but the corresponding tax rates on long term capital gains (from the sale of capital assets held more than 12 months) are substantially lower. Also there is a limit to how much capital loss can be deducted from ordinary income, but no limit on how much capital lost can be deducted from capital gains. In addition, if you are a sole proprietor or partner whose timber holdings are considered a business, your ordinary income is subject to self-employment tax, but capital gains income is not subject to this tax.

Capital gains are categorized as long-term or short-term. To qualify for long-term capital gains, you must have owned timber (or the contract right to harvest timber) for more than one year prior to sale. If you sell timber acquired by gift the holding period starts on the same day the donor's holding period started. For inherited timber, no holding period is required to qualify for long-term capital gains status.

Whether your timber sale income is a capital gain depends on your primary purpose for holding timber and your sale method. Sale methods are: (1) a lump-sum sale, (2) a pay-as-cut sale, or (3) harvesting the timber yourself and selling cut products, such as logs.

Lump Sum Sale: When you hold timber for at least 12 months and sell it for a fixed amount agreed upon in advance of the harvest (i.e., a lump sum sale), you may treat the income as a capital gain. This rule applies whether you manage timber as a business, investment, or for personal use.

Pay-As-Cut Sale: Timber harvested under a contract that requires payment at a specified amount for each unit of timber harvested (such as $18 per cord), is a disposal with an economic interest retained. Advance payments are permitted, but the contract must clearly state that adjustments will be made so that the total amount paid will be determined by multiplying the volume actually cut by the specified unit price. The income is considered a capital gain under IR Code Section 631(b) whether the timber was held primarily for personal use, investment, use in a business, or sale to customers in the ordinary course of a business so long as it meets the minimum holding period requirement.

Harvest Timber, Then Sell Products: If you harvest standing timber and then sell the logs or other timber products, report the income as ordinary income, unless you make a Section 631(a) election. You may make a Section 631(a) election only if you held the timber primarily for investment or for sale or use in your business (not for personal use), you met the minimum holding period requirement for a long-term capital gain (more than 1 year), and you owned the timber (or the contract right to harvest timber) on the first day of the tax year. Report a Section 631(a) transaction in two parts:

(1) Net income from harvesting timber: For the timber that was cut, determine its fair market value as standing timber on the first day of the tax year in which it was cut. Value the timber as it existed on that date regardless of any changes to it between that date and the harvest date. Subtract from this fair market value, the allowable basis for the timber that was cut. The difference qualifies as a long-term capital gain (or loss) under Section 631(a) and is reported as a Section 1231 transaction.

(2) Net income from selling sawlogs: From the gross log sale income, deduct the fair market value of standing timber on the first day of the tax year in which it was cut and the logging expenses. The difference is ordinary income (Example 6).

Example 6. You held timber for more than one year, then personally harvested timber and then old the cut logs to a sawmill. Your depletion allowance for the standing timber was $3,000. Based on sales of comparable timber in the area, a forester estimated the fair market value of the standing timber on the first day of the tax year in which it was harvested as $11,000. Your logging expenses were $2,000. The sawmill paid you $14,000 for the logs. Since you had owned the timber longer than the one-year minimum holding period, you may report part of your earnings as a long-term capital gain. Determine the income from harvesting timber separately from the income from selling sawlogs as follows:

Transactions	$ Amount
Net Income From Harvesting Timber:	
Fair market value of standing timber on first day of tax year	11,000
Allowable basis	-3,000
Long-term capital gain (Section 1231)	8,000
Net Income From Selling Sawlogs:	
Gross log sale income	14,000
Fair market value of standing timber on first day of tax year	11,000
Logging expenses	-2,000
Ordinary income	1,000

Report $8,000 as a long term capital gain. Then report ordinary income of $14,000 and ordinary expenses of $13,000.

Installment Sale: Installment sale provisions apply when you sell timber either:

- for a lump sum agreed upon in advance of the harvest, and receive payments in more than one year (such as down payment and final payment), or
- on a pay-as-cut basis and held the timber for less than one year, and receive payments in more than one year.

You may elect out of the installment sale provisions by reporting the full fair market value of the contract in the year of the sale. Refer to IRS Publication 537 to report an installment sale. Installment provisions do not apply toward a loss. A loss must be reported in full in the year incurred.

Other Timber-Related Income

Report the sale of products derived from trees as ordinary gains or losses. This rule applies to all wood products derived from harvested trees, such as logs, lumber, pulpwood, poles, fence posts, crossties, fuelwood, and chips. It also applies to maple syrup, fruit, nuts, bark, and nursery stock. Income from sale of limbs and tops left after logging is ordinary income, even if the timber was subject to a 631(a) election and subsequently eligible for capital gains treatment.

Form 1099, Information Return

When you sell timber, the purchaser may file Form 1099 with the IRS showing the payment made to you. Whether you receive a Form 1099 or not, you still are obligated to report timber sale and cost-share income to the IRS.

Cost-Share Payments

How you treat cost-share payments depends on whether they were received for timber stand improvement or for reforestation.

Timber Stand Improvement

Timber stand improvement (TSI) includes such practices as weed or brush control after stand es-

tablishment, pruning, culling, and pre-commercial thinning. If you received a government cost share payment for TSI, you must report it as income. Then deduct or capitalize the full cost of the practice as you would other operating expenses.

Reforestation

Reforestation means to seed or plant trees on forest or open land or to perform site preparation work that stimulates natural tree regeneration. A government cost-share payment for reforestation may be partially or totally excluded from taxable income if two provisions are met: (1) the Secretary of Agriculture determines that the reforestation practice is primarily for conserving soil and water, protecting or restoring the environment, improving forests, or providing wildlife habitat; and (2) the Secretary of the Treasury determines that payment does not substantially increase your annual income from the property. Ask the agency that provides the cost-share payment whether it has been approved for the exclusion or check with the IRS.

Include Cost-Share Payment: Report the cost-share payment that you choose or are required to include in your gross income as ordinary income. When you receive cost-sharing to plant trees for timber production you may be qualified to currently deduct up to $10,000 in reforestation expenses, including the cost-share amount, plus you may amortize any remainder above $10,000.

Exclude Cost-Share Payment: You may exclude from income your cost-share payment for reforestation, subject to limits set by the Secretary of the Treasury. According to Treasury rules, the maximum cost-share payment that may be excluded is the present fair market value of the right to receive annual income from the affected acreage equal to the greater of: (1) 10 percent of the prior average annual income from the affected acreage or (2) $2.50 times the number of affected acres (Example 7).

IRS regulations do not describe how to determine the present fair market value of the right to receive annual income. A common method for determining the value of annual income over an indefinitely long period is to divide the current annual income by the interest rate that you could expect to earn in your next best investment alternative over a time period similar to the timber investment. IRS regulations do not specify an appropriate interest rate to use, however, a procedure is described in IR Code Section 2032A (e)(7)(A) for valuing farm and forest lands for estate tax special-use valuation purposes, which specifies the Farm Credit Bank interest rate. Technically the Farm Credit Bank interest rate does not apply to calculating the exclusion for reforestation cost-share payments, but it has been informally accepted by the IRS.

Prior average annual income is defined as the average gross receipts from the reforested acreage for the three tax years immediately preceding reforestation.

Example 7. You harvested $12,000 worth of timber from 20 acres and then within three years you reforested that same 20 acres at a cost of $3,800. You received 50% government cost-sharing, or $1,900, for reforestation from a program approved for exclusion. To calculate your cost-share exclusion:

(1) **Calculate average annual income from the three previous years:**
$$\$12,000 \div 3 = \$4,000$$

(2) **Calculate 10% of average annual income from the three previous years:**
$$\$4,000 \times 0.10 = \$400$$

(3) **Calculate $2.50 times the number of reforested acres.**
$$\$2.50 \times 20 = \$50$$

(4) **Select the larger amount ($400) from steps 2 and 3, and calculate its present value over an indefinitely long time period:**
$$\$400 \div 0.0736 = \$5,435$$

[Note: 0.0736 was the average annual effective interest rate on Farm Credit Bank loans at the time of this writing.]

(5) **Compare the cost-share payment to the value from step 4 and determine which is larger:**
$5,435 exclusion is larger than $1,900 cost-share payment.

(6) **Since the cost-share payment is less than the exclusion limit, you may exclude the entire cost-share payment.**

Note: If you had no income from the reforested acres within the previous three years, then the maximum exclusion would have been $2.50 times the number of reforested acres, divided by the Farm Credit Bank interest rate:
$$(\$2.50 \times 20) \div 0.0736 = \$679$$
$679 qualifies for exclusion; the remaining $1,221 portion of your cost-share payment must be included in income.

If you exclude any portion of your cost-share payment, attach a statement to your tax return showing the amount of the cost-share payment you received, date you received it, amount of cost-share payment that qualifies for exclusion, amount you choose to exclude, and how you determined that amount.

Payments excluded from taxable income may be subject to taxation as ordinary income if trees are disposed of within 20 years of establishment.

Casualty Loss

You may be able to claim a deduction for a casualty loss to timber if you have determined a basis in the timber. A casualty results from a natural or other external force acting in a sudden, unexpected, and unusual manner. Examples include fire, windstorm, tornado, hail, sleet, and airplane crash. Losses from insects, disease and drought usually do not qualify as a casualty loss because the damage is not sudden and such losses are expected over the life of a timber stand, but there are exceptions among Revenue Rulings.

Your deductible loss is the reduction in value of the timber damaged or destroyed, up to its allowable basis, less any insurance, salvage, or other compensation received. Every reasonable effort must be made to salvage timber, such as by offering it for sale. If a gain results from the salvage activity, there is no casualty loss. The identifiable property for purposes of claiming a casualty loss is any unit of property containing the damaged timber that has an identifiable adjusted basis.

Example 8.
A wildfire damaged or destroyed 15 acres of timber on your 40 acre tract. The fair market value of timber on this 15 acres immediately before the fire was $7,000, but your adjusted basis in the 15 acres destroyed was just $5,000. You offered the timber for sale and received $3,500 for trees that could be salvaged. Your reportable casualty loss is your adjusted basis, minus the salvage value:

$5,000 - $3,500 = $1,500 casualty loss

Property Taxes

Property taxes may be deducted from taxable income on your federal income tax return if you itemize deductions. This deduction is available to all taxpayers whether you hold timber for personal use, for an investment or for a business. But, property taxes still must be paid and constitute a substantial annual cost of forest land ownership. To reduce property taxes get information from your state or local taxing authority or from a forester about special property tax programs in which you may enroll your woodland. In some states forest land may be eligible for more than one classification, depending on its use, and each classification may carry a different tax rate. Discuss your use of the land with your taxing authority and ask about any special tax breaks for managed forest land. If any tax breaks exist, they may require you to follow a forest management plan prepared by a forester with your input, and approved by a government agency.

Financial Analysis of Woodland Investments

Whether its stocks, bonds, mutual funds, or savings accounts, as an investor you are interested in getting the greatest return on each dollar invested. Forest land is no exception. Many landowners,

however, overlook the potential opportunity to increase the return on their forest land investment. In addition to providing important wildlife, recreation, and aesthetic values, investing in forest management can add to your financial bottom line. Because management is a long-term proposition, the investments you make need to be carefully considered. When properly applied, modest investments in management early in a life of a forest stand can have a substantial impact on financial returns through increased forest growth, improved wood quality, and greater economic yields in the future. In addition, investing in forest management often compliments many other reasons individuals own forests such as improving wildlife habitat.

Forestry investments generally require a long-range commitment of money, land, time, and other resources. Because such resources are limited, you should identify and evaluate various investment alternatives to determine how these resources can best be used to meet your demands. This process, called financial analysis, is described in this chapter. Keep in mind, however, that a financial analysis offers one input toward deciding which alternative is best. Your decisions also may depend on other factors that are not easily quantified or profit-motivated.

There are a number of factors to consider when investing in forest management. These include:

Tolerance for risk– Future rates of return cannot be predicted with certainty. Investments that pay higher rates of return are generally subject to higher risk and volatility. The actual rate of return on investments can vary widely over time, especially for long-term investments such as forest management, as there is often a large degree of uncertainty that anticipated returns will be fully realized. This includes uncertainty about future prices for your products ("What markets will exist when my products are ready for sale?"), management costs ("What will be my annual property tax liability for the property?"), and future forest conditions ("Will forest growth increase in response to management as expected?" "Will the forest be affected by insect or disease infestation or wildfire?").

Investment timelines– Landowners need to consider the timeframe associated with their forest management investments. The income or benefits from these investments may not be realized for years or even decades. In some cases, it may be your heirs that realize the investments you make today in your forests.

Portfolio diversification– For many individuals, investing in forest management provides added diversification that complements an existing investment portfolio.

Stand suitability for potential practices– The existing condition of your forest (such as tree types, sizes, ages) will often dictate the opportunities to invest in forest management, as well as the specific practices that can be applied.

Financing– Depending on your access to capital to fund investments in forest management, you may need to secure outside funding. The terms of outside financing (that is, the interest rate charged by the lending institution, repayment period, the amount of financing obtained) can vary considerably and have a substantial impact on the financial feasibility of an investment.

When to sell your products– How will you know when your timber and other forest products are ready for harvest? What criteria will you use to make this determination? From a strictly financial perspective, you will want to sell your products when they no longer increase in value at a rate that exceeds your next best investment opportunity (such as your opportunity cost). For example, if you could invest the proceeds from the sale of your forest products into an account earning an eight percent annual return, you would want to let your forest grow until its value increases at a rate that is less than eight percent per year. The timing of any income-generating activities can also be affected by other factors such as the immediate need for money, anticipation of an insect attack, or cleanup following a windstorm.

Marketing– When your forest products are ready for sale, there will likely be costs associated with preparing your stand for sale and finding a market for the products. Many landowners use a consulting forester to oversee the sale of forest products. They will typically collect a fee that represents a percent of the gross sale value.

Importance of benefits which are difficult to quantify– Forest management may involve selling timber or other forest products to markets which pay for delivered material. It can also provide other benefits that may not have a well-defined market (such as aesthetics, bird-watching). As the significance of these non-market benefits varies from one landowner to another, it may be important to weigh them in any management decisions.

Taxes– Property taxes are usually the single largest recurring annual cost of forest management. What are the expectations about the future level of property taxes? Additionally, how will federal and state income tax provisions (such as treatment of timber income and management expenses) affect the performance of my investment?

Record keeping– Important, but often overlooked is keeping complete and detailed records of your forest management activities. These records are not only important for tax purposes, but they also enable you to better document the timing and types of treatments applied to your stand.

Government and other support or incentive programs– There are several government-sponsored programs that provide technical and/or financial assistance to landowners interested in managing their forest. This includes cost-share funds to help with certain management practices such as tree planting or other silvicultural activities. A consulting forester or your local department of natural resources office can help you identify the programs applicable for your situation.

Steps in a Financial Analysis

Investments require costs and produce benefits or income at various points over time. The timing and amounts of these cash flows determine the profitability of an investment alternative.

A financial analysis requires identifying objectives, potential projects and your level of involvement;

determining the schedule of activities for each objective; attaching a dollar value to each activity; and discounting those dollar values to the present (Figure 14-1). Your consulting forester can help you with many parts of this process.

Figure 14-1. Flow chart of financial analysis steps.

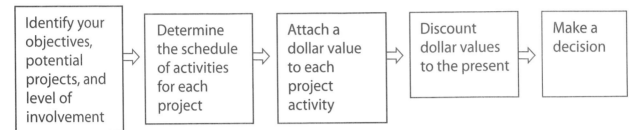

1. Identify your objectives, potential projects, and level of involvement

Sound planning begins with determining your objectives, identifying potential projects which might help you achieve those objectives, and deciding the level of involvement you want to have with on-the-ground management of your forest. When identifying your objectives, it may be useful to write a short description of the situation or to describe the desired outcome in a clear, concise statement. Develop a list of potential solutions or investment alternatives which might help achieve your objectives. To reduce the number of alternatives to a manageable few, start by considering your resources such as:

- Technical-equipment, species, etc.
- Economic-relationship between benefits and costs (timing, amount, etc.).
- Commercial-availability of markets.
- Financial-amount of available funds and other financial obligations.
- Personnel-adequacy of staffing (number, capabilities, etc.).
- Legal/Ethical-relationship with accepted standards and expectations.

You probably lack data to predict outcomes for many alternatives. Many otherwise promising options may be discarded because there is little or no information regarding benefits.

While being actively involved in the on-the-ground management activities, can save you money, it takes time. Do you anticipate doing those activities as a hobby when time permits or do you plan to make it a major line of your work? Because the amount of involvement often depends on the perceived returns, leave room for flexibility. You can rerun your analysis to evaluate how different levels of personal involvement or hired services will impact your profitability.

2. Determine the schedule of activities for each project

Each project that you might undertake has an associated schedule of activities during its life. The events should be placed in the appropriate year(s) on a time line to help you track these activities over time. A sample time line for a Christmas tree farm is shown in Figure 14-2.

Figure 14-2. Sample time line.

Years in the Future	Activity
0	Site preparation, tree planting, weed control, spraying, taxes
1	Spraying, fertilize, weed control, taxes
2	Spraying, fertilize, shearing, taxes
3	Spraying, shearing, taxes
4	Spraying, shearing, taxes
5	Spraying, fertilize, shearing, taxes
6	Spraying, shearing, tree sales, taxes
7	Spraying, shearing, tree sales, taxes

In this case, site preparation, planting, weed control, spraying, fertilizing, shearing, payment of property taxes, site cleaning, and marketing are needed during various years. While site preparation and tree planting would occur now according to the timeline (Figure 14-2), the marketing of trees (sale) would occur six and seven years in the future. Make sure your timeline include all activities, including your own investment of time that the project will require.

3. Attach dollar values to each project activity

Identify those activities from your time line that involve a cash transaction where you are either receiving income (a benefit) or paying someone (a cost). For each of those activities, determine the associated dollar value. Do not include the cash flow from an existing or completed project as an initial benefit in an analysis. However, that income may be used as available funds to cover investment costs.

As the economic environment is constantly changing and your financial analysis is heavily influenced by your assumptions about the timing and dollar amount of financial transactions, it is very important to have the best and most current information available. Some products have grower associations such as a Christmas tree grower's association or a maple syrup producers association. These associations may be of some assistance in determining dollar values, growth rates, insurance costs, etc. Some products however do not yet have well-defined markets and prices. In these cases, foresters and extension educators may be of some assistance. When defining dollar values, make sure that they are all expressed in the same units (such as $/acre, $/year).

4. Discount values to the present

If you deposit funds into a saving account, you expect your investment to grow over time through a process called compounding. Compounding occurs when interest is paid on the original principal and on the accumulated past interest. Assuming a 5 percent interest rate and compounding once a year, a $100 investment would grow to $105 ($100 X 1.05) at the end of the first year and $110.25 ($105

X 1.05) at the end of the second year. Before you can compare your alternatives and make a decision (Step 5), you must convert the cash flows on your time line into comparable values. This is done through a process called dis¬counting, which is just the opposite of compound¬ing; it starts with a future value and finds its worth today. The formula for calculating the present value of a future value is:

$$PV = \frac{FV}{(1 + i)^n}$$

Where:
   PV = Present value
   FV = Future value
i = Alternative rate of return or interest rate (expressed in decimal form)

n = Number of years in the future when the transaction occurs.

Fortunately, computer spreadsheet programs contain built in functions for determining the present value of future financial transactions. The key factor when discounting values to the present is determining the discount rate or alternative rate of return (i). This is the cost of borrowing money or the best rate of return available in other investments. These other investments may be alternative land uses, what you can earn through financial markets, or the rate of return available in a savings account or money market fund.

Using the formula above, the present value of $110.25 in two years is $100 using a discount rate of 5 percent.

$$\$100 = \frac{\$110.25}{(1 + .05)^2}$$

Or, suppose that a future transaction will provide $250 in 10 years. If your savings account pays 7 percent interest, then FV = $250, i =.07 (for 7 percent), and n = 10. The calculated present value is $127.09. You would do the same for all financial transactions which occur in the future, discounting them to the present.

Depending on an individual's financial resources, tolerance for risk, and investment preferences (such as stock market vs. savings account) the discount rate applied may vary from one individual to another. As a result, the present value for a future transaction can vary considerably among individuals. For example, the present value of the same $250 transaction in 10 years is $139.60 using a 6 percent interest rate.

5. Make a decision

There are many economic decision rules that can analyze the financial feasibility of investment opportunities. One of the more common is net present value (NPV), the difference between a project's discounted benefits and discounted costs. A positive NPV indicates that a project is a better use of your resources when compared to the rate of return you could get from your next best investment opportunity (i.e., your discount rate).

The investment alternative with the highest positive NPV is generally the preferred alternative. You need to consider additional factors such as the amount of risk, investment timelines, the amount of uncertainty associated with future cash flows, tax implications, non-market benefits provided or affected (such as aesthetics, bird-watching), your labor, etc. before making a final decision.

As an example, suppose you identified the two investment options shown below with an alternative rate of return of 7 percent. Neither option provides net income until the third year. The NPV for Option A is $16.61 and $17.62 for Option B. Because both options have a positive NPV, we know that they will each return more than the alternative rate of return (7 percent). Based solely on financial criteria, Option B would be preferred because it has the largest NPV. But, because a financial analysis only incorporates project costs and benefits that can be quantified, consideration of other factors may result in Option A being preferred.

Option	Net benefit ($) by year				Net present value ($)
	0	1	2	3	
A	-100	-10	-10	165	16.61
B	-250	-10	-10	350	17.62

Example

The farm you grew up on is now being sold by your parents who are retiring. Your siblings and you decide to purchase the farm to keep it in the family. While your brothers and sisters decide to keep their part of the farm in production, you are going to establish pheasant habitat on the 100 acres you purchased, with the intent of leasing the hunting rights once the habitat is suitable. Your estimated costs and returns are as follows:

- $750/acre purchase price of land, paid back annually in equal installments over 5 years at 9% annual interest.

- $200/acre wildlife habitat establishment costs incurred one year after purchase.

- $50/acre habitat maintenance costs in years 2 to 3.

- $10/acre habitat maintenance costs in years 4 to 10.

- Annual recreation leases of $140/acre beginning in years 4 to 9.

- $5/acre/year in property taxes and liability insurance, beginning immediately.

- You plan to sell the land in year 10 for $1,300 per acre.

- Your alternative rate of return is 7%.

Cash Flow Table ($/acre)

	0	1	2	3	4	5	6	7	8	9	10
Costs											
Purchase		193	193	193	193	193					
Wildlife Est.		200									
Habitat Maint.			50	50	10	10	10	10	10	10	10
Prop. Taxes	5	5	5	5	5	5	5	5	5	5	5
Total Costs	**5**	**398**	**248**	**248**	**208**	**208**	**15**	**15**	**15**	**15**	**15**
Returns					140	140	140	140	140	140	
Rec. Lease											1,300
Total Return					140	140	140	140	140	140	1,300
Net Return	**-5**	**-398**	**-248**	**-248**	**-68**	**-68**	**125**	**125**	**125**	**125**	**1,285**

Discounted Cash Flow Table ($/acre)

	0	1	2	3	4	5	6	7	8	9	10
Costs											
Purchase	0	180	169	157	147	137	0	0	0	0	0
Wildlife Est.	0	187	0	0	0	0	0	0	0	0	0
Habitat Maint.	0	0	44	41	8	7	7	6	6	5	5
Prop. Taxes	5	5	4	4	4	4	3	3	3	3	3
Total Costs	**5**	**372**	**217**	**202**	**159**	**148**	**10**	**9**	**9**	**8**	**8**
Returns	0	0	0	0	107	100	93	87	81	76	0
Rec. Lease	0	0	0	0	0	0	0	0	0	0	661
Total Return					**107**	**100**	**93**	**87**	**81**	**76**	**661**
Net Return	($5)	($372)	($217)	($202)	($52)	($48)	$83	$78	$73	$68	$653

Adding numbers in the Net Return row of the Discounted Cash Flow table above, we find, the net present value is $59/acre (rounded to the nearest dollar). Because that value is positive, this alternative will provide a 7 percent rate of return plus an additional $59 acre. Assuming that the level of risk, investment timelines, the amount of uncertainty associated with future cash flows, tax implications, non-market benefits provided or affected (such as aesthetics, bird-watching), your labor requirements, etc. are acceptable, you would prefer this alternative to the one which yields a 7 percent rate of return.

Carbon Credits for Forestry

Global climate change may result in severe changes in temperature, precipitation, and melting polar ice caps. In the Lake States climate change may lead to changes in vegetation, wildlife habitat and habitat ranges, and even economic opportunities.

More than 40 years ago scientists around the world recognized that global climate change may be related to increased concentrations of "greenhouse gases" such as carbon dioxide (CO_2) that enters and circulates in the atmosphere. Human-induced activities contributing to greenhouse gas concentrations include deforestation, urbanization, emissions from burning fossil fuels, and industrial agriculture.

Carbon sequestration (extracting and storing carbon from the atmosphere) has been proposed as one means among many to help mitigate climate change. Growing plants extract CO_2 from the atmosphere and convert it to biomass—a process referred to as "terrestrial carbon sequestration." New tree plantings provide a net gain in carbon sequestered. A managed forest both maintains a stock of carbon and continuously sequesters more carbon. If trees are harvested and converted to long-lived forest products, the carbon is stored in those products until they are discarded and decay, releasing the stored carbon.

Market for Forest-based Carbon Credits

Since trees sequester carbon over a relatively long time period, the scientific community recognizes the role of forests in mitigating climate change. Farmers and landowners who use practices that sequester carbon from the atmosphere may be eligible for carbon credit payments for this ecological service. Carbon credits for forestry aim to 1) prevent or reduce carbon emissions produced by human activities from reaching the atmosphere, and 2) remove carbon from the atmosphere by planting trees and securely storing it in tree biomass and the soil.

The carbon credits, also called offsets, are being traded on greenhouse gas markets and exchanges, much like a stock exchange. Current United States markets are voluntary, member-based organizations comprised of large companies, municipalities, and institutions that allow greenhouse gas sequestration benefits from conservation practices to be quantified, credited and sold. The greenhouse gas exchanges purchase carbon sequestration credits from landowners who have implemented carbon sequestering practices on their lands, and in turn, sell those credits to carbon emitting companies and industries, thereby allowing the carbon emitters to reduce their net carbon emissions. The greenhouse gas exchanges offer carbon credits for the following forestry practices: managed reforestation, new plantings on afforested lands, existing sustainably managed forests, substitution of renewable fuels for fossil fuels, and long-lived forest products.

Landowner Enrollment Procedures

The amounts of carbon sequestered per acre are determined either by rate tables organized by species or species groups or by direct measurement of biomass. In the Lake States those values range between one and two metric tons of CO_2 equivalent per acre. The greenhouse gas exchanges currently require that credits be sold in increments much larger than what the average landowner might be able to offer. For example, one exchange requires that at least 12,500 metric tons of CO_2 equivalent be available to trade. That equates to around 4,000 acres of land.

In order for most forest landowners to sell their credits to the carbon exchange, they need to work with an aggregator. An aggregator is a company that will combine a landowner's carbon credits with those of other landowners to create a large enough bundle to sell to the greenhouse gas exchange.

Before enrolling in the program, the landowner must demonstrate that the land is or was degraded before the restoration or sequestration project began, and demonstrate a long-term commitment to maintain the land in trees. The landowner must also demonstrate that they would not have undertaken the forestry activity without the credit. This is called "additionality," meaning that any credits must support activities that are "in addition" to what the landowner would have done without the credit. The current greenhouse gas exchange stipulates that to receive credits for managed forests, the forest must be certified through an organization (see Forest Certification, page 120), or through a conservation easement, letter of intent, or U. S. Department of Agriculture Conservation Reserve Program contract. The aggregator is responsible for preparing all documents required for the landowner to get started in the program. The landowner must provide to the aggregator a legal description of the acreage and practice(s) employed on the land.

Verification

A third party verification of sequestration levels is generally required for projects that sequester large amounts of carbon (for example, more than 2,000 metric tons of carbon annually). This verification guarantees transparency, rigor, and integrity, and provides members with standardized procedures for managing greenhouse gases. Verifiers use information provided by the landowner or aggregator, combined with potential site visits, to accurately assess a project's actual, annual greenhouse gas sequestration or loss. A carbon offset project is subject to initial verification, as well as annual verification for the duration of its enrollment.

Trading Carbon Credits

Once the carbon offset is verified, the aggregator will trade the carbon to the greenhouse gas exchange. The aggregator usually conducts trading when the price is favorable to the aggregator and landowner. A landowner participating in the program usually receives payment once or twice a year. The amount of money received depends on the amount of credits being enrolled or sold through the aggregator, the price of carbon at the time of trading, the fees deducted by the aggregator (usually 8 to 10 percent of the gross amount) and other fees, such as insurance, that will protect the participant in case of events might affect the enrolled credits (such as fire and drought).

Estate Planning

After managing a woodland for many years, you want to preserve its financial and other values for the benefit of future generations. Discuss your goals for the property with family members and others that have a stake in it. Listen to their concerns and expectations. Then fine-tune your goals and work with professional advisors (attorney, accountant, and forester) to find the right mechanism for passing on this legacy.

Get an accurate appraisal of your woodland and other assets. State and/or federal estate taxes may be due upon the death of an owner. Property owned in different states is subject to estate laws in those states. If there is not enough cash available from liquid assets to pay estate taxes, it may be necessary to sell land to pay those taxes.

Wills and Trusts

Prepare a will to insure that taxes and creditors are paid and assets are transferred to heirs as you wish. A will does not control distribution of some assets, such as property held in joint tenancy, life insurance, and retirement plans. Designate beneficiaries on financial accounts (such as retirement accounts, bank accounts, life insurance) to keep them out of probate.

A trust can be written to specify how assets will be managed and distributed after death. Assets can be transferred to the trust during the lifetime of the trustor or at death. The trustee is obligated to manage the trust's assets for the benefit of beneficiaries. A trust can be written to last a specified number of years, a lifetime, or multiple generations. The trustee must file income tax returns and pay taxes on income retained in the trust while beneficiaries pay income taxes on funds distributed to them.

A revocable living trust enables the creator to become both the trustee and beneficiary. This trust may be amended or revoked at any time. The trust is not subject to income tax. By designating an alternate trustee, it provides financial protection in case of disability and assets transferred to the trust during the trustor's lifetime avoid probate at death. Estate taxes cannot be avoided by this trust.

Types of Business Ownership

To keep your woodland intact and managed as a business after your death, discuss these forms of business ownership with your professional advisors.

Sole Proprietorship

This business has one owner. Startup costs are low, income and taxes are reported on the owner's tax return, one person makes all decisions, and no documents are required to describe the business or its management. The owner is not protected from liability and the business ends when the owner dies. Upon death of the owner, the business's value is its fair market value at the date of death.

Joint Tenancy and Tenants-in-Common

More than one individual owns the business. The business pays no tax, but does file a tax return to report income or loss. Partners report their share of the income on individual tax returns. Partners are not employees so no payroll tax is reported. Partners can pool finances and share management with few legal restrictions. Every partner shares liability for his or her own actions, for actions of other partners, and for actions of employees. The joint ownership terminates at the death or bankruptcy of any partner. Written buy-sell agreements are important to determine what happens to the business and land when an owner dies. Individual owners in the land can demand their share of the fair value of the property at any time, and force the sale of the property to get their value out. This creates an unpredictable situation for remaining owners. When the death of a partner occurs,

- Under joint tenancy, ownership passes automatically to the remaining partners.
- Under tenants-in-common, ownership passes to the heirs of the partner that died if there is no buy-sell agreement between partners.

Family Limited Partnership

The partnership is composed of family members. One or more general partners manage the business for the benefit of all partners and have general liability for the business. Limited partners are treated as investors with no active role in management and no liability. The business pays no tax, but does file a tax return to report income or loss. Partners report their share of the income on individual tax returns. Partners are not employees so no payroll tax is reported. This arrangement allows selected family members that are most interested and competent to manage the business to the benefit of all while allowing other family members to transition into management over time. This partnership may be required to terminate at the death of a general partner or at a specified time. At the death of a partner, buy-sell agreements control how partner interests are valued and transferred. Valuation is based on the business's assets and cash flow, reduced by any restrictions in the partnership agreement.

Limited Liability Company

This entity combines features of a partnership and corporation. Owners are called members. The business pays no tax, but does file a tax return to report income or loss. Members report their share of the income on individual tax returns. Members are not employees so no payroll tax is reported. One or more general members manage the business for the benefit of all members. General members have limited liability for business actions and debts. Limited members are treated as investors with no active role in management and no liability. Profit distribution is flexible. LLCs can be created with unlimited life. At the death of a member, buy-sell agreements control how member interests are valued and transferred. Valuation is based on the business's assets and cash flow, reduced by any restrictions in the membership agreement. Each state has different laws and regulations concerning LLCs. This is a popular business entity for ownership and transfer of land between generations.

S Corporation

This is an Internal Revenue Service designation for a small corporation. The business itself pays no tax, but does file a tax return to report income or loss. Shareholders report their share of the income on individual tax returns. Shareholders who manage the corporation are employees and payroll reporting is required for their salaries. All shareholders have liability protection. Self-employment tax may be lower than under a partnership. Only one class of stock is permitted and distributions to stockholders must be equal. Corporate structure is defined by state law. All appreciation in the value of assets, including land, is taxed if land is sold or the corporation is dissolved, making the S Corporation less suitable for small woodlands.

C Corporation

This entity may have one or more shareholders that pool capital and resources to conduct business. The corporation pays taxes on its income at corporate tax rates. Money comes out of the corporation through salaries or dividends. Dividends are not deductible to the corporation, but are taxable to shareholders, creating a double tax burden. Corporate tax rates vary, but may be lower than rates for a sole proprietor or partnership. Both common and preferred shares can be issued with different rights for each class. Shareholders are protected from liability. Corporate structure is defined by state law. C Corporations are less suitable for small woodlands because 1) all appreciation in the value of assets, including land, is taxed if land is sold or the corporation is dissolved, and 2) C corporations do not qualify for reduced capital gains tax rates. Transfer of stock is controlled by corporate statute and limited by any buy-sell agreements between shareholders.

Land Protection Options

Many woodland owners invest a great deal of time and money into managing their woodland and wish to preserve the features they value about their land for future generations. But pressure to develop that woodland for residential or business use may lead a future landowner to sell the property for such development. Woodland can be protected from development by a conservation easement or donation to a conservation organization.

Conservation Easement

A conservation easement is a legally enforceable land preservation agreement between a landowner and a land protection organization, such as a nonprofit land trust or public agency. The owner typically gives up the right to develop the land while retaining other rights, such as the right to sell the property, live on the property, manage timber, recreate, and mine subsurface minerals. All rights are negotiable between the landowner and the entity holding the easement. The receiving organization is obligated to prevent future development of the property and may have other rights to use it for conservation purposes stipulated in the agreement.

There are several benefits of a conservation easement to the landowner, foremost of which is that the land will continue to be managed and used as the current owner specifies. If the fair market value of the land declines as a consequence of the easement, the landowner may deduct this "loss" as a charitable contribution on federal income taxes [Internal Revenue Code Section 170(h)]. The reduced land value also may result in lower property taxes. Lowering the property value also lowers the estate value, thus reducing estate taxes when the property owner dies. A conservation easement does not always result in a lower property value since the property's value as "green space" in a rapidly developing area may sustain or raise the property value.

Search for natural resources-oriented state and federal agencies and nonprofit land trusts that may offer conservation easements. Some easements are for fixed-time periods while others are perpetual. Work with an attorney experienced in such easements to help you write the agreement.

Land Donation

Another means to protect your land is to donate it to a public agency, nonprofit organization, or college that shares your values. Such organizations may accept land for natural areas, parks, forestry, hunting and fishing, research or other uses that you value.

References

Bentz, C. J.; M Green; R Irvin; C. Landgren; C. Lync; S. Watkins; B. Withrow-Robinson. 2006. *Ties to the Land: Your Family Forest Heritage.* Austin Family Business Program, Oregon State University, Corvallis, OR. 76 p.

Haney, L. Jr.; W. Hoover; W. Siegel; J. Green. 2001. *Forest Landowners' Guide to the Federal Income Tax* (U.S. Department of Agriculture, Forest Service, Agriculture Handbook No. 718; (ISBN 0-16-042794-0). U.S. Government Printing Office, Washington, DC; http://bookstore.gpo.gov/. 157 p.

Potter-Witter, K. and C.W. Ramm. 1999. *Depletion Accounts: Guide for Consulting Foresters and Landowners*. North Central Region Extension Bulletin NCR 609.

Web Sites:

Internal Revenue Service: www.irs.gov

Small Business Administration: www.sba.gov

National Timber Tax Website: http://www.timbertax.org/

For details on how to incorporate family discussion and succession planning into your land transfer plans, visit the Ties to the Land website at http://www.familybusinessonline.org/resources/ttl/home.htm

Appendix A:

Forestry Measurements and Conversions

Land Measurements

Linear

1 link = 7.92 inches
100 links = 1 chain
1 chain = 66 feet
80 chains = 1 mile
1 rod = 16.5 feet
4 rods = 1 chain
1 mile = 5,280 feet

Square

1 square rod = 272.25 square feet
10 square chains = 1 acre
1 acre = 43,560 square feet; a square acre measures about 209 feet on each side
1 square mile (section) = 640 acres
1 township = 36 sections

Tree and Log Measurements

1 board foot = 144 cubic inches of solid wood
1 cubic foot = 1,728 cubic inches of solid wood or about 5 to 6 board feet (because of losses in sawing)
1 cunit = 100 cubic feet of solid wood
1 cord = a closely stacked pile of wood containing 128 cubic feet of wood, bark, and air spaces. Usually measured as 4 feet x 4 feet x 8 feet. Usually contains 70 to 90 cubic feet of solid wood or about 500 board feet.

Approximate English to Metric System Conversions

English to Metric

1 inch = 2.540 centimeters
1 foot or 12 inches = 30.480 centimeters
1 yard or 3 feet = 0.914 meters
1 U.S. statute mile or 5,280 feet = 1.609 kilometers
1 acre or 43,560 square feet = 0.405 hectares
1 cubic foot or 1,728 cubic inches = 0.028 cubic meters

Metric to English

1 centimeter or 10 millimeters = 0.394 inches
1 meter = 39.370 inches
1 kilometer or 1,000 meters = 0.621 U.S. statute mile
1 hectare or 10,000 square meters = 2.471 acres
1 cubic meter or 1,000,000 cubic centimeters = 35.315 cubic feet

Appendix B:

Site Index Curves for Selected Tree Species

Interpreting Site Index Curves

Site index is the height to which trees will grow over a given period—usually 50 years in the Lake States. Trees are expected to grow taller on good sites than on poor sites. Site index curves can be used to estimate relative site quality from the average age and average total height of dominant and codominant trees on a particular site. Each tree species has its own set of site index curves.

To use the site index curves in this appendix, first measure the age and total height of several dominant and codominant trees of a single species on a site. Calculate the average total age and average total height of those same trees. Then refer to the site index curves for that species.

For example, refer to the site index curves for quaking aspen in Appendix B-1. If the average age of aspen trees in your stand of interest is 40 years (horizontal axis) and the average total height is 62 feet (vertical axis), then those two lines converge closest to the site index curve for 70. This means that aspen trees in your stand are expected to be 70 feet tall when they are 50 years old. They are growing on a good site.

B-1. Quaking Aspen
B-2. Balsam Fir in the Lake States
B-3. Black Spruce
B-4. Black Walnut
B-5. Green Ash
B-6. Eastern Cottonwood
B-7. Eastern White Pine
B-8. Hardwood Comparisons
B-9. Jack Pine
B-10. Northern White-Cedar
B-11. Red (Norway) Pine
B-12. Tamarack
B-13. Northern Red Oak

B-1: Quaking Aspen

Note: Add 4 years to age at DBH to obtain total age.

Source: Carmean, W. H., J. T. Hahn, and R. D. Jacobs. 1989. *Site Index Curves for Forest Tree Species in the Eastern United States (General Technical Report NC-128)*. USDA Forest Service, North Central Forest Experimental Station, 1992 Folwell Avenue, St. Paul, MN 55108. p. 46.

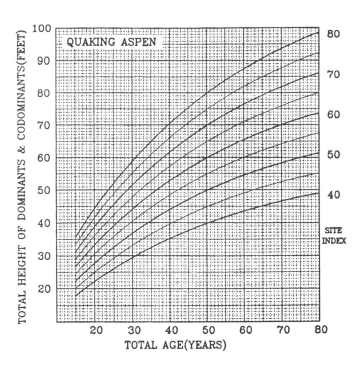

B-2: Balsam Fir in the Lake States

Note: To obtain total age, add years to age at DBH according to the table below.
Site Index: 20 30 40 50 60 70
Add Years: 15 13 11 10 9 8

Note: Curves are based on plots in the Lake States.

Source: Carmean, W. H., J. T. Hahn, and R. D. Jacobs. 1989. *Site Index Curves for Forest Tree Species in the Eastern United States (General Technical Report NC-128)*. USDA Forest Service, North Central Forest Experimental Station, 1992 Folwell Avenue, St. Paul, MN 55108. p. 70.

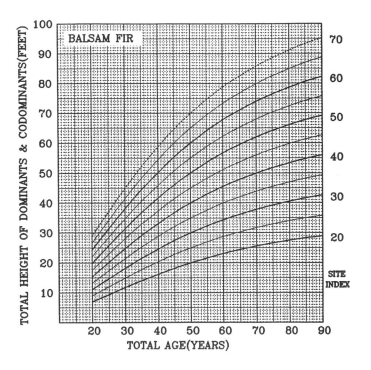

▲

B-3: Black Spruce

Note: To obtain total age, add years to age at DBH according to the table below.
Site Index: 20 30 40 50 60 70 80 90
Add Years: 15 13 11 10 9 8 7 6

Note: Curves are based on plots in northeastern Minnesota—Superior National Forest.

Source: Carmean, W. H., J. T. Hahn, and R. D. Jacobs. 1989. *Site Index Curves for Forest Tree Species in the Eastern United States (General Technical Report NC-128)*. USDA Forest Service, North Central Forest Experimental Station, 1992 Folwell Avenue, St. Paul, MN 55108. p. 85.

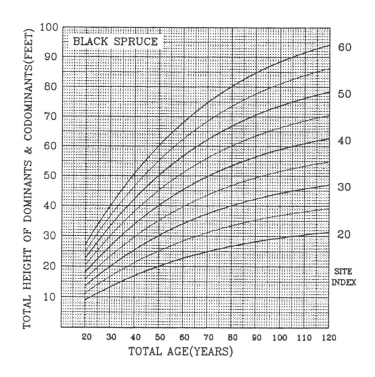

B-4: Black Walnut

Note: Determine total age from stumps or planting records; do not damage trees by using an increment borer.

Note: Curves are based on plots in southern Illinois.

Source: Carmean, W. H., J. T. Hahn, and R. D. Jacobs. 1989. *Site Index Curves for Forest Tree Species in the Eastern United States (General Technical Report NC-128)*. USDA Forest Service, North Central Forest Experimental Station, 1992 Folwell Avenue, St. Paul, MN 55108. p. 33.

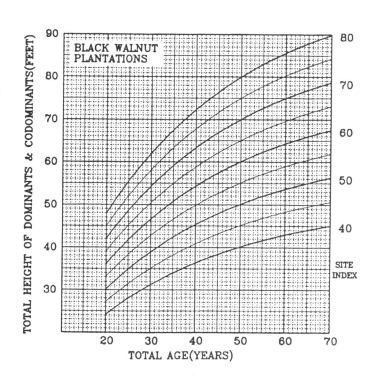

202

B-5: Green Ash

Note: Add 2 years to age at DBH to obtain total age.

Note: Curves are based on plots in Mississippi Valley alluvium in Louisiana, Mississippi, Arkansas, and Tennessee.

Source: Carmean, W. H., J. T. Hahn, and R. D. Jacobs. 1989. *Site Index Curves for Forest Tree Species in the Eastern United States (General Technical Report NC-128).* USDA Forest Service, North Central Forest Experimental Station, 1992 Folwell Avenue, St. Paul, MN 55108. p. 30.

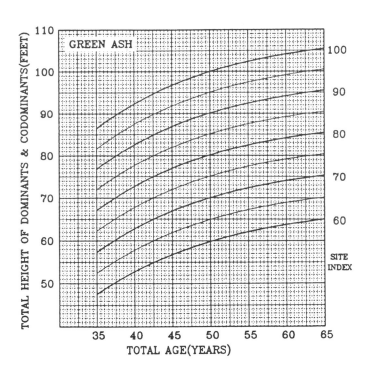

B-6: Eastern Cottonwood

Note: Add 2 years to age at DBH to obtain total age.

Note: Curves are based on plots in Iowa bottomlands.

Source: Carmean, W. H., J. T. Hahn, and R. D. Jacobs. 1989. *Site Index Curves for Forest Tree Species in the Eastern United States (General Technical Report NC-128).* USDA Forest Service, North Central Forest Experimental Station, 1992 Folwell Avenue, St. Paul, MN 55108. p. 45.

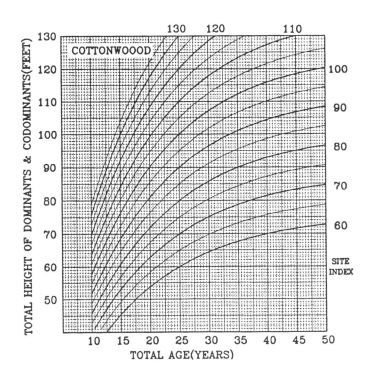

B-7: Eastern White Pine

Note: To obtain total age, add years to age at DBH according to the table below.
Site Index: 40 50 60 70 80
Add Years: 12 12 10 8 6

Note: Curves are based on plots in northern Wisconsin.

Source: Carmean, W. H., J. T. Hahn, and R. D. Jacobs. 1989. *Site Index Curves for Forest Tree Species in the Eastern United States (General Technical Report NC-128)*. USDA Forest Service, North Central Forest Experimental Station, 1992 Folwell Avenue, St. Paul, MN 55108. p. 118.

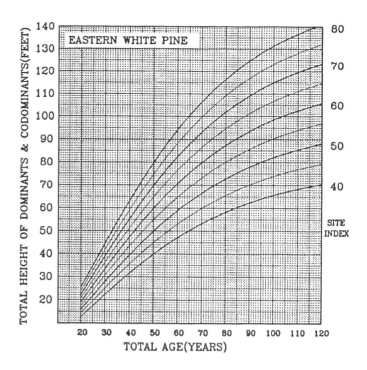

B-8: Hardwood Comparisons

Note: If you know the site index for one species, you can determine the site index for another species on the same site by moving vertically up or down to the curve for each species of interest. For example, if you know the site index for aspen is 72, find that number on the aspen curve. Then read directly downward to the white ash curve to find the corresponding site index of 68 for white ash.

Source: USDA, Forest Service. 1985. *Northern Hardwood Notes (Note 4.02)*. U.S. Government Printing Office, Washington, DC 20402.

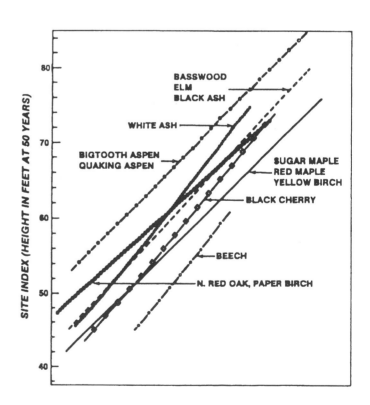

B-9: Jack Pine

Note: To obtain total age, add years to age at DBH according to the table below.
Site Index: 30 40 50 60 70 80 90
Add Years: 9 8 7 6 5 4 4

Note: Curves are based on plots in the Lake States.

Source: Carmean, W. H., J. T. Hahn, and R. D. Jacobs. 1989. *Site Index Curves for Forest Tree Species in the Eastern United States (General Technical Report NC-128)*. USDA Forest Service, North Central Forest Experimental Station, 1992 Folwell Avenue, St. Paul, MN 55108. p. 89.

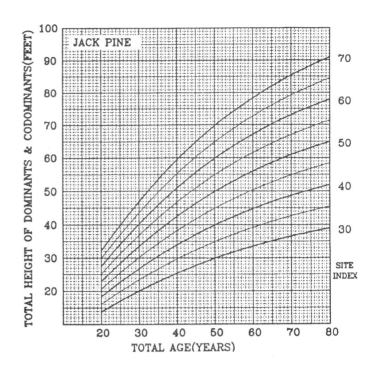

B-10: Northern White-Cedar

Note: To obtain total age, add years to age at DBH according to the table below.
Site Index: 20 30 40 50 60
Add Years: 20 15 15 10 10

Note: Curves are based on plots in the Lake States.

Source: Carmean, W. H., J. T. Hahn, and R. D. Jacobs. 1989. *Site Index Curves for Forest Tree Species in the Eastern United States (General Technical Report NC-128)*. USDA Forest Service, North Central Forest Experimental Station, 1992 Folwell Avenue, St. Paul, MN 55108. p. 141.

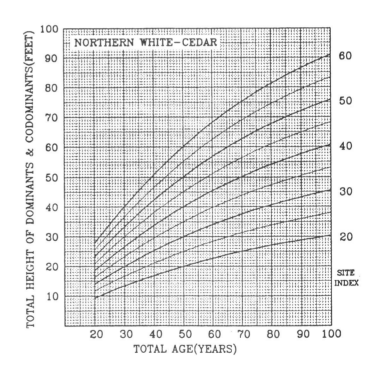

B-11: Red (Norway) Pine

Note: To obtain total age, add years to age at DBH according to the table below.
Site Index: 40 50 60 70+
Add Years: 8 6 5 4

Note: Curves are based on plots in Minnesota.

Source: Carmean, W. H., J. T. Hahn, and R. D. Jacobs. 1989. *Site Index Curves for Forest Tree Species in the Eastern United States (General Technical Report NC-128)*. USDA Forest Service, North Central Forest Experimental Station, 1992 Folwell Avenue, St. Paul, MN 55108. p. 110.

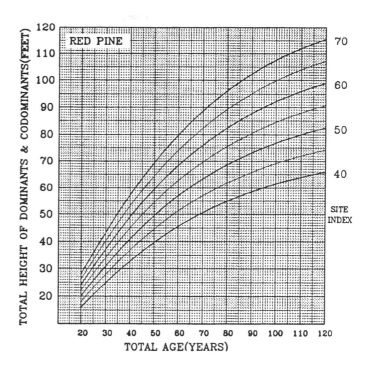

B-12: Tamarack

Note: To obtain total age, add years to age at DBH according to the table below.
Site Index: 20 30 40 50-90
Add Years: 12 10 7 5

Note: Curves are based on plots in Minnesota.

Source: Carmean, W. H., J. T. Hahn, and R. D. Jacobs. 1989. *Site Index Curves for Forest Tree Species in the Eastern United States (General Technical Report NC-128)*. USDA Forest Service, North Central Forest Experimental Station, 1992 Folwell Avenue, St. Paul, MN 55108. p. 75.

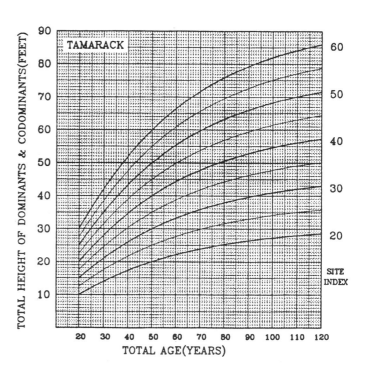

B-13: Northern Red Oak

Note: Add 4 years to age at DBH to obtain total age.

Note: Curves are based on plots in southwestern Wisconsin.

Source: Carmean, W. H., J. T. Hahn, and R. D. Jacobs. 1989. *Site Index Curves for Forest Tree Species in the Eastern United States (General Technical Report NC-128).* USDA Forest Service, North Central Forest Experimental Station, 1992 Folwell Avenue, St. Paul, MN 55108. p. 62.

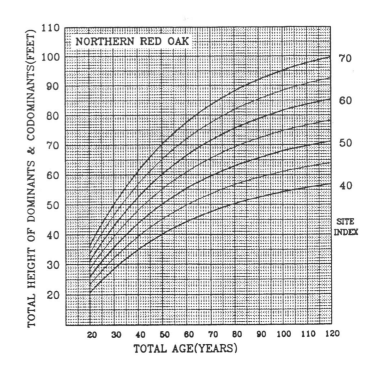

Appendix C:

Stocking Charts for Selected Tree Species and Forest Types

Stocking charts are useful thinning guides. If you know the square feet of basal area and number of trees per acre in a stand, you can refer to a stocking chart for the species of interest and determine whether the stand is overstocked, fully stocked, or understocked. Stands above the A level on a stocking chart are overstocked and should be thinned back to near the B level to increase tree growth rate.

For example, refer to Appendix C-2. If your stand had a basal area of 110 square feet and 200 trees per acre, it would be at the A level where it is nearly overstocked. Trees in the stand would grow faster if the stand were thinned. Trees in this sample stand have an average stand diameter of 10 inches. Follow the line for 10 inches diameter down to the B-level curve. It intersects the B-level curve where the basal area is 68 square feet and there are 125 trees per acre. The residual trees would grow best if the stand were thinned back to this stocking level.

However, a stand that is heavily thinned may be subject to windthrow and epicormic branching. As a rule of thumb, do not remove more than one-third of the basal area from a stand at any one time. Applying this principle to the example above, the stand should be thinned down to 74 square feet of basal area and approximately 135 trees per acre.

C-1. Even-Aged Spruce-Balsam Fir Stands

C-2. Elm-Ash-Cottonwood

C-3. Nearly Pure Even-Aged Eastern White Pine

C-4. Jack Pine

C-5. Even-Aged Management of Northern Hardwoods

C-6. Red (Norway) Pine

C-7. Upland Central Hardwoods

C-1: Even-Aged Spruce-Balsam Fir Stands

Source: Johnston, W. F. 1986. *Manager's Handbook for Balsam Fir in the North Central States (General Technical Report NC-111)*. USDA Forest Service, North Central Forest Experiment Station, 1992 Folwell Avenue, St. Paul, MN 55108. p. 8.

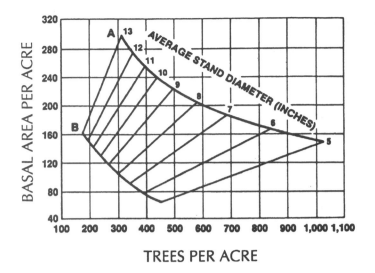

C-2: Elm-Ash-Cottonwood

Source: Myers, C. C. and R. G. Buchman. 1984. *Manager's Handbook for Elm-Ash-Cottonwood in the North Central States (General Technical Report NC-98)*. USDA Forest Service, North Central Forest Experiment Station, 1992 Folwell Avenue, St. Paul, MN 55108. p. 9.

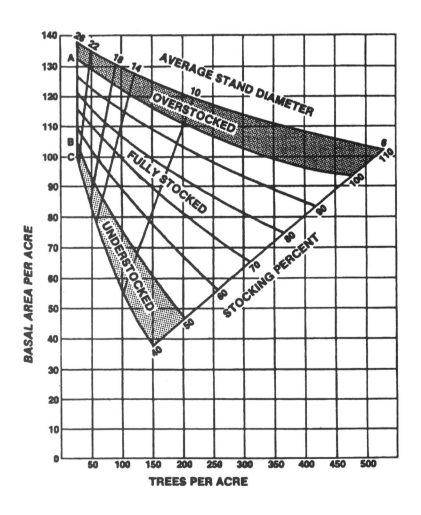

C-3: Nearly Pure Even-Aged Eastern White Pine

Source: U.S. Department of Agriculture, Forest Service. 1990. *Silvics of North America, Volume I Conifers (Agricultural Handbook No. 654)*. U.S. Government Printing Office, Washington, DC 20402. p. 482.

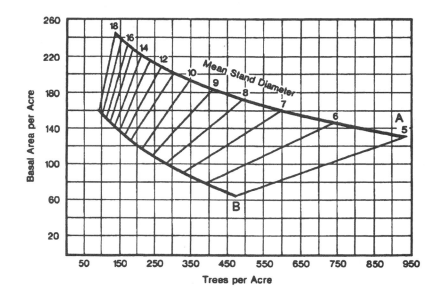

C-4: Jack Pine

Source: Benzie, J. W. 1977. *Manager's Handbook for Jack Pine in the North Central States (General Technical Report NC-32)*. USDA Forest Service, North Central Forest Experiment Station, 1992 Folwell Avenue, St. Paul, MN 55108. p. 11.

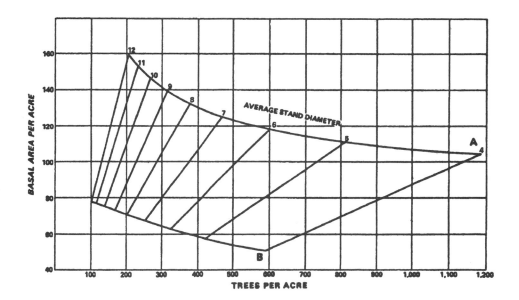

C-5: Even-Aged Management of Northern Hardwoods

Source: U.S. Department of Agriculture, Forest Service. 1985. *Northern Hardwood Notes (Note 4.03)*. U.S. Government Printing Office, Washington, DC 20402.

Note: Find the current basal area per acre of your stand on the vertical axis and the number of trees per acre on the horizontal axis. Where these lines meet is the average tree diameter. Next extend a line paralleling the average tree diameter line to the appropriate specie curve. (Use the hemlock and basswood curves labeled 100 percent only if the stand you are thinning is at least 80 percent stocked with that particular species. Use the dashed curves for stands that are about 50 percent stocked with that particular species.) Go horizontally from the intersection of the average tree diameter line and species curve to the vetrical axis and read the residual basal area that is optimum for that stand.

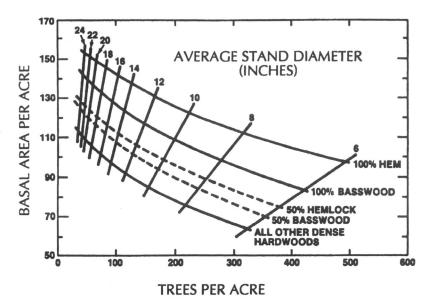

C-6: Red (Norway) Pine

Source: Benzie, J. W. 1976. *Manager's Handbook for Red Pine in the North Central States (General Technical Report NC-33)*. USDA Forest Service, North Central Forest Experiment Station, 1992 Folwell Avenue, St. Paul, MN 55108. p. 13.

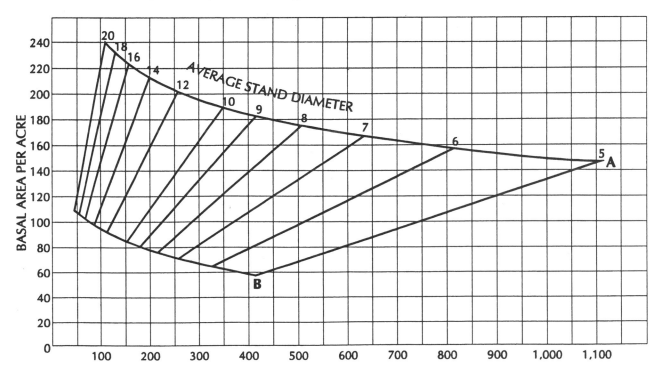

▲ ———————————————————————————

C-7: Upland Central Hardwoods

Note: For average tree diameters of 7 to 15 inches, use Chart A.
For average tree diameters of 3 to 7 inches, use Chart B.

Source: Sandler, I. L. 1977. *Manager's Handbook for Oaks in the North Central States (General Technical Report NC-37).* USDA Forest Service, North Central Forest Experiment Station, 1992 Folwell Avenue, St. Paul, MN 55108. p. 29.

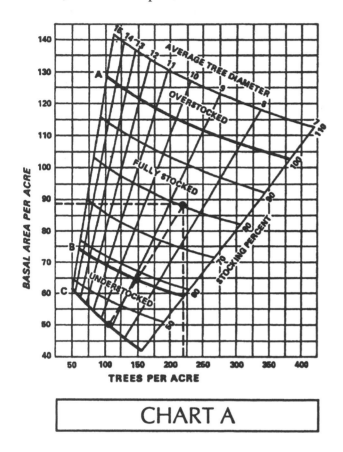

CHART A

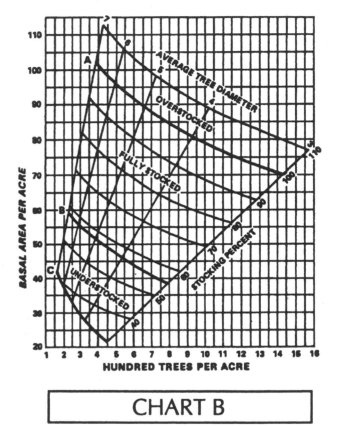

CHART B

Glossary

Acre– An area of land that contains 43,560 square feet.

Advance regeneration (reproduction)– Seedling-size trees present in a stand before a harvest aimed at regenerating the stand.

Age class– A year or defined period of years within the life of a tree stand.

All-aged stand– A stand that contains trees of all, or almost all, age classes. Also called "uneven-aged" stand. Contrast with an "even-aged" stand.

Alluvial soil– Soil deposited when flowing water slows down and suspended sediment drops to the bottom.

Artificial regeneration (reproduction)– See regeneration.

Aspect– The compass direction toward which a slope faces.

Basal area– 1) Of a tree: the cross-sectional area (in square feet) of the trunk at breast height (4.5 feet above the ground). For example, the basal area of a tree 14 inches DBH is approximately 1 square foot. 2) Of an acre: the sum of basal areas of the individual trees on the acre. A well-stocked northern hardwood stand might contain 80 to 100 square feet of basal area per acre.

Block– An area of woodland based on geographic boundaries, tree species composition, timber products, accessibility, or other stand characteristics.

Board foot– A unit for measuring wood volumes equaling 144 cubic inches. It commonly is used to measure and express the amount of wood in a tree, sawlog, veneer log, or individual piece of lumber. For example, a piece of wood 12 inches x 12 inches x 1 inch and one measuring 12 inches x 3 inches x 4 inches each contains 1 board foot of wood.

Bole– The main trunk or stem of a tree.

Bolt– A short log or a squared timber cut from a log, commonly 8 feet long.

Broadcast burn– A controlled fire that is set purposely to burn across an area and eliminate woody debris and undesirable small trees and shrubs.

Browse– Growing leaves, shoots, or twigs used as animal fodder. As a verb, to feed on leaves, shoots, or twigs.

Buck– The process of cutting a tree stem into logs.

Burl– An abnormal growth of woody tissue protruding outward from a tree stem. Usually rounded in shape.

Canopy– The highest horizontal layer of vegetation in a forest made up of tree crowns.

Certification– Forest certification is a voluntary process by an authorized forester that verifies whether your forest management, including harvesting timber or other products, is environmentally appropriate, socially beneficial, and economically viable.

Chain– A distance of 66 feet.

Cleaning– See release cutting.

Clearcut– A harvesting method that removes all the trees on an area in one operation. Regeneration occurs from seed or seedlings present before cutting, from dormant seed on the ground, from seed that disperses from adjoining stands, or from artificial planting or seeding. Clearcutting is used most often with species that require full sunlight to reproduce and grow well. Produces an even-aged forest stand.

Clone– A group of plants derived from a single individual through asexual (vegetative) reproduction.

Codominant– See crown classification.

Commercial cut– A timber harvest for which the value of cut timber exceeds the cost of cutting.

Conifer– A tree belonging to the order Coniferales that usually is evergreen, cone-bearing, and has leaves that are needle-, awl- or scale-like, such as pine, spruce, fir, and cedar; often referred to as softwood.

Conservation– The protection, improvement, and wise use of natural resources to assure the attainment of their highest economic and social values over a long time period.

Cord– A stack of logs containing 128 cubic feet of wood, bark and air space. Normal dimensions of a standard cord are 4 feet x 4 feet x 8 feet. In the Lake States, pulpwood cords usually are 4 feet x 4 feet x 100 inches.

Crop tree– A tree that will be grown to economic or physical maturity. Usually selected on the basis of its species, location with respect to other trees, and quality.

Crown– The leaves and branches of a tree.

Crown classification– Ranking of individual trees in a stand according to the size and height of their crowns. In descending order of crown height and size, the classes commonly used are dominant, codominant, intermediate, and suppressed.

Crown ratio– Percentage of total tree height that is occupied by living branches.

Cruise– Process of collecting stand inventory information such as tree volumes.

Cubic foot– A wood volume measurement containing 1,728 cubic inches, such as a piece of wood measuring 12 inches on a side. A cubic foot of wood contains approximately 6 to 10 usable board feet of wood.

Cull– A tree or log of merchantable size but no market value because of serious wood quality defects.

Cutting– A segment of a tree stem, usually about 12 inches long, that can be planted to grow a new tree. The practice of severing a tree stem to fell it.

Cutting cycle– The planned time interval between major harvesting operations in a stand. The term usually is applied to uneven-aged stands. For example, a cutting cycle of 10 years means that a harvest would be carried out once every 10 years in a stand.

DBH– The diameter of a tree stem at breast height (4.5 feet) above the ground.

DIB (d.i.b.)– Diameter inside bark. Diameter of a log at its small end, measured inside the bark.

Deciduous tree– A tree that loses its leaves during the winter.

Defect– The portion of a tree or log that is unusable for the intended product. Examples are decay, crook, and excessive limbiness.

Diameter– See DBH or DIB.

Diameter class– A tree stem diameter category that may include 1 or more inches of diameter.

Direct seeding– See seeding.

Dominant– See crown classification.

Duff– Undecomposed organic matter (such as leaves, twigs, moss, pieces of bark and wood) that litters a forest floor.

Ecosystem– A system of plants, animals, and microorganisms interacting with their environment of soil, water, and climate.

Endangered species– A plant or animal that is in danger of going extinct throughout all or part of its range.

Environment– The prevailing conditions of climate, soil, topography, and biological (other plants and animals) factors in an area.

Epicormic branch– A branch that develops by chance or from a dormant bud beneath the bark in an unusual location, usually on hardwood tree stems and major limbs. It typically arises after a stand has been heavily thinned, apparently in response to additional sunlight. Also called "water sprout."

Even-aged stand– A stand in which the age difference between trees forming the main canopy does not exceed 20 percent of the age of the stand at maturity.

Evergreen tree– A tree that retains some or all of its leaves throughout the entire year, for example, red pine, white spruce, white-cedar.

Financial analysis– An analysis that estimates the profitability for an investment from the point of view of the decision maker(s) involved in the investment.

Foliage– Leaves on a tree or other plant.

Forb– An herbaceous flowering plant that is not a grass, sedge, or rush.

Forest– A plant community in which the dominant vegetation is trees and other woody plants.

Forest management– The process of giving a forest care so that it remains healthy and vigorous and provides the products and amenities the landowner desires; also, the application of technical forestry principles, practices, and business techniques to the management of a forest.

Forest type– A group of tree species which, because of their environmental requirements and tolerance for shade and moisture, often is found growing together. A forest type is named for one to three dominant tree species occurring in it, for example, silver maple-American elm forest type.

Forestry– The science, art, and practice of managing trees and forests and their associated resources for human benefit.

Frilling– Completely encircling the stem of a tree with ax cuts that sever the bark and cambium (actively growing layer of cells) with the intent of killing the tree. Herbicide often is injected into the frill.

Full-tree skidding– See whole-tree skidding.

Fungicide– A chemical that kills fungi.

Geotextile fabric– A very tough, coarsely-woven fabric used as underlayment for road and trail beds to strengthen the bed.

Girdling– Completely encircling the trunk of a tree with a cut that severs the bark and cambium (actively growing layer of cells) and usually penetrates into the sapwood to kill the tree by preventing the conduction of water and nutrients.

Grading (trees or logs)– Evaluating and sorting trees or logs according to wood quality.

Habitat– The local environment in which a plant or animal lives.

Haul road– A roadway that provides access for trucks to specific points in the woodland for hauling logs or other materials.

Hardboard– A panel of wood formed from wood fibers compressed together under heat.

Harden off– A natural physiological change that a plant goes through late in the growing season to prepare it for winter survival. It involves thickening of cell walls and other physiological changes.

Hardwood– A broadleaf, usually deciduous, tree such as oak, maple, ash, and elm.

Harvest– The felling and removal of final crop trees on an area to 1) obtain income, 2) develop the environment necessary to regenerate the forest, or 3) achieve objectives such as development of wildlife habitat. Contrast with intermediate cut.

Height, merchantable– The length of a tree stem from the top of the expected stump to the maximum height above which no usable wood products may be obtained. For example, if the minimum usable diameter of pulpwood sticks is 4 inches, the merchantable height of a straight tree would be its height from stump height up to a trunk diameter of 4 inches.

Height, total– Height of a tree from ground level to the top of its crown.

Herb– A nonwoody plant.

Herbicide– A chemical that kills herbaceous (nonwoody) plants. In common usage, often used interchangeably with phytocide (plant killer) and silvicide (tree killer).

Humus– any organic matter which has reached a point of stability, where it will break down no further and might, if conditions do not change, remain essentially as it is for centuries.

Increment borer– A hollow, auger-like instrument used to bore into the stem of a tree to remove a pencil-sized cylinder of wood containing a cross-section of the tree's growth rings.

Insecticide– A chemical that kills insects.

Intermediate– See crown classification and shade tolerance.

Intermediate cut– The removal of physically or financially immature trees from a stand to improve the quality or growth of remaining trees. An intermediate cut may generate income (commercial cut) or may cost the forest landowner (a noncommercial cut). Contrast with harvest.

Kerf– The width of a saw blade. The cut made by a saw blade. The wood converted to sawdust as a saw cuts lumber from a log.

Landing– Small area in or near a woodland that is used for processing (such as sorting products, delimbing, cutting logs to shorter lengths, debarking) and loading timber products onto trucks.

Layering– Process of regenerating a tree by covering a lower branch with soil or organic matter, after which the branch develops roots and can stand alone as a new tree.

Liberation– See release cutting.

Live-crown ratio– The percentage of total tree height that has live branches on it (see Figure 3-2).

Loess soil– Soil deposited by wind.

Log– A cut piece of the woody stem of a tree. A 16-foot long piece of a tree stem.

Logger– An individual whose occupation is cutting timber.

Mast– Tree-produced nuts (hard mast) and fleshy fruits (soft mast) that are edible to wildlife.

Mature tree– A tree that has reached the desired biological size or age or economic value for its intended use.

Muskeg– A bog, especially a sphagnum bog of the northern U.S., often with tussocks.

Natural forest stand– A stand of trees that originated from seed, seedlings, root suckers, or stump sprouts that were naturally present on the site.

Noncommercial cutting– A cutting that does not yield a net income, usually because the trees harvested are too small, of poor quality, or of nonmerchantable species.

Overstory– The highest horizontal layer of tree crowns in a stand of trees. Contrast with understory.

Plantation– A tree stand established by planting or direct seeding.

Planting stock– Tree seedlings or transplants that will be planted to reproduce a tree stand.

Plot– An area of land, usually less than one acre, on which trees and sometimes other vegetation are measured during a cruise (or inventory).

Pole stand– A stand of trees where DBH ranges from 4 inches up to approximately 8 to 12 inches.

Poletimber– See pole stand.

Precommercial cutting– See noncommercial cutting.

Pruning– The removal of live or dead branches from standing trees. With forest trees, pruning generally means removing limbs from the lower 17 feet of the main stem to produce higher quality (knot-free) wood.

Pulpwood– Wood cut primarily to be converted

into wood pulp, chips, or fiber for the manufacture of paper, fiberboard, or other wood fiber products.

Range– 1) Commercial range is the geographic area in which a species is harvested for commercial purposes. 2) Natural range is the geographic area where a species is known to occur under natural conditions without human interference. 3) Home range is the geographic area within which a wildlife species spends most of its time throughout the year.

Reforestation– Reestablishing a stand of trees on an area where forest vegetation has been removed.

Regeneration– The process by which a stand is replaced by natural seed fall, stump sprouts, root suckers, or layering, or by artificial planting of seed or seedlings. Also, young trees.

Release cutting– A cutting operation to release seedlings or saplings from competition with other trees of the same size (a "cleaning") or from larger and overtopping trees (a "liberation").

Reproduction– See regeneration.

Risk– The chance of a loss. In some cases, risk can be estimated using probability principles. In other cases, the risk cannot be quantified. The terms "risk" and "uncertainty" are sometimes used interchangeably.

Root collar– The place on a tree seedling stem that differentiates the above-ground stem from the below-ground roots. The stem may be slightly swollen at the root collar.

Root sucker– A shoot that arises from a dormant bud on a lateral tree root, but grows above ground as a new tree. Root suckers usually develop when the parent tree is harvested or is severely damaged.

Roots– That portion of a tree that generally is underground and that functions in nutrient absorption, anchorage, and storage of food and waste products.

Rotation– The number of years required to establish and grow trees to a specified size, product, or maturity.

Salvage cut– Harvesting trees that have been killed or are in danger of being killed by insects, disease, fire, wind, flood or other unexpected cause to recover their economic value.

Sanitation cut– The harvesting or destruction of trees infected or highly susceptible to insects or diseases to prevent spreading the pest to remaining trees in the area.

Sapling– A small tree, often defined as being between 1 and 4 inches DBH.

Sawlog– A log large enough to produce a sawn product—usually at least 10 to 12 inches in diameter, 8 feet long, and solid.

Sawtimber– Standing trees large enough to produce sawlogs.

Scalping– Removing a patch or strip of sod to expose mineral soil in preparation for planting trees.

Scarification– Churning the soil surface to expose mineral soil and uproot vegetation to prepare a seedbed for natural or artificial seeding.

Seedbed– The ground surface on which tree seeds will naturally fall or be artificially seeded.

Seed cut– A harvest in a shelterwood system that is designed to encourage the growth of desirable seed-producing trees, create a good seedbed for germination, and eliminate undesirable trees, shrubs, and herbaceous plants that may produce seed.

Seed tree– A tree left standing after a timber harvest as a source of seed for reproducing a new stand.

Seed tree harvest– A harvest in which all trees are removed from the harvest area except for a few scattered trees that provide seed to establish a new stand. Produces an even-aged stand.

Seeding– Scattering tree seeds over an area by hand or machinery to establish a new stand of trees.

Seedling– A tree, usually defined as less than 1 inch in DBH, that has grown from a seed (in contrast to a root sucker or stump sprout).

Selection harvest– A harvest in which individual trees or small groups of trees are cut at periodic intervals (usually 8 to 15 years) based on their physical condition or degree of maturity. Produces an uneven-aged forest.

Self-prune– The ability of a tree to naturally lose its lower branches as the tree ages, thus enabling knot-free wood to grow on the stem.

Shade tolerance– Relative ability of a tree species to reproduce and grow under shade. Tree species usually are classified in descending order of shade tolerance as very tolerant, tolerant, intermediate, intolerant, or very intolerant.

Shelterwood harvest– A harvest in which trees are removed in a series of two or more cuttings to allow the establishment and early growth of new seedlings under the partial shade and protection of older trees. Produces an even-aged forest.

Shrub– A perennial plant with a persistent woody stem(s) and low-branching habit that usually grows less than 10 feet tall. Contrast with tree.

Silviculture– The art, science, and practice of establishing, tending, and reproducing forest stands of desired characteristics based on knowledge of species characteristics and their environmental requirements.

Site– A contiguous (connected) area with a more or less uniform combination of biological, climatic, and soil conditions.

Site index– A measure of site quality for growing trees based on the total height that dominant and codominant trees are expected to grow in a given time period, usually 50 years in the Lake States. Trees are expected to grow taller on good sites than on poor ones in the same time period.

Site preparation– A set of practices (for example, brush clearing, chemical vegetation control, and prescribed burning) that improve a seedbed or suppress competing vegetation, to increase the chances for successfully establishing a new stand of trees.

Skid trail– Usually a temporary, unimproved roadway that enables skidders or forwarders to transport logs from the interior of a woodland to a landing.

Slash– Residue such as tree tops, branches, bark, and unmerchantable wood left on the ground after logging, pruning, or other forest operations.

Snag– A standing dead tree.

Softwoods– See conifer.

Soil texture– The particle composition of a soil based on the proportion of sand, silt, and clay.

Species– One of the basic units of biological classification—a group of organisms capable of interbreeding and producing fertile offspring.

Species composition– The mix of tree species occurring together in a stand.

Stand– A group of trees occupying a given area and sufficiently uniform in species composition, tree size distribution, stocking, and soil characteristics so as to be distinguishable from the adjoining forest. If 80 percent or more of the trees are of the same species, it is a pure stand. Otherwise, it is a mixed species stand.

Stand density– See stocking.

Stocking– A measure of the degree of crowding of trees in a stand, also known as stand density. Commonly expressed by the number of trees per acre or percentage of crown cover.

Stocking chart– A chart usually based on one or more tree species, number of trees per acre, and tree stem diameters that shows the best stocking for timber growth, considering the species present and stem diameters.

Stratify seed– Subjecting seed to cold temperatures and regulating moisture for a period of time to break seedcoat dormancy and improve seed germination.

Structural board– A wood panel made from chips or flakes that have been formed into a panel by heat, pressure, and sometimes an adhesive. Frequently used in construction for underlayment on floors, roofs, and walls.

Stumpage– The dollar value of a standing tree or group of trees.

Stump sprout– A young tree that has grown from a dormant bud on a tree stump. It is an exact genetic replica of the original tree.

Succession– The process by which one plant community is gradually replaced by another due to environmental conditions and species characteristics, such as shade tolerance.

Sucker– See root sucker.

Suppressed– See crown classification.

Sweep– A C-shaped curvature in a tree stem or log.

TSI (Timber Stand Improvement)– The practice of removing undesirable trees, shrubs, vines, or other vegetation to achieve the desired stocking of the best quality trees.

Thinning– Cutting scattered trees or rows of trees to reduce the stocking and concentrate growth on fewer, higher quality remaining trees.

Threatened species– A plant or animal that may soon become endangered throughout all or part of its range.

Till– Unstratified glacial drift consisting of clay, sand, gravel, and boulders intermingled.

Timber– Standing trees, usually of commercial size.

Timber inventory– A collection of information about a stand made by measuring tree and stand characteristics such as tree volume and grade and stand density.

Tolerance– See shade tolerance.

Tract– A contiguous (connected) area of land (and water).

Transplant– A tree seedling that was transplanted at least once in the nursery.

Tree– A woody plant with a well-defined stem and a more or less definitely formed crown, which usually grows more than 10 feet tall.

Tree farm– A privately owned woodland dedicated to the production of timber crops and other environmental benefits. It may be formally recognized by the Tree Farm program of the American Forest Council.

Tree length skidding– When a tree is felled, the process of removing the top and limbs, then moving (skidding) the entire tree stem in one piece to the landing.

Trunk– The main stem or bole of a tree.

Understory– A low-growing, horizontal layer of woody or herbaceous vegetation that forms beneath an overstory of taller trees.

Uneven-aged forest– A forest or stand in which there are more than two age classes of trees present. There usually is a minimum age difference of 20 percent of the rotation length in years.

Veneer– Thin sheets of wood (usually less than $1/4$-inch thick) produced by slicing or peeling a log. A tree or log suitable for cutting into veneer because of its species, size, and good quality.

Volume table– A table that estimates the volume of wood in a standing tree (cords or board feet), usually based on DBH and merchantable height.

Water table– The highest point in a soil profile at which water saturates the soil on a seasonal or permanent basis.

Weeding– The practice of removing undesirable tree species that take up valuable growing space in a stand.

Whole-tree (full-tree) skidding– The process by which an entire tree, including the stem, limbs, and top, is brought to the landing in one piece.

Whorl (of branches)– A set of branches arising from one year's growth that occur at the same height on a tree stem and are distributed around the stem at relatively even spacing.

Windthrow– A tree uprooted or broken by wind.

Wolf tree– A tree with a large crown, but poor form and low wood product value that occupies more space in the forest than its timber value justifies.

Wood pulp– Mechanically ground or chemically digested wood used in the manufacture of paper.

Woodland management– See forest management.